TEACHING

With Love & Logic®

Taking Control of the Classroom

Jim Fay & David Funk

The Love and Logic PRESS Inc.
800-338-4065
www.loveandlogic.com

*The Love and Logic Press, Inc. gratefully acknowledges
the contributions of Betsy Geddes and Jim McKee.*

First edition
First printing, 1995
Printed in the United States of America

Library of Congress Cataloging-in-Publication Data
Fay, Jim
        Teaching with love and logic: taking control of the classroom /
by Jim Fay and David Funk.—1st ed.
            p. cm.
        Includes bibliographical references and index.
        ISBN 0-944634-29-X (hc)
        1. School discipline—United States. 2. Classroom management—
United States. I. Funk, David, 1946-   . II. Title.
        LB3012.2.F39 1995
        371.5'0973—dc2

                                                        95-14613
                                                        CIP

Editing by Adryan Russ, Burbank, CA
Design by Bob Schram, Bookends, Boulder, CO
Jacket design by Barry Eisenoch, Phoenix Design, Arvada, CO

Published and printed in the United States of America

▼

Acknowledgments

*T*eaching a classroom of difficult students is the easiest thing I do nowdays. I am reminded of this every time I have a chance to do demonstration teaching. I didn't always have this ability. Earlier in my teaching career there were days where the students took over control of the classroom I went home frustrated and angry, wondering why I should go back to the next day.

The difference now is that I have a set of effective skills that I acquired over a very long period of time. I was exposed to these new skills as a result of having the opportunity to work with some very special people who possessed these skills. These people also shared and demonstrated valuable beliefs and attitudes about people, which became valuable to me in my work with students.

I was fortunate to meet these people at times in my life when I was highly motivated. These were times in which I was desperate, making the types of mistakes that virtually shouted to me that there must be a better way.

Dr. Gus Profit, principal of Asbury School, in Denver, Colorado believed in me. He was gentle with me, and constantly urged me to try new teaching approaches. Gus had a strong belief in the value of people and modeled the importance of treating others with respect. He was the first of my mentors who demonstrated the value of sharing control.

Gene Cosby, Mountain Area Superintendent of Schools in Jefferson County, Colorado, hired me to be a principal in a school that was to undergo a difficult transition. Gene believed in me and he believed that people are important and that they should be treated with dignity. He ranks high on my list of mentors and models. I grew under his guidance, as he gave me the freedom to develop and acted as a fine example to follow.

Foster W. Cline, M.D. came into my life at a perfect time. He was a psychiatrist in Evergreen, Colorado. He generously donated time to help the teachers at my elementary school. He was always available to help me learn about many innovative child management techniques. Foster has a well of knowledge that is so deep that it has no limits. This combined with his creativity has helped him become one of the most effective psychiatrists in America.

Foster later became my best friend, partner and co-founder of the Cline/Fay Institute, inc. There has never been an end to his mentoring. Love and Logic is a combination of his expertise in psychology, my adaptating these concepts and experimenting with school children, and my years of experience in the schools.

An acknowledgement for *Teaching With Love ana Logic* would not be complete without thanking Nancy Henry and Carol Core. Nancy is my wonderful daughter who is the Executive Vice President of the Love and Logic Companies. Carol Core is Vice President of Marketing. This book would not be in print had it not been for their belief in my ability to write it, their constant encouragement and Nancy Henry's editorial skills.

I didn't learn Love and Logic on my own and I did not produce this book on my own. My sincere thanks go to to all of you who contributed to my growth as an educator over the last 42 years of working with children. I can't begin to name you all or there would be no space for the text of this book.

Other Titles From Love and Logic

- *Meeting the Challenge*

- *Hope for Underachieving Kids: Opening the Door to Success with Love and Logic*

- *Pearls of Love and Logic for Parents and Teachers*

- *Quick and Easy Classroom Interventions: 23 Proven Tools for Increasing Student Cooperation*

- *9 Essential Skills for the Love and Logic Classroom: Low Stress Strategies for Highly Successful Educators*
  This professional development multimedia training curriculum gives you classroom management skills.

- *Parenting With Love and Logic: Teaching Children Responsibility*

- *Parenting Teens With Love and Logic: Preparing Adolescents for Responsible Adulthood*

- *Grandparenting With Love and Logic: Practical Solutions to Today's Grandparenting Challenges*

- *Love and Logic Solutions for Kids with Special Needs*

For a complete Love and Logic catalog please contact us at 800-338-4065 or visit our website at www.loveandlogic.com.

Dedication

To my wife, Diane,
our children, Aleshia and Jaben,
and grandson, Edrik,
who have taught me
about life's highest values.

David Funk

Preface

*A*re you looking for practical solutions to the day-to-day frustrations and challenges common in today's classroom? Are you seeking tried and true techniques that reduce the time and energy you spend maintaining discipline in your classroom?

Are you searching for ways to relate to students that increase the level of student cooperation so that you can enjoy teaching? Have you been hoping to find ideas and strategies that put some fun into teaching?

Love and Logic is an approach to working with students that:

- Puts teachers in control
- Teaches kids to think for themselves
- Raises the level of student responsibility
- Prepares kids to function effectively in a society filled with temptations, decisions, and consequences.

The techniques offered in this book were born out of practical application. Many of these strategies were developed over a period of 31 years of teaching and school administration. For the past 17 years, I have been teaching these techniques to teachers and administrators who have found them effective. Over a period of time, this collection of techniques and the philosophy that guides it have become known as "The Love and Logic Approach to Discipline."

The Love and Logic Institute was first created during the early 1980s and since then has taken a unique approach to research in the area of discipline and behavior management. At the Institute, we have observed many proficient teachers in action, and identified their most effective strategies. We then analyzed these strategies to verify that they were consistent with the findings of research and literature of psychology.

At the end of this book, you will find supportive research and readings that will help you continue your study of discipline. This collection of research was compiled by Charles Fay, at the University of South Carolina. While Charles was working on his Ph.D. in psychology, he spent considerable time working with me in the analysis of Love and Logic and was instrumental in verifying the concepts taught in this book.

Many educators have applied Love and Logic effectively in their schools and classrooms and have been instrumental in bringing about system change resulting in exemplary teaching and learning environments. Several of them have been chosen as examples of practical application for this book.

David Funk applied Love and Logic in his work in the New Berlin Public Schools (New Berlin, Wisconsin) first as a teacher and later as an administrator. He then applied his new strategies at the university level and developed an outstanding teacher-training facility. You will read his analysis of the principles of Love and Logic as well as his suggestions for practicing these principles, all born out of his day-to-day use and experience, in Part Two: The Four Key Principles of Love and Logic.

Dr. Betsy Geddes used the principles of Love and Logic to turn around an inner-city school in Portland,

Oregon. She was so successful that she later became a highly effective and popular educational consultant and public speaker. Among her strengths is her ability to provide practical techniques. She addresses the challenge of implementing a school-wide discipline plan based upon Love and Logic in Chapter 14: Implementing School Discipline: Systems vs. Principles.

Jim McKee is a counselor at Walled Lake High School in Walled Lake, Michigan. His contribution to this book is an outstanding example of systems change, which he describes in Chapter 15: Walled Lake Central High School: One School's Approach To Love and Logic. He and his committee implemented The Four Key Principles of Love and Logic to move an entire staff to develop a Love and Logic school.

This book is truly based on practical experience. The total years of school experience represented by the authors and contributors is in excess of 105. We hope you enjoy our book and find that the application of Love and Logic increases your ability to have fun and feel satisfaction in the classroom. We also invite you to become acquainted with the Love and Logic Institute and some of our other books, training programs, and materials, such as *9 Essential Skills for the Love and Logic Classroom* curriculum, *Becoming a Love and Logic Parent* curriculum, and the books *Parenting With Love and Logic, Parenting Teens With Love and Logic,* and *Grandparenting With Love and Logic.* We value your feedback and hope you will let us know how this book helps you.

Please enjoy . . .

Jim Fay

Contents

PART FIVE:
Love and Logic Experiments, Charts, and Tips

PART ONE

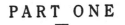

How Does Love and Logic Work?

▼

CHAPTER ONE

The Purpose of Love and Logic

A Master Makes It Look Easy

*I*sn't it great to watch a master at work? The masters always make things look so easy. They stay calm. They avoid taking on ownership of another person's problem. They set firm limits without waging war. Able to maintain their dignity in rough situations, they can help others and, at the same time, maintain their self-respect. Masters get the job done.

I watched Parley Jacobs, a wise middle-school principal and master of Love and Logic, handle a very difficult situation. He not only made it look easy but, even better, the student involved solved the problem and left with his dignity intact.

I saw an angry teacher coming down the hall with a student in tow. She delivered him to Parley with, "Here, do something with him! I'm not having him back in class. He stole the bobbin out of the sewing machine." She left, and the master principal went to work.

PARLEY: Have a seat, pal.

STUDENT: I didn't do it! I hate her!

PARLEY: Bummer.

Parley walked away with me to visit classrooms.
We returned in about ten minutes. The boy looked up
at Parley. He still appeared to be angry.

STUDENT: What!

PARLEY: What do you think?

STUDENT: I didn't do it!

PARLEY: Bummer.

Parley walked away again, but returned in about
five minutes.

PARLEY: What do you think?

STUDENT: She doesn't have any right to throw
            me out. I didn't do it!

PARLEY: Bummer.

Parley walked away, but returned again in about
five minutes.

PARLEY: What do you think?

STUDENT: I told you, I didn't do it. She hates me. She's always blaming me for everything that happens!

PARLEY: Bummer.

Parley left and returned fifteen minutes later.

PARLEY: What do you think?

STUDENT: I told you. I didn't steal it . . . but I know where it is!

PARLEY: Wow.

Parley walked away and returned in about ten minutes.

PARLEY: What do you think?

STUDENT: What if I get it back for her?

PARLEY: I don't know.

Parley walked away again and returned in another ten minutes.

PARLEY: What do you think?

STUDENT: What if I get it back and apologize?

PARLEY: I don't know.

Parley walked off again.

By now, I could see that Parley was "milking" this situation for all he could get out of it. The next time he walked past the student, he didn't even stop. The next thing I heard was the student yelling at Parley to get his attention.

STUDENT: Well, can I?

PARLEY: Can you what?

STUDENT: Can I go get it for her and try to apologize?

PARLEY: It sounds like a good idea to me. Do you want to give it a try?

STUDENT: Yeah. Can I go now?

PARLEY: I'll give you a pass. Hope it works out for you. Good luck, pal.

At last report, this student worked things out with his teacher and they got on with their lives.

Creating A Higher Standard of Behavior

I asked Parley if he had always handled discipline problems this way. "No," he laughed. "This is a new way of working with students. My life used to be filled with angry students and stressful situations. I used to make all of these problems my own. I used traditional methods of lecturing and punishing with limited success. Now that I've discovered the Love and Logic methods of discipline, I'm having more fun on the job. We're able to hold students to a higher standard of behavior.

"I used to work with kids immediately," he continued, "while they were still upset, angry, emotional. Now I give them time to cool down. I used to stop whatever I was doing to work on the problem. Now they have to wait for me so I can work with them on *my* terms. I used to do most of the talking, letting them know what they had done wrong and telling them what I was going to do about it. Now I use a lot of questions.

"Questions force the youngsters to do the thinking and to come up with their own solutions," Parley added. "I used to own the problems. Now the kids own the problems. I used to go home angry and tired from doing all the thinking. Now the kids are the ones who go home tired from thinking. I used to take on all of the responsibility. Now the kids learn to take responsibility. I used to be the bad guy. Now it's their problems and consequences that are the bad guys and I'm the good guy. Life is good again!"

"The Love and Logic approach has also given me new understanding," Parley Jacobs said. "Love and Logic concepts help me develop better relationships with kids. And the great thing about improved relationships is that they lead to improved cooperation. Now, that is what school is all about."

"The bottom line is: students at our school are more responsible now. Love and Logic enables us to hold kids to higher standards of behavior."

Great Educators Are Experimenters

The purpose of this book is not to motivate you to care more for kids. Nobody would do the job teachers do for the little appreciation received if they didn't already care a lot about children. Nor is the purpose of this book to ask you

---

✎ **LOVE AND LOGIC TIP #1:**
Dealing with Power Struggles

Power is a major issue between children and adults. While still very young, some kids realize they don't have much control over anything. A toddler unconsciously thinks, "I'm the smallest. They tell me what to do, and I don't get to make decisions. I need to find a way to get some control." Then, winning the power struggle becomes all-important—more important than making good decisions.

When we offer kids a choice instead of making a demand, no power struggle ever begins. When we make a demand, we own the wise choice, leaving the child with only one way to win the power struggle—by making a foolish choice. Given a range of choices, a child has endless opportunities to choose wisely.

---

to change. Our research indicates that demands for change tend to raise anxiety and increase resistance to change.

I am, however, going to ask you to do what great educators do. Great educators are experimenters. They read and attend workshops looking for special techniques to experiment with in their schools. When they identify a potentially helpful technique, they play with the concept. They begin to visualize experimenting with it on one of the students: "I could use that on Larry in my fourth-hour class."

Pretty soon, they relish the idea of this student giving them a hard time, just so they can experiment. They think, "Come on, Larry. Give me trouble! Make my day! I can't wait to try my new techniques on you!" If the experiment is successful, it was a good experiment. If not, the technique is set aside. The self-worth of the teacher is never in question, only the value of the technique.

Are you a teacher who looks for distinct ways to create growth and new dimensions in the classroom? If so, this book will be valuable. It is loaded with specific techniques. Before the specifics are presented, however, we want to talk about some of the roadblocks that can prevent working effectively with students—such as existing myths about teaching and discipline.

PEARL

▼

You want your students to know that making it through a tough situation is always an option.

CHAPTER TWO

Confronting the Myths About Discipline

To Warn or Not to Warn

*D*o you have a rules list in your classroom? This seems to be standard in American classrooms. In fact, most of the district discipline plans I have seen are built around identification of all the possible infractions kids can think of. Do you also have a list of consequences? This, too, is standard. Usually this second list includes consequences for the first offense, second offense, and third offense, if not more.

Myth:
Students must be warned in advance of the consequences for violating rules.

I have asked thousands of teachers, those who are in the trenches every day with students, the following question: "Is it effective to warn kids in advance of consequences? Does this act as a deterrent?"

The answer is a resounding "No." Advance warning of consequences has never had a positive effect on school discipline. Yet, we continue each year to refine these strict discipline plans even though the results do not change.

I also ask teachers these questions:

1. Have you ever known a child to think, "Teacher says that if I break the rule, he is going to . . . I wonder if he really will do it. Well, I guess there's only way to find out."?

2. Have you ever known a child who thinks, "Teacher says that if I break the rule, she is going to . . . I wonder if it's worth it. Yeah, I think it is!"?

3. Have you ever known a child so polite that he/she breaks the school rules exactly the way they are supposed to be broken so that the prescribed consequence fits the crime? Does that *ever* happen? No! Kids are great "loophole" artists. Their job is to break the rule slightly off-center so that the consequence doesn't fit and the teacher either overreacts or underreacts. This provides the opportunity for the child to complain, "Not fair!" And in many cases, this brings parents racing to school to help fight for the child's rights.

4. Do you need the aggravation of these kinds of problems?

I wonder if we hold on to the concept of warning children of consequences in advance because we have heard parents complain so often, "You didn't warn my child that he would face these consequences. It's not fair."

To respond to this, I must say that all school districts have some ironclad rules, laid down by the Board of Education, that have prescribed consequences. These have to do with issues such as violence, drugs, alcohol, tobacco, and weapons. The consequences for these major violations should be spelled out clearly and levied in a consistent manner.

Many classroom infractions, however, can be handled in a much simpler manner. One of the most effective teachers I have ever known started out each school year with the following discussion:

TEACHER: Class, here is a list of the rules I use in my classroom. Please look them over and tell me if there is anything that seems unreasonable.

STUDENT: Where does it tell what's going to happen if we break the rules?

TEACHER: I don't expect you to break the rules. But if that does happen, I'll do something.

STUDENT: Something? What is something?

TEACHER: I don't know. It will depend on how you break the rules. I treat everyone in this room as a unique individual and each situation as a unique case. So, I will think of something based

on the situation. I'll try to be fair.
In fact, if I come up with something
you believe is not fair, I want you to tell
me why it's not fair. If you present a
good case, I'll change the consequence
to something fair.

STUDENT: Oh, right. I bet!

TEACHER: To show you that I mean it, I'll even
teach you the words I want you to say
if you think I've done something that
isn't fair. Repeat after me: "I'm not sure
that's fair." Let's practice this until
you're sure you have it.

*Now, kids, if you don't think you are getting a fair deal,
what are you going to say to me?*

CLASS: I'm not sure that's fair.

TEACHER: Great. Won't it be fun to find out how
this works for you?

In the event that this teacher is confronted by a parent who complains about the fact that kids are not warned about consequences in advance, the teacher can inform the parent in a three-point discussion:

1. "I've taught all the kids in my class the words to say if they feel that my consequences are not fair. I'm surprised that your youngster goes to you to complain instead of expressing his feelings of unfairness to me."

✎ **LOVE AND LOGIC TIP #2:**
How to Destroy the Teaching Value
Of a Logical Consequence

• Say, "This will teach you a good lesson"
• Display anger or disgust
• Explain the value of the consequence
• Moralize or threaten
• Talk too much
• Feel sorry and "give in"
• Contrive a consequence for the purpose of "getting even"

---

2. "I've even told them that if they can present a good case, I'll change the consequences. I do this because every student and every situation is unique, and in this class I treat them as such."

3. "I'd be glad to meet with both of you so that you can hear your youngster present his particular case to me."

Immediate Consequences vs. Delayed Consequences

The preceding example usually encourages the reaction: "How can you individualize consequences? This takes time. If we cannot deliver an immediate consequence, we'll lose the teaching moment. We were taught in college that consequences must be immediate to be effective."

Myth:
When students break the rules,
consequences must follow immediately.

The teacher in the preceding example would indeed have difficulty with individualizing her discipline program had she not learned the concepts demonstrated in the story about Parley Jacobs and the stolen bobbin.

During my days as a teacher, I spent considerable time worrying about the possibility that students would cause some kind of new problem for which I didn't have an immediate consequence. This constant, low-level anxiety kept me on edge about discipline and, as a result, I was often frustrated and angry when a student acted out. Once I learned that student/teacher problems did not have to be solved on the spot, a tremendous load was lifted from my shoulders.

Delaying the Consequence
A Missouri teacher experimented with this approach. One of his sixth grade students "talked back" to him. His immediate response was, "That kind of talk is not acceptable in this classroom. I'm going to have to do something about that. I don't know what it will be because I'm busy teaching right now. I'll let you know what I decide in the morning. Don't worry about it tonight."

As you can imagine, the student worried about it overnight and returned to class the next morning and said, "What about yesterday?" His teacher was now having so much fun with this approach that he couldn't stop. Turning to the student, he replied, "I'll tell you about it after lunch. Don't worry about it this morning."

After going to the teachers' lounge during his planning period, meeting with some other teachers, and getting some advice, he returned to talk with the student, to whom he said, "You and I have a relationship problem. I don't know what I did to upset you, but it has to be worked out."

The student refused to come in after school because of basketball practice. His teacher said, "I talked with your mom, and she suggests you stay so that we can work this out to our mutual satisfaction. You can call her afterward and she will come to drive you to basketball practice. She also told me to tell you not to feel guilty about it. She has some chores for you to do to make up for her inconvenience.

When they met after school, the following conversation took place:

TEACHER: What have I done to make you so upset?

STUDENT: You're always trying to make me look bad.

TEACHER: No, I don't.

STUDENT: Oh yes, you do! You just wait until I don't know the answer and then you call on me so I'll look bad.

TEACHER: Wait! I don't know when you don't know the answer. And, I don't want you to look bad. I have an idea. How would it work if when I call on you, and you don't know the answer, you just look away, and I call on someone else right away?

STUDENT: Yeah. I guess that would help.

TEACHER: Good. Have we got a deal? If so, let's get on with the important things we both have to do. See you tomorrow, pal.

I later asked this teacher about his thoughts concerning this interaction.

"You know, Jim," he replied, "what surprised me the most was that when I told him I *would* do something about his smart mouth, but not until *tomorrow*, that was the first time this year he didn't argue with me. He couldn't argue with me, because he couldn't figure out what to argue about.

"I realized that in the past I have always given the kids plenty to argue about when they're upset.

"I also discovered that this kid was reasonable with me after school—the first time he has ever been reasonable.

"My mistake in the past was trying to solve problems with kids while they were upset, instead of waiting until they were calm."

Experienced teachers know that there are times when students can calm down and stay in the classroom while doing so. There are also some children who are so volatile that they must be removed until they are calm. This is an individual, professional decision that is made at the time of the incident.

Do Students Need to Like Their Teachers?

Kids work harder for some teachers than they do for others. Our research indicates that some teachers bring out the best in kids, and others bring out the worst.

Myth:
It is not necessary for students to like
their teachers. However, they should respect them.

Have you ever gone camping? Do you remember that first time being the worst time of your life? You couldn't sleep. The ground was hard. You were cold. The mosquitoes chewed on you, and you were still awake at 2:14 a.m. At 3:01 a.m., you discovered that sleeping bags were designed for people who weigh 85 pounds. At precisely 3:09 a.m., you rolled over and said to yourself, "Never again. Not for anyone on the face of the earth will I ever do this!" You returned home, held a garage sale, sold all of the camping gear, sat back and said, "That's the end of camping."

Then a wonderful thing happened. You fell in love. That wonderful person you've always dreamed of entered your world. Life was great. The sky was bluer. The grass, greener. You were filled with that warm feeling called love. Then your loved one called you one day and said, "Let's go camping next week."

What did you do? You went out and bought new camping gear—of course. And as you signed the credit card slip, you said to yourself, "Not for anyone else would I do this!"

Many kids feel the same way about their teachers. They say, "I'll do it for that teacher, but not for anyone else!" Great teachers know that you cannot overpower students, but you can get them to behave, or do their assignments, because they want to please their teacher.

A great salesperson said to me once:

"You can't make people angry
and sell them something at the same time."

"The only people who think you can," he said, "are highly educated people, like teachers, who think you can get into an adversarial position with students and then sell 'em on the idea of doing what *you* want."

Great teachers have discovered that a large part of their success is due to their ability to establish positive relationships with children. These teachers are not afraid to say to students, "Will you do that just for me? Thank you." Many teachers are uncomfortable with asking kids to do something for them, for a variety of reasons. One is that many university programs taught us that we should get students to do their studying, assignments, and hard work solely for themselves.

One of the rules of the psychology of self-concept states:

"Human beings will perform for the person they love."
If a person loves himself, he will do it for himself.
If he does not have that high self-esteem or belief
in self, he will have to do it for someone else
until the time comes that he does love himself.

This psychology also teaches us that it takes *years* to remediate a damaged self-concept. In the meantime, a student with such a self-concept will most likely do school assignments when doing them for someone he or she loves.

Relationship-Building Experiment

Experiment with one of your most uncooperative students. Go to that student six times over the next three school weeks and use a "one-sentence intervention." This should take a few seconds each time.

Each intervention should consist of only one sentence, and that sentence should start with the words, "I noticed . . ." Then, you fill in the blank with something personal about the student—something positive and true. It is important that your statement *not* focus upon school activities. This is strictly about the student's personal life.

An example might be, "I noticed that you are interested in dinosaurs." That is the sum total of the intervention. If the student wants to visit with this interest, do so. However, do not praise or judge. If you feel compelled to say something, you might add, "Well, I noticed that."

Your next intervention might be, "I noticed that you really stand up for yourself." Be cautious. Don't use the phrase, "I like." Kids who have low self-esteem often feel manipulated when the teacher says, "I like." They may turn off from the adult. Remember to spread these interventions over a three-week period.

After experimenting with this type of intervention, check to determine if the student is more cooperative than before you started by going to the student at an appropriate time and asking, "Will you try that just for me?" Or, "Will you stop doing that just for me?"

The one-sentence intervention was developed and researched to provide specific help to teachers who are dedicated to building better relationships with children.

This intervention is based upon research that shows that a student's improved behavior or cooperation can be traced and linked to the personal connection he/she developed with a special adult.

As you read on, you will become more and more aware of how Love and Logic techniques are designed to enhance relationships between students and teachers. The structural setup of these techniques is based on three basic "rules."

PEARL
▼

Saying the following to a student gives you the opportunity to model a good response to any critique you might get as a result of the question:
"We've been around each other a lot, and I'm wondering if anything I do gets on your nerves.
If so, I'd really like to know."

Love and Logic Experiment #1

STUDENT:

I'm not staying after school and you can't make me!

TEACHER:

Don't worry about it. We can do it any time.

Let's call your parent and see which day this week

would be convenient.

CHAPTER THREE

The Three Rules
of Love and Logic

*L*ove and Logic is designed to provide a beacon or guide as you attempt to solve the vast spectrum of behaviors that confront you in the classroom. It is not a system designed to replace your present system. Nor should it complicate your life.

After attending many seminars and reading many books promoting complicated systems, I would often return to school overloaded with new methods—most of which were complex, required additional study on my part, and called for an exceptional memory. Unfortunately, my memory is at its worst when I'm faced with a problem child in the midst of everything else that goes on in a classroom. In spite of the books and seminars, when a problem situation arose, I would immediately find myself in the emotional state and, as a result, reverting to my old habits of lecturing and threatening.

I had an additional problem. The consultants who brought their ideas to our school often approached us by telling us that everything we had been doing so far was wrong and strongly advised that we immediately switch to their new system. This usually left me feeling guilty and unsure of my position as an authority figure in the classroom. The result was that when students acted out, I was rendered ineffective—unsure that I should rely on my old system and not able to remember the new one.

People Learn from Their Own Decisions

Our institute was eventually motivated to study the psychology of behavior in a way that was new for us. We analyzed the writing and research to look for common threads and made an important discovery: All effective systems allow people to learn from the results of their own decisions.

We created the Four Basic Principles of Love and Logic, which you will probably agree are present in most success-ful human interactions: 1) share the control, 2) share the thinking, 3) balance consequences with empathy, and 4) maintain self-concept. These principles will be covered more thoroughly later in this book.

Since some of these principles are still somewhat avant-garde, we are constantly searching for ways to make them easy to practice and simple to remember. At the time of this book's writing, I remember best how to use them by thinking of Love and Logic as having three basic rules:

- Use enforceable limits
- Provide choices within limits
- Apply consequences with empathy

Use Enforceable Limits

The effective application of limits requires that chil-dren have implied choices and be forced into the thinking mode. It is impossible to set limits by ordering, "Don't you talk to me in that tone of voice! You get a civil tongue in your mouth right this minute!" Telling kids how to run their lives usually makes things worse.

Love and Logic limit-setting is a matter of telling kids how you will be running your life. Handling the same situation, a Love and Logic teacher would say, "I'll be glad to listen to you when your voice sounds like mine."

I knew one teacher who, for years, tried to order kids around about turning in their assignments. One day she discovered that it just didn't create the desired effect and she decided to experiment with the Love and Logic approach to setting this limit.

The next day, the students saw two wire baskets on the teacher's desk. There was a sign on each one. One sign read, "Papers to be graded tonight." The other sign read, "Papers to be graded during the summer."

STUDENTS: What's this?

TEACHER: Just what it says. I'll be grading all the on-time papers tonight and the late papers during the summer.

STUDENTS: If you grade the late papers during the summer, how are we supposed to graduate?

TEACHER: I don't know.

The teacher reports that the number of on-time papers increased dramatically when she quit telling the kids how to run their lives and started telling them how she was going to run hers.

This approach to setting limits forces students into the thinking mode, implying that there are choices to be made. Each has its own consequence. Love and Logic teachers refer to this technique as "the enforceable statement."

Our words can be either garbage or gold in a child's life. "Garbage" statements are idle, useless words that tell someone else what to do, yet give us no power to enforce them. Although these statements may be based on positive principles, they do not produce positive results. "Gold" statements are based on positive principles, but show empathy and encourage children to think and work things out for themselves. Their power lies in putting responsibility where it belongs—on the person with the problem—while showing that you care.

Provide Choices Within Limits

Human beings have a strong need for control. A great many of the issues we deal with each day have to do with control. There is a basic rule in psychology that says, "I either give the other person control on my terms, or he will take it on his terms."

Have you ever seen a teacher try to take control of a situation with, "You get yourself to the time-out area right now! And you stay there until I tell you to come back!"?

How long does it take the student to regain control? It's almost immediate, as the student moves as slowly as he/she possibly can toward the time-out area. And once the youngster is in time-out, what happens? Tapping, rocking of the chair, humming, belching, and often the production of noxious fumes. The teacher can no longer work with the other children, having become totally involved with the offending student, who now has, on his/her *own* terms, total control.

TURN YOUR GARBAGE INTO GOLD

GARBAGE	GOLD
Unenforceable Statements:	*Enforceable Statements:*
• Open your books to page 54.	• I'll be working from page 54.
• I'm not going to line you up until everyone is quiet.	• I'll be lining people up as soon as it's quiet.
• Don't sharpen your pencil while I'm talking.	• I allow people to sharpen pencils when I am not giving directions.
• You can't go to the rest room until I finish the directions.	• Feel free to go to the rest room when I'm not giving directions.
• Don't be bothering your neighbors.	• You're welcome to stay with us as long as you and others are not bothered.
• Turn your assignment in on time or you'll get a lower grade.	• I give full credit for papers turned in on time.
• Don't try to turn in sloppy papers to me.	• I'll be glad to accept all papers that meet the neatness standard for this room.
• Raise your hand if you want to talk to me.	• I'm sure you're anxious to talk, and I listen to people who raise their hands. Thank you.

Compare this situation to one in which the teacher knows how to share control. She offers the student a portion of the control upfront, on her terms, so that the student's self-respect remains intact. "Would you rather work quietly with us, or would you rather be in the time-out area? It's really up to you. If you decide to go to time-out, please come back as soon as you can handle it. I'd love to have you back. Thank you."

It's obvious which teacher brings out the best in students. It's also obvious which teacher goes home most angry and tired at the end of the school day and which has the most fun.

The name of the game in teaching is getting kids to cooperate. Love and Logic teachers agree that they get the best cooperation when they remember to provide a lot of choices throughout the day.

Caution! Never offer one choice you like and one you don't. A student will invariably go for the one you don't like. Be sure to offer two choices—either of which will make you deliriously happy. *Consider the following examples:*

- "Would you guys rather wear your coats out to recess, or would you rather carry them?"

- "This assignment needs to be completed this week. Would you rather make the deadline Thursday or Friday? It's up to you."

- "Today you have your choice of working alone or with a friend. You decide."

✐ "Would you rather play by the rules, or learn about the game by watching the others play? Let me know what you think."

For years I taught teachers and parents that when they found themselves in a difficult situation with kids, it was best to offer some choices. While this looks good in print and seems excellent in theory, I finally realized that I was asking others to do something that was also difficult for me. Very few people find it easy to think of choices when they are upset. When I get into the emotional state, the only choice I can think of is, "Do you want to live or die?" Not a very professional thought.

The Savings Account Approach

Love and Logic teachers approach choices and the sharing of control in a slightly different manner:

✎ **LOVE AND LOGIC TIP #3:**
Rules for Giving Choices

1. Always be sure to select choices that *you* like. Never provide one you like and one you don't, because a child seems to have a sixth sense in selecting the one you don't like.

2. Never give a choice unless you are willing to allow the child to experience the consequence of that choice.

3. Never give choices when the child is in danger.

4. Never give choices unless you are willing to make the choice for the child in the event he/she does not choose within ten seconds.

5. Your delivery is important. Try to start your sentence with:
  • You're welcome to—or—.
  • Feel free to—or—.
  • Would you rather—or—?
  • What would be best for you—or—?

---

*The time to offer choices is when you are happy
and everything is going smoothly.*

It is relatively easy to think of choices during these times. Love and Logic teachers try to offer as many choices as possible when there are no problems, at those times when it's simple to create a "savings account" of control, using such phrases as "That's your choice" and "You decide."

Keep in mind that in each of these situations the student is not making decisions that have a direct effect upon the teacher. The kids are making decisions about issues that affect only their own lives. The teacher has already made appropriate adult decisions before giving the kids their choices.

The concept behind the "savings account" approach is that as each student develops a sense that control is shared in a healthy way by the teacher, there is no longer a need for the student to fight for control. This opens the door for the adult to take withdrawals from the account when necessary.

A withdrawal from the account would be, "Hey, team. Aren't I usually pretty reasonable? Don't I let you make a lot of your own decisions? I do, don't I? Well, it's my turn this time. Thanks for understanding that I need to decide this time."

*The easiest student to boss around
is one who believes that the teacher is reasonable
and takes control only when necessary.*

I once had a parent approach me during a parenting course. The conversation went like this:

PARENT: Are you saying that kids are happy with decisions whether they are big ones or little ones?

JIM: Yes.

PARENT: Are you saying that if I let them decide about a lot of little decisions, I create a "savings account" from which I can make withdrawals?

JIM: Yes again.

PARENT: How about little decisions, such as "Do you want to wear red socks or blue socks?" Or "Do you want to go to your room with your feet touching the ground or not touching the ground?"

JIM: Right again.

PARENT: Are you saying I should not let them make decisions that affect others, but only ones that directly affect them? And, if I do that often enough, I should be able to boss them around more easily?

JIM: You've got it.

"Oh, rats!" she said before departing. "Now I have to go home and apologize to my husband. I've been telling him that he was a wimp. I don't know how many times I have said to him: 'Be a man. Let those kids know who's boss. I

get sick and tired of all those choices you give the kids!'
Now that I understand the savings account approach, I
know why the kids always behave better for him. He is a
master at collecting deposits."

She had seen him do it the previous night, right in
the middle of the kids' favorite television program.

HUSBAND: Okay, guys. Turn off the TV. Go to bed.

KIDS: Oh, no! We want to see the end of the
                program!

HUSBAND: Well, do you want to go to bed now or
                wait until the show is over?

KIDS: We want to wait till it's over.

HUSBAND: Well, you have to decide things like that.

Later, when the show was over, he collected a whole
series of deposits by encouraging the kids to make a
series of decisions:

HUSBAND: Now, do you want a drink of water
                before you go to bed, or no water?

KIDS: Water! We need water!

HUSBAND: Good. Do you want kitchen water or
                bathroom water?

Then they had to decide about a piggyback ride, whether they had a story or not, whether they went to sleep with the light on or off, whether or not they had the door open and whether they went to sleep with the blankets on or off.

By that time, the kids were begging to stay up a little longer. But this is when he took his withdrawal from the account, saying, "Wait a minute. Who's been making all the decisions around here tonight? You guys, right? Don't I get a turn once in a while? Thanks for understanding. Time for bed!"

Translating this example to the classroom, is it more fun to sit around the teachers' lounge complaining about how bad kids are today? Or is it more fun to sit around dreaming up all the choices kids in your school can make?

You can't take a withdrawal from an account when there have been no deposits.

Apply Consequences with Empathy

The concept of logical and natural consequences has been around for many years. However, many teachers have experimented with this idea and abandoned its use, reporting disappointment with the results. These teachers commonly say that many kids don't seem to learn from consequences.

After observing hundreds of teachers applying consequences in behavior management, it has become obvious to me that some teachers are effective in their use of consequences and others are not. The reason for the success of the technique employed by the effective teacher is obvious even to the casual observer.

The effective teacher administers consequences
with empathy and understanding,
as opposed to anger and lecture.

The concept of balancing consequences with empathy was first reinforced for me after a speech I gave in Vail, Colorado. A woman rushed up to me after the speech to say, "Jim, I want you to know that I got up at 4:00 this morning and drove 135 miles just to hear you speak." You can imagine how proud I felt hearing this, until she added, "Yes, because you ruined our school. I'm a parent at a school where you conducted one of your seminars. The teachers applied your techniques, and they didn't work. Now the kids, teachers, and parents are all angry."

She went on. "I came here to give you a piece of my mind, but now that I heard your presentation today, I know what went wrong. Those teachers must have heard every word you said that day except for the most important one—empathy. They applied consequences all right, but with anger and intimidation. They didn't apply consequences with understanding and empathy."

She said that she wanted to help them understand this new concept but first wanted to be certain that she understood what I was teaching that day. She proceeded to recapitulate: "The attention of children is easily captivated by emotion. When the teacher displays anger, the child gets caught up in the anger. Since humans can only think of one thing at a time, the child is so busy thinking about the adult's anger, there is little thought about the mistake or new plan of behavior. The result is that the consequence does not register in the child's mind the way it should.

"When the adult uses empathy in describing the consequence, however," she continued, right ontrack, "the child's mind tends to focus on the mistake with more intensity. This leads the child to build a thought process about the mistake, perhaps including an awareness that it was his or her own decision that caused this mistake."

This wise woman from Colorado said that she now understood the concept and was prepared to go back to her child's school to let the teachers know what was wrong with them. My parting words to her should probably have been, "Be sure to use some empathy while you explain to the teachers!"

✎ **LOVE AND LOGIC TIP #4:**
Consequences with Empathy

Children learn from their mistakes when:
- They experience the consequences of their mistakes; and
- Adults in their environment provide empathy.

Bad choices have natural consequences. If David fails to wear a coat, he gets cold. If Jan misses the school bus, she stays home with an unexcused absence for the day.

Adults are tempted to scold and reprimand, but may be surprised to learn that children actually learn best from consequences when adults empathize:
- "I'm so sorry you're cold, David."
- "What a bummer that you missed an after-school party on the day you were absent, Jan."

If adults reprimand them, children may transform sorrow over their choice into anger with the adult—and the lesson may be lost.

If adults express sorrow, children have a significant learning opportunity. David may think, "Tomorrow I'll wear my coat." Jan may decide, "I'll get up fifteen minutes earlier tomorrow."

Consequences + Empathy = Learning

This experience concerned me so much that I went back to discuss the importance of the role of empathy in the application of consequences to behavior problems with Foster W. Cline, M.D., psychiatrist and cofounder of the Love and Logic Institute.

His position was that all great counselors, teachers, and parents rely heavily upon the consequence/empathy formula to help others create healthy problem-solving and decision-making. He also reminded me that in spite of its successful use, very little is written on the subject of the role of empathy in consequence application.

I have since been motivated to write and teach on the subject. Since that time, thousands of teachers have consciously applied this technique and enjoyed the dramatic results attained through balancing consequences with empathy.

Years into Minutes

A good example of the use of this technique was reported by a father who lives in Kansas. He called to tell about his daughter, who was having academic problems at school. He had become frustrated with her apparent lack of motivation. Each time she brought home a poor report card, he had become more enraged. He threatened, scolded, and punished with increased severity, none of which brought improvement in her school performance.

In desperation, he tried the consequence/empathy approach. The next time she brought home a report card with two F's, two D's, and a C. This time, he put his arm around her shoulder and said, "Aw, honey. This must feel awful for you, getting grades like that. I can't imagine how much it hurts. It must feel terrible to bring home a report card like that. I can't think of anything I could do to make you feel worse than to have a report card like that. I tell you what. You go back to school tomorrow and tell those teachers I will love you regardless of the number of years it takes you to get through seventh grade. Now, give me a hug."

His daughter looked up at him and screamed, "Years!? I don't have years to get through seventh grade! My friends are going on to eighth grade!"

"I know," Dad said. "But maybe they won't dump you just because you're a year behind them in school. Besides, you don't need them. You have me for a friend."

Dad reported that this was the first time he had seen his daughter concerned about her own grades. As soon as she owned the problem and had no other person to blame or fight, she did something about her grades.

A mistake can be a great teacher, provided the child is allowed to experience the consequences of the mistake. However, it is the empathy expressed by the adult that drives the pain of the consequence into his or her heart and turns experience into long-term memory and wisdom.

Another fine example of the empathy/consequence formula can be seen in the two different approaches used by these high school principals dealing with a fight resulting in a school suspension.

Situation A.

PRINCIPAL: You know better than to fight at this school. You knew before you did it that anyone who fights gets a three-day suspension. You're out of here until Friday. Don't come back on campus before that!

STUDENT: But you don't understand!

PRINCIPAL: I don't want to hear it. You heard what I said. Now get out!

What's happening as this student leaves the room? What's happening to the door? What's happening to the kids who are in his way as he leaves the office? What happens to the lockers as this kid goes down the hall? And what about the spray paint this evening? This principal brought out the worst in this youngster while enforcing the rule about automatic suspension for fighting in school.

Situation B.

PRINCIPAL: Wow! That must have been some fight. That kid must have really made you mad. Tell me about it.

STUDENT: Hey, man. He was calling down my mother. Nobody talks that way about my mother.

PRINCIPAL: Yeah, I guess I would have been pretty mad, too. And . . . a fight

around here will get you how many
days' suspension?

STUDENT: Three?

PRINCIPAL: There you go, Jed. I guess we'll get
to see you again on Friday. I'll look
forward to it. See you then.

What's happening as this student leaves the room? Is
he more angry, or is he confused? Which would you
rather have?

Whereas the first principal brought out the worst in
the student, the second brought out the best. Both principals applied the same consequences. One principal used
anger; the other, empathy. Which principal do you think
is the most tired at the end of the day? Which has the
most arguments each day? Which receives the most parent complaints? Which principal goes home with energy
to enjoy the evening?

PEARL
▼

*Sending students in the emotional state
to a new location gives them the underlying
message that they are capable of handling
their situation on their own.*

Love and Logic Experiment #2

STUDENT:

I shouldn't have to memorize all this stuff.
It's irrelevant, because I'm gifted.

TEACHER:

Nice try, pal.

(Grin while you say this.)

⊖ ⊖ ⊖

Love and Logic Experiment #3

STUDENT:

I can't do it. It's too hard.

TEACHER:

Aren't you glad I don't believe that?

▼

CHAPTER FOUR

Finding Time for
Love and Logic Discipline

*I*t is tempting for educators to resist new techniques or approaches to working with children. One of the avoidance techniques employed by some teachers is, "I don't have time to work with children in the Love and Logic way."

I agree that teachers don't have the time they need to do their jobs. Society expects more from schools each year. Experienced Love and Logic teachers, however, consistently report that they spend less and less time on discipline and classroom control as their skills increase. The reason is that they deal with discipline problems on their own terms.

You control the discipline problems.
They do not control you.

Dealing with Discipline on Your Own Terms

The trick to controlling the time you spend on discipline is related to your ability to:

1. Build positive relationships with your students.

2. Set enforceable limits through enforceable statements.

3. Share control.

4. Implement disciplinary interventions that stop undesirable behaviors in their infancy, avoiding the need for consequences.

5. Delay consequences.

The first story in this book was about a principal who worked on a problem in very short sessions, each consisting of between five and twenty seconds. Parley Jacobs conducted each of these sessions on his terms, when he had the time. The student waited for Parley, who did not allow his schedule to be affected by the child's problem.

Compare this to what happens in many schools in which the staff believes that consequences must be applied instantly. In these situations, the adult feels a need to stop whatever he/she is doing and work with the child until a solution is found or consequences are applied.

This approach can be more time-consuming for several reasons:

- The student is in an emotional, rather than a thinking, state.

- The adult is more than likely stressed, having to take time away from present activities.

✍ The student gains a certain amount of power
by controlling the activities of the adult.

I have known children who prefer involving their
teachers in problem-solving rather than academics. In
these classrooms, teachers become increasingly frustrated, and kids spend less and less time learning.

The trick to finding time and being efficient with discipline is to follow Parley Jacob's example:

*Meet with kids on your time, on your terms,
with short, sweet interactions.
Ask brief questions.*

Short, Sweet Interactions

Consider this situation in which a student displayed
an obscene gesture when the class photograph was being
taken. Nobody knew it until the pictures were developed.
Parents were angry.

TEACHER: Alex, on a scale of 1 to 10, how great
a decision was that for you?

ALEX: I don't know.

TEACHER: What a bummer not to know. Well, I'm
busy right now. I'm going to have to give
some thought to what I'm going to do
about it. Go back to your seat, please.
When I have some time, I'll get back to
you. In the meantime, you might want
to try not to worry about it too much.

That was a twenty-two-second session. Later that day, while the other kids were doing seat work, the teacher went back to Alex and spent a total of fifteen seconds:

TEACHER: Do you have enough money to pay the photographer to come back and take another picture?

ALEX: No way!

TEACHER: Well, paying for a new picture is one option. Maybe you can think of another one you like better. I'll get back to you on that.

At the end of the school day, the teacher went to Alex and spent another fifteen seconds:

TEACHER: You might want to talk with your parents about this soon, just in case I need to call them. I'm sure they'd rather hear it from you. I'll look forward to seeing you in the morning. Try not to worry about this. I'm sure you'll think up a solution. I hope it all works out for you.

Needless to say, Alex couldn't help but worry about the problem. The teacher was not giving it a rest. Besides, what do kids do when you say, "Don't worry about it."? They worry about it.

The next morning the teacher went to Alex while he was doing his seat work. This time, she spent about twenty-five seconds:

TEACHER: Alex, I've talked to the principal about your problem, and she thinks it would be best for you to bring us a solution before you return to school. Since you're already here, you can stay for the rest of the day. But a solution will be your ticket to return to school tomorrow.

Alex: I've got a solution.

Teacher: That's great, but I'm busy teaching right now. Maybe you can tell me your solution later.

Later that day, Alex suggested that he could write a letter of apology to each of the kids and their parents. He thought that if each one signed and returned the letter, his apology would be accepted. If that didn't work, he could try something else.

This is an example of a problem that, in the past, has consumed many hours of teacher, parent, and administrator time in other schools. No school I have known has escaped kids acting up in school pictures.

This teacher handled the problem efficiently, exerting a minimum of time and effort. At the same time, she applied the three rules of Love and Logic. She set enforceable limits, provided choices within limits, and allowed the consequences to do the teaching. Furthermore, she was understanding and compassionate. The self-concepts of both the student and the teacher were enhanced.

Discipline situations can become
self-concept builders—for everyone involved.

Dealing with Kids Who Feed off Each Other

Teachers often find themselves in the frustrating situation in which more than one student is misbehaving. The teacher in this situation finds him/herself unable to deal effectively with one child because others are interrupting or supporting the misbehaving youngster.

The following process has been effective for many Love and Logic teachers. You will notice that it involves several of the concepts presented in preceding chapters. When there are classroom disruptions caused by children who feed off each other, the way to solve the problem is:

1. Make a list of the students involved and prioritize the list. Put the most compliant of the students at the top of the list and the least compliant at the bottom.

2. Divide and conquer. Arrange with fellow teachers to provide a chair in the rear of their classrooms so that you can send the students, one at a time, to separate classrooms to sit and think out their behavior. You will need one room for each student. Your student will not be expected to participate with the other class. Each student goes with the understanding that he/she may return to class when that will not result in any form of disruption.

3. Meet with the principal to describe your solution and ask for support. "I am doing this because I cannot allow these children to continue to disrupt the class. I don't want to make a problem for you, so if any one of these children acts out in the temporary classroom, I'd like him/her to come to you for a 'cool-down' period. Please don't feel a need to do anything other than allow the student to cool down and then return to my class when ready."

4. When the disruption starts, you have two options, depending upon the strength of the leader of the group. In the event that you can move the group leader out to another location, do that first and then say to the other group members, "Do you guys think you can get yourselves back together, or do I need to find another place for you?"

In the event that you question the ease with which you can remove the leader:

☞ Go to the first student (most compliant) on the list and say, "That is not acceptable. Mr. Sawyer has a place in his room for you until you can get yourself back together. You may return when you know that you can be here without causing a problem. Thank you."

☞ As soon as this one has left the room, go to the next student on the list and say, "Mrs. Babcock is expecting you in her room. You may return as soon as you can be here without causing a problem. Thank you."

☞ Continue this process until you get to the last student (least compliant) and say, "Now, do you think you can behave here, or would you rather go to a different room until you can? Thank you."

You may find it helpful to send another student to make sure the individuals have gone to their assigned rooms.

5. Implement the "One-Sentence Intervention" with the children who are troublemakers:

✏ Start noticing positive and personal attributes of the student. Mention them in private. For example, "Jeremy, I notice you are really interested in baseball cards."

✏ Do this a couple of times per week for three weeks. Each time, notice something different. Be careful not to judge. Remember that troubled children feel manipulated when teachers say, "I like . . ."

✏ Experiment with the following when this student starts to misbehave: "Jeremy, will you stop doing that, just for me? Thank you." Children who have fallen in love with their teacher are far more cooperative.

6. Start having "heart to heart" talks with these students after school. Meet with them one at a time. The idea here is not to solve the problem all at once, but to plant some seeds of thought in the student's mind:

TEACHER:	Jeremy, I noticed that you've been having a hard time behaving when you're around your friends. Are you aware that this makes it hard for me to teach?
JEREMY:	I guess.

TEACHER: There are several different reasons why this happens with some kids. Sometimes it's because they hate the teacher, sometimes they're afraid that the work is too hard, sometimes it's because the kids are part of organized crime, sometimes it's because things aren't going well at home, and sometimes it's because the kids need friends so badly that they're willing to act out in class to be part of the group. Does anything sound familiar to you?

JEREMY: I don't know.

TEACHER: Well, that's sad not to know. Thanks for giving it some thought. I'll see you. By the way, do you think this behavior is going to change by tomorrow?

JEREMY: Yeah, I guess.

TEACHER: Thanks, Jeremy. I'm sure that would be best for all of us.

7. Continue the "heart to heart" talks until a better relationship is developed between teacher and student. In the event that things are not better the next day, the following conversation may be helpful:

TEACHER: Say, Jeremy, I didn't see a great improvement in your behavior today. Do you hate me?

JEREMY: No.

TEACHER: Guess what it looks like to me.

JEREMY: I don't know.

TEACHER: I'm thinking that either I have done
             something terrible that you don't
             want to tell me about, or that you
             need your friends so badly, you have
             to continue to act up just to look
             good to them. I'm wondering if
             you'd be happier with a different
             teacher, or a different place to sit in
             the classroom, or what? (You would
             not make this statement if you had
             concerns about actually making a
             change in seating assignments.)
             What are your thoughts?

8. These techniques usually solve the problem. In the event that they don't, consider reassigning one or more of these students. There are times when the best solution is to break up the group. It never serves the best interests of the child, the class, or the teacher for a group to stay together when it has become dysfunctional. This is a time when the teacher needs to set aside personal feelings of "not wanting to give up" on the child or problem.

Although this section looks at eight different concepts, the most important aspect of this problem remains the quality of the relationship between teacher and students. Students who have a strong level of caring for their teachers usually become more cooperative when invited to do so.

A coercive or adversarial classroom climate tends to encourage negative group behavior when there are several students who lack the confidence to be successful in the classroom.

The following chapter deals with norms teachers must face in their day-to-day attempts to discipline and control, as well as internalized control, external enforcement, and learning to see the difference between the source and the symptom.

PEARL
▼

When they state the standards themselves, students do better than when they simply listen to you lay down the law.

Love and Logic Experiment #4

STUDENT:

We get to chew gum in the other classes.

TEACHER:

I'm sure that's true.

And what's the rule in *this* room?

STUDENT:

But it's not fair.

TEACHER:

I know, and what's the rule in this room?

✏ ✏ ✏

Love and Logic Experiment #5

STUDENT:

Do we have to do this assignment?

TEACHER:

Only if you want credit for it.

CHAPTER FIVE

▼

Discipline
and Control

*A*s a student in the Iowa public schools, I (David Funk) experienced discipline a bit differently than students experience it now. I vividly remember sitting on the porch with my best friend and discussing the world as a ten-year-old sees it. That discussion was the beginning of my understanding of societal norms.

Once we discussed at length whether adults could make kids do things that kids didn't want to do. We examined our experiences and could list a number of times this had happened. For instance, parents could make you eat what you didn't want to, or make you go to bed when they decided it was time. Our conversation then turned to teachers. They could make kids either do their work or stay in from recess.

After a lengthy discussion, we came to our conclusion: Yes, adults can make kids do things that kids don't want to do. This was generally accepted by all kids, because I can't remember any who thought they had "rights." I do recall bringing this up once with my dad, who simply replied, "You'll have rights when you pay the rent." At the time, that seemed reasonable, and the subject didn't come up again.

Norms Teachers Must Face

Norm #1: Do Kids Have Rights? Today, things are different. There are lots of students who give teachers lots of trouble. Moreover, there are many students who feel they are entitled to do so. A fairly common phrase teachers hear from students is "I've got rights." The fact is, they do. Students may indeed have more rights than any teacher in the school situation. The problem this creates is that old techniques that worked years ago with kids who had no rights simply do not work with kids who do. Kids today not only know they have them; they flaunt the fact that they have them.

One educator who relies upon a set of core Love and Logic beliefs is David Funk, who wrote this chapter and who has spent many years analyzing Love and Logic principles and applying them in his teaching and in his work as a school administrator in the New Berlin Public Schools, in New Berlin, Wisconsin. He also serves as professor and administrator for Aurora University.

We can no longer argue whether or not youngsters have rights. In some instances they do, and in others they don't.

The important thing to remember is:
Students who believe that their rights are
being violated do not respond positively
to teachers' requests.

This is especially true when teachers rely on orders and threats that were effectively used on *them* by teachers when *they* were children.

Norm #2: The Future As an Extension of the Past. Teachers need to face another societal norm that may insidiously sabotage effective discipline and teaching. If you believe that the future is an extension of the past— and you have a tendency to look at what once worked and think, if it worked before, it should work again if we simply intensify or refine it—it's time for you to revamp your thinking.

If you believe that old techniques would work if people would just act the way they used to, you already have a discipline problem difficult to solve.

An example related to discipline involves the concepts developed from operant conditioning, the basis of behavior modification applied extensively to education. B. F. Skinner laboriously studied the behavior of animals (primarily rats and pigeons) and contributed significant insights to how behavior is shaped. Not long after this, some educators decided that students were just like rats and pigeons. B. F. Skinner's observations were then translated for application to education, and a generation of students was exposed to behavior modification and programmed learning.

To a large degree these methods were accepted because, at least in certain circumstances, they worked. They also came at a time when teachers needed help. In the turbulent 1970s, teachers could no longer simply rely on the fact that since they were the teachers, kids were compelled to obey them. Teachers needed new techniques that would cause kids to behave.

Eventually, old behavior modification techniques of reward, variable schedules of reinforcement, and token economics lost their effectiveness. My suspicion is that students realized they were being manipulated. Once this awareness is in place, behavior modification doesn't work.

Faced with the ineffectiveness of behavior modification in the classroom, many educators who still subscribed to the "future is an extension of the past" mindset attempted to refine and extend behavior modification instead of giving it up. Thus, a plethora of commercialized discipline programs were developed. They sold well because they were built on the operant conditioning premise that was already accepted by a significant number of professionals within education.

Norm #3: It's Not My Fault. The concept of "external locus of control" is simple graduate-level vocabulary for "it's not my fault." It takes little research to confirm that we humans live by this concept.

People excuse all sorts of inappropriate behaviors by placing the blame on something or someone outside themselves.

Look at these phrases. They may seem familiar. Perhaps they have been spoken by people you know well— very well:

- No wonder I drive so fast, living with someone like her.
- I drink too much because I have the disease alcoholism.

- I'm a fiery redhead—I lose my temper easily.
- I couldn't possibly lose weight without my counselor.
- I got an F because the teacher doesn't like me.

The ultimate case involved the defense of a girl who had killed another child while stealing the victim's coat. Her defense attorney offered the plea that the girl was suffering from "urban stress syndrome" and, therefore, was not responsible for her actions. The jury denied this defense, but who knows when such a plea might become acceptable?

This norm strongly affects discipline in our society today because many of our "helping professions" depend upon our believing this. People search for and find extraordinary reasons to explain why people do what they do and find more "disabilities" than one might think possible. This greatly affects discipline when we are working to help students learn to take responsibility for their own behavior and internalize controls.

When the "normal" thing is to blame someone or something outside ourselves, it is a challenge to interact with students in ways that will orient them to an internalized locus of control.

Norm #4: Achievement Determines Worth. Here is a norm that greatly affects a student's performance. As educators, we want students to achieve, not only for school standards but because we know that achievement can increase students' positive feelings about themselves. However, when many students engage in *competitive* achievement, we end up with winners and losers. The winners function fine. The losers invariably become the source of significant discipline problems. It is only natural that students who cannot achieve and relate this inability to their sense of personal worth will compensate in ways to relieve the accompanying emotional overlays that come with the pain of failure.

> *When achievement is considered an extension of ourselves rather than a measure of our worth, there are usually no discipline ramifications.*

Later, we will discuss how to help students achieve their own potential without harboring negative emotions for those achieving at a different level.

Norm #5: I See, I Want, I Believe I Deserve. Another norm we have to contend with in the classroom is represented by the phrase "I see, I want, I believe I deserve." People who believe they *deserve* something will react differently than those who feel they have *earned* something. Personally, I think it is far easier to appreciate what you have earned than to appreciate what you believe you deserve.

Students today are much more accustomed to having privileges. They are fed this need by radio, television, billboards, and other commercial entities. There are advertisements for fast food enticing us to not wait for a meal, the cosmetic industry convincing us we deserve to have luxurious hair, automobile manufacturers persuading us that we merit a car that will put us a step above everyone else.

Those who lock in to this cultural norm can become terminally egocentric. After all, if all these things accrue to me, I start to expect them—without any thought of expending any effort to get them. To the extreme, those in this mind-set become resistant to having controls exerted over them. They believe that because they are special, they don't have to follow rules applicable to "little people" or be responsible for their own behavior. If things don't work, well, obviously it's someone else's fault.

Other Factors That Affect Discipline

In addition to societal norms, there are other circumstances within our culture to be considered when developing an overall discipline plan.

Legal Aspects. Discipline is one of the major areas in which teachers are susceptible to litigation. Teachers today must be aware and prepared for such factors as disciplining students within a due process procedure, malpractice accusations, and pressures from special interest parent groups. In addition, there are legal considerations to keep in mind when disciplining special education students, because of limits on disciplinary measures for behaviors related to or resulting from the condition that handicaps them. (See Chapter Thirteen for an important discussion of legal considerations.)

Changes in Family Dynamics. Children need stability and security in which to develop. In today's world, family stability is not as prevalent as it once was. With the disruption of divorce, rising abuse and neglect statistics, drug and alcohol issues, loss of trust, and a host of other social maladies, many children grow up in an atmosphere of confusion with resulting maladjustment and behavior problems that show up at school. It takes a community to fully raise a child.

Effects of the Media. The classic comment, "The medium is the message" was more than a simple observation—it was a prophesy. Movies and television consume hours of the typical student's day; as a result, their influence is great. Kids see thousands of acts of violence, mistreatment of women, and erotica. Perhaps even more subtly, they see major interpersonal conflicts resolved in a half hour—fifteen seconds in commercials—and other non-real-life situations. Many students have grown up with children's programming that offers changes every few seconds, strongly affecting their attention span. All of these factors form perceptions that lead to certain expectations. When our expectations are not met, negative behavior often follows.

Effects of Technology. Technology has opened a world of learning and enables significantly increased output. However, there have been technological boomerangs that have disrupted the environment, invaded our privacy, and betrayed the promise of a better quality of life. We consider many things commonplace that were in the realm of science fiction only a few years ago, but there is a price to pay. We increasingly demand more speed, so we lose the opportunity to contemplate. We require perfection, so we lose the opportunity to develop experience and wisdom and learn from our mistakes. Students who feel disenfranchised as persons often seek to assert their humanity by displaying aberrant behavior and disrupting the system.

In addition to factors that directly affect discipline, other aspects confront educators on a daily basis. There are always new ideas to try. Curricula become outdated. New technological skills become necessary to learn. Students feel unprepared for school.

Seldom does anyone suggest that we stop awhile to reflect on a constant that has worked for most of humankind for as long as there has been human history: interaction dynamics between people.

Although this will be explored more fully later in this book, we want teachers to know, early on, that effective interaction between teacher and student is a primary goal of Love and Logic. Great teachers are always looking for ideas that can improve their relationships with kids. When they hear a new idea, and associate it with a particular student, sometimes a workable solution is born. Many top-notch teachers actually look forward with great anticipation to a kid messing up so the experiment can continue. "Come on, kid. Make my day. Have I got a surprise for you," the teachers think. If the plan works, they use it. If it doesn't, they retool.

Internalized Control vs. External Enforcement

Before we go further in this book, our understanding of the word "discipline" needs to be established. In many of my classes and workshops, we ask participants to indicate what they associate with the word "discipline." Commonly, the words "rules," "punishment," and "enforcement" are used. From the time of the pilgrims, the idea has been perpetuated that discipline is the breaking of a person's will—a tearing-down process.

In fact, there is another aspect of discipline—a building-up process. If I were an athlete—and for those who have ever seen me, you know that I am not—would I not have to build *up* my body in order to succeed? Would I not have to build myself *up* in a healthy way to make the team or participate in the Olympics?

Love and Logic says that discipline involves building students *up* so they feel more capable—better about themselves, in a healthy way, even after a discipline situation. For this to be accomplished, we must consider internalized control vs. external enforcement.

When I was in seventh grade, I went to a small school in rural Iowa. Our teacher was a former Marine drill sergeant and he ran his class the way he ran his troops. Had you walked into his class you would have seen kids reading books and writing on paper in a well-controlled classroom—that is, while he was in the classroom. When Mr. Fowler left the room, do you suppose we continued sitting in our seats engaged in our schoolwork? Not on your life! All students (except the one kid who always did right) were out of their seats, testing the limits of what could be done without getting caught.

We became very creative. We assumed roles we never could play when Mr. Fowler was present. On a rotating basis, one of the boys would take guard duty. This was a solemn position because the welfare of the other students was at stake. It was a job that required diligence and concentration and the consequences for failure were severe. Our school was two stories tall and had wooden floors that squeaked. We had refined our auditory perception to the point that we could tell where someone was on the basis of those squeaks—down the hall, coming up the stairs, or just around the corner. The duty of the sentry was to listen for these and warn other compatriots in time for them to return to their work before Mr. Fowler returned.

When I look back on this, I see a contradiction:

*Although we were controlled when Mr. Fowler
was present, we were far from being a
"disciplined" group.*

Wouldn't it be nice to have a class of kids that you know could be left for a time and would honor your request to work on their math or to continue their free reading? *That* would be a disciplined class.

For this to be accomplished, something more powerful than external enforcement must exist. That something consists of internal controls and values. They are much more powerful.

Let me use a family experience as an example. Since the time our own children were in elementary school, my wife, Diane, and I have been foster parents to pre-adoptive infants. That is, we care for babies from the time they leave the hospital to the time they are adopted or returned to their birth mother. As foster parents, we are obligated to follow a plethora of regulations, and there are penalties for violations. Simplistically, the state says, "If you don't take good care of those children, we will do something bad to you." This is the "law of the land," waiting out there to exert external controls should we breach some regulation.

However, there is another factor to consider in this case. For lack of a better term, we will call this the "law of love." This is internal, and my observation of my wife is that this internal law is much more powerful than the external, that the external is really of little effect. Because Diane loves those babies, she will do far more for them than the state would ever require.

Although we get a stipend (we figure a whopping 7.5 cents per hour), she spends more on clothes, decorations, occasional babysitters, and diapers than we could ever

— 65 —

expect to recover. She nurtures the babies, comforts them when they are sick, and makes sure each has his or her own individually selected stuffed animal as a present when it is time to go to a permanent home.

She does much more than the state law requires
with little consciousness of it.
Her behavior is compelled by internalized love,
not externalized law.

So, are we as teachers going to rely on external controls to maintain student behavior, or are we going to orient ourselves toward working with students to develop internalized controls? Do we want to *make* kids behave, or get them to *want to* behave?

There is another aspect to consider. Within the framework of Love and Logic, discipline is an integral part of the teaching process. I recall several years ago hearing a high school English teacher say, "If it weren't for those three boys in my class, I could do some real teaching." There was the distinct impression that she considered discipline an intrusion.

There may be another way of looking at discipline. It can be what we do *with* kids rather than what we do *to* them. I recall many years ago listening to a talk show interview with a famous feminist. As the conversation focused on male/female relationships, the speaker said, "When men realize sex is not something they do to women, lovemaking will be a whole lot better."

I think the same can be said about discipline: When we realize that discipline is not something we do *to* students, teaching will be a whole lot better.

*When we are actively engaged with students
in our overall instructional philosophy,
discipline can actually become
one of the most rewarding parts of teaching.*

The Source or the Symptom?

When I was heavily invested in behavior modification, I recall reading the comments of one author who said that internal drives would be changed if the behavior were altered. I remember questioning this at the time, but my involvement with operant conditioning was such that I tentatively accepted the premise and incorporated it into my philosophy of classroom management. To a very large degree, the classroom management strategies I was utilizing concerned only behavior. I gave precious little attention to the sources of those behavior problems.

Since my involvement with Love and Logic, my opinion of what needs to be addressed has significantly changed. From personal experience and the wisdom of others, I have concluded that if we address only the symptoms of behavioral problems rather than the source of those problems, we will be hard-pressed to have any long-term effect.

This was illustrated for me some years ago. I get migraine headaches and for years I treated this malady with medications that dealt with the symptoms of the problem: pain and nausea. As happens to many people taking pharmaceuticals, however, I built up a tolerance and had to take increasing amounts to obtain relief. Eventually I reached the point where I was "over-using" (a polite term for abusing) these medications and, as a result, damaged my kidneys. I mentioned this to my brother and he recommended a headache clinic.

My response was instantaneous: I had gone to doctors and clinics before; what was this one going to do that the others couldn't? Besides, the place was about 100 miles away. He then looked me in the eye and said, "Dave, if you don't go, I'm going to tell Mom about your kidneys!" Well, I didn't want that, so I acquiesced.

I'm glad I did because, after a thorough checkup, the doctors at that clinic determined that my headaches were triggered by a body chemistry imbalance and prescribed a medication, not to deal with the pain and nausea, but with the imbalance—the source of the problem. Did it work? It sure did. My headaches went from two to three a week to perhaps one per month, and even those were not nearly as severe as my headaches used to be. My lesson: Deal with the source of a problem, not the symptoms.

In relating this to discipline, I recalled what Foster Cline, one of the originators of Love and Logic, mentions in one of his works:

Avoidance of pain is the source of misbehavior.

That is a key to dealing with discipline problems in the classroom. For the most part, we can reduce misconduct by responding to its psychological origin.

Autonomy and Self-Concept. Although there may be several of these sources, two that significantly impact classroom performance are the issues of autonomy and self-concept. We all want to have some control over our own lives and when we feel we are losing that control, we will fight to the end to get it back. Likewise, if our sense of self-worth is being attacked, we will rise at all costs to defend it. Our needs for autonomy and self-concept are so powerful that we will sometimes engage in conduct that is detrimental to ourselves in order to hang onto them. Consider the teenager who drives recklessly to show how tough he is, or the student who fails a class to prove the teacher can't make her do anything she doesn't want to do.

For teachers to be successful in today's classroom, we must have a different set of skills and expectations than our teachers had. Today's educators need to teach more than just academic skills for our students to be successful. We must rely on development of inner wisdom and deal with kids at an interpersonal level.

PEARL
▼

When a student's or a teacher's need is unspoken, there is fertile ground for resentment.

Love and Logic Experiment #6

STUDENT:

(Enters class with a negative look on his face, throws himself down into his chair and rolls his eyes toward the ceiling.)

TEACHER:

(With a whisper in his ear)

Looks like a rough morning. Any way I can help?

Let me know if there's anything I can do.

Would it be better to wait a little while before starting your work?

☙ ☙ ☙

Love and Logic Experiment #7

STUDENT:

I'm not doing this assignment, and you can't make me.

TEACHER:

(Whisper in student's ear)

Would you try it just for me? Thank you.

(Walk away before student can answer.)

▼

CHAPTER SIX

Perception
and Behavior

*E*very culture has identifiable behaviors that are gender, role, and age appropriate, which, to a large
degree, "control" a society. Whereas one culture, for example, will consider older people useless, another will emulate
them. Because the school is a microcosm of its culture,
there are similar forces working in every classroom.

Our Perception Is Our Reality

Consider the following concept: Perception is the driving
force of behavior. This idea may be so subtle that we don't
bring it to consciousness when addressing student performance, but it is a fundamental idea that we would do well to
explore in managing today's classrooms. Within the Love
and Logic philosophy, we believe that to affect disruptive,
volitional behavior on a long-term basis, we need to change
the perceptions that drive that behavior.

Not only is perception the driving force of behavior,
but it appears, from observing human behavior, that perception *becomes* reality.

A significant danger we all face is to interpret another person's behavior based on our own perceptions.

I (Dave Funk) recall one of the first times I went shopping with Diane, at the time my wife-to-be. She asked if I would go with her to buy a pair of slacks. I had purchased slacks before and had an experiential base and, therefore, an estimate of the time it would take. I calculated the distance to the mall and back, added a liberal amount of time for parking and thought to myself, "Sure, I've got half an hour to kill. Why not?"

You see, my record for buying slacks is 7 minutes, 56 seconds. That was part of my perception. Needless to say, Diane had a different experiential base and, therefore, a different perception. On that first shopping trip, I got a real education. When I buy slacks, they are usually a "replacement" pair. If I wear out my black slacks, that's what I usually look for at the store.

In this and the following chapter, David Funk presents essential concepts that are strong factors in determining forces that occur in every classroom.

I'm not into high fashion, so, although I deal with some of the same options as Diane (color, size, and style) I have fewer variables to consider. How many colors are there to choose from in men's dress slacks? Besides, as mentioned before, I usually am *replacing* a color.

Size is no problem. My in-seam has been the same since eighth grade. If I have purchased a 36-inch waist before, that's probably what I would be getting again. And style? For me there are two styles: pleated and unpleated. And I don't like pleated.

To my chagrin, when I went with Diane, the first thing we had to find was the right "department." We weaved in and out of sections labeled "misses," "juniors," "women's," and others I can't remember, until we came to "petites." I then realized that women's clothes are not determined by waist and in-seam (a common-sense idea as far as I am concerned), but, rather, size. And colors! Dozens of colors!

As Diane shopped, I studied, hoping I could accelerate the process with some analysis. I noticed once that she had picked a pair of slacks close to a little sign that said "5." That must be the size, I thought, and was rather pleased that I was learning the system so quickly. When Diane was in the dressing room, I went to a rack of slacks, mentally checking off the two variables I now knew (petite, 5). I picked a pair that seemed reasonable to me and, as Diane came out of the dressing room, handed them to her and said, "Here, I like these."

I was confident that she would acknowledge my insight and fast study. Instead, she took them and, to my surprise, looked at the manufacture's label. "These won't work," she said. "This brand runs large." I was stumped.

Eventually I was able to put this experience into a perspective that helped me with kids in my classroom. You see, there is the gender-bias wisecrack about how long it takes women to shop. Many males will believe that it's because women can't make decisions. After all, men can do in an hour what it takes women all day to accomplish, right? But the honest truth is that women may be making many more decisions. When men are confronted with as many variables (watch men at a hardware store looking for a new power tool), the behavior equalizes.

When we interpret another person's behavior through our own perception, we can run into some impassible barriers. As teachers, especially when disciplining students, an understanding of the student's perception, as well as our own, will be vitally important to not only be effective in our disciplining but to avoid the pitfalls of power struggles, passive-resistive behavior, and perpetuation of the offending perception.

Self-Worth and the Desire to Avoid Pain

When we are dealing with perception in relation to discipline, the following phrase, coined by James Rafini, comes to mind: "If I can't win, at least I can avoid losing." This is a perception that drives much of the misbehavior we see in kids. Almost all behavior has a positive spin in the perception of the person committing the offense.

A "positive spin" in the case of student misbehavior is often related to a desperate attempt to maintain a sense of self-worth.

Every day teachers see students engaging in behavior that allows them to avoid a sense of failure. Our society places inordinate value on ability, and the perceptual set of many of our students is that they must avoid any appearance that they have low ability. Failure to learn or perform to expectations is countered with failure-avoiding tactics that will "put the blame" on something other than the student's ability. When this blame is accomplished, there is no threat to self.

For instance, a student who anticipates failing a course may do absolutely nothing in class. The F can then be attributed to "I didn't do any work." Perhaps the student will misbehave to the point of being removed from the class. Then the reason for failure is that "the teacher got mad and kicked me out of class." Whatever the tactic, the source of the behavior is the same: Avoid the pain of insult to the sense of self-worth by putting blame anywhere other than on self.

So, we return to the principle that the source of most misbehavior is the desire to avoid pain.

It seems contrary to logic, then, to engage in discipline strategies that inflict more of what the student is trying to avoid.

How often have we seen teachers belittle students, embarrass them in front of their peers, take things away, and, generally, try to "break them down?"

In my experience, it seems that the more we work to change behavior rather than perception, the more the "fight or flight" principle comes into play. Students become aggressive or passive—in either case, using failure-avoiding tactics.

We all want to protect our sense of self-worth and avoid facing any lack of ability. Here are some tactics we are all certainly familiar with:

Blaming Others. It's easy to avoid personal pain by making a situation someone else's fault. Statements like "The teacher doesn't like me" or "They were unfair" are heard in schools everywhere. At the extreme, there are people who blame God, who seldom participates in these conversations. I remember one girl who blamed God for her pregnancy. To the best of my knowledge, only one person could legitimately make this claim. This girl blamed God because other girls were having sex and they didn't get pregnant.

Procrastination. Have you ever known someone who is given an assignment on Monday, due Friday, who does not work on it until late Thursday night? If a good job is not done, who's to blame? Time, of course! There was not enough time. "That's why the work was not up to my usual standard."

Discounting the Value. "This is a stupid class," can be a defense for a student who doesn't feel capable of performing. I remember one student I was testing some time ago who said, "Why should I have to learn how to read? I'm going to be an ophthalmologist." I'm not sure where he got his reasoning, but he believed it, nevertheless.

Noninvolvement. Have you ever had a student whose performance in your class was just above that of a fresh carrot? Many kids will perform at zero level and then blame the "F" on: "They didn't do nothin' in that stupid class."

Blaming Emotions. This is sophisticated, but sometimes blatantly offensive. Surely we have known people who blow up just as they realize failure is imminent and blame their lack of skill or perseverance on their "short temper" or the stress of their job.

Faulting Circumstances. Many years ago, one of my teaching peers, in a teacher's lounge conversation, said that he couldn't be expected to do his best teaching because the Board had not allocated enough money for his equipment needs. When it was pointed out to him that adequate, if not downright good, teaching could take place without this equipment, he made a defensive comment about our heads being in the clouds. And where did we get off telling him how to teach?

Our Field of Awareness

If we are going to teach and discipline in a manner that will be dealing with causal factors such as perceptions, we need to interact with students in such a way that sidesteps these responsibility-avoiding tactics. We must: (1) focus on the problem at hand and (2) give the offender no opportunity for displacement.

Focus on the Problem at Hand. We maintain our focus on the problem at hand by not being led on a "birdwalk"—a distracting departure from where we want to go. Here is an example of such a scenario:

TEACHER: Johnny, I want to talk to you about your behavior on the playground today.

JOHNNY: Yeah, well, Jamie hit me first and you never punish her because you like girls better, and that makes me so mad!

TEACHER: Johnny, I do not like girls better and I didn't know Jamie even hit you, and . . ."

And the birdwalk is on. The teacher allows the focus to be shifted from Johnny's behavior to gender preference. The teacher would have done better dealing only with Johnny's behavior until that situation was resolved:

TEACHER: Johnny, I want to talk to you about your behavior on the playground today.

JOHNNY: Yeah, well, Jamie hit me first and you never punish her because you like girls better, and that makes me so mad!

TEACHER: What we are talking about now is your behavior on the playground. We can address those other issues later.

Leaving No Room for Displacement. When dealing with failure-avoiding tactics, we can learn to give no opportunity for displacement. That is, we help the student being disciplined focus, in that moment, only on the behavior in question and who is responsible for changing it.

One of the most common ways teachers allow students to displace their responsibility is by giving them a high emotional overlay to react to. Teachers who get angry when disciplining give students the opportunity to focus on the anger instead of their behavior. Then, students ask questions such as, "Why is she so mad?" rather than, "Am I the one who needs to change my behavior? What do I need to do?"

Martin Covington and Richard Beery, in their book *Self-Worth and School Learning,* demonstrate that self-enhancement and protection are motives for human behavior. They establish two concepts:

*To protect that which is "us" is our primary goal,
and we will go to great lengths to do this.
People strive to be the best they can be,
given their field of awareness.*

These concepts are vital components in dealing with discipline situations. We can all probably think of several instances when someone we know has engaged in behavior that was detrimental, just to maintain an image. People lie about how much money they have, avoid situations in which they may appear to be inadequate, and cheat to appear more competent.

But the second concept, dealing with the field of awareness (how the world is viewed), can be far more powerful for teachers in dealing with students. Awareness relies on motivation. How many times have teachers been told that they must motivate their students to do their best, whether in academics, athletics, or behavior? I often wonder how many ergs of energy have been expended in this frustrating and often hopeless task. How do you make someone motivated? This becomes a moot question because people *are* motivated to enhance their sense of self-worth.

When I understood this, a great burden, bestowed upon me by the history of teacher training, was lifted. I no longer had to perform an impossible duty (i.e., motivate someone else), because I suddenly understood that people will motivate themselves.

What is my responsibility, and well within my abilities, is to change my students' field of awareness. I need to give my students information that will cause them to think differently about a situation.

Changing field of awareness is easy and it happens to us all the time. Have you ever said something in anger to a loved one and, as soon as you have said it, regretted saying it? The very process of saying something in anger triggers a response in you that causes you to think differently about the situation. At first, as you were saying the words, it seemed the only thing to do, given your field of awareness (i.e., your understanding of the situation, given your current perceptions). In this case, you may have been hurt and wanted to hurt back. But then, you hear yourself or see the effect on a loved one—an effect, perhaps, you didn't expect. Maybe you were anticipating the other person's anger, and saw that person's deep hurt instead. What matters is that your field of awareness has changed.

When your field of awareness is changed,
so is your motivation and subsequent behavior.

If you have ever apologized for an intentional act, this change in your motivation/behavior changed because of a change in your field of awareness.

Consider this generalized classroom scenario:

1. A student believes personal worth depends on accomplishments (e.g., grades, athletic achievement).

2. Ability is perceived as a critical component for attaining these accomplishments.

3. Ability, therefore, becomes a primary component of self-worth.

4. If success is unlikely or unanticipated, behaviors are utilized that minimize implications of lack of ability.

5. Student chooses apathy, aggressiveness, passive-resistive behavior to protect self.

There are several factors within the "system of education" that contribute to students maintaining their sense of self-worth through behaviors considered misconduct.

Achievement. In our schools, achievement is often the major criterion for measuring success. And our society tends to prefer success that comes from achievement that is the result of ability rather than effort. In other words, would you rather be known as "brilliant" or a "good little worker"? Since we all have varying abilities, this perception gives ample opportunity for failure.

Evaluation. Another factor that contributes to behavior and achievement problems is the extensive use of norm-referenced evaluation (i.e., comparing an individual student's performance with the performance of others, rather than with him- or herself or an objective standard or goal). From early on, parents compare their baby's development with that of the neighbor's kid. Worse, some parents engage in a desperate attempt to make sure their child has an "edge up" on neighboring children and start a frantic, competitive cycle of clubs, lessons, and enrichment activities. This attitude puts kids in jeopardy, because they begin to believe "I am good only if I am better than someone else." Here lie the foundations for racism, sexism, and a variety of emotional problems.

By comparing people with other people to determine who is acceptable, we run headlong into a number of problems related to discipline.

Norm-referenced situations severely limit students' experiences of success. Only the A's and B's are considered successful. C is average, which in our society is negative. Who wants to be known as an average lover, or be nominated as Average Teacher of the Year? In the same way, a D means the student tried, but was too dumb to make it. That leaves F as the only way some students can avoid a sense of failure. As we've already learned, they can attribute such a grade to many situations that have nothing to do with ability. In addition, norm-referenced evaluation generally eliminates significant rewards for effort, which is the only component of achievement under a student's control.

> *When I am no longer in charge of my learning,*
> *it becomes less worthwhile to pursue.*

So what are we as teachers to do? To do nothing is to perpetuate the system. To believe we can change the whole system is fantasy. What we can change are those aspects within our own sphere of influence, and that's where we need to focus our work.

Our Sphere of Influence

We have engaged in a discussion of perception, but to be practical, we need to concentrate now on how perception effects change. We need to have a global look at how perceptions are established. To do this, let's get a bit theoretical and discuss the cycle of influence.

At the top of the cycle we begin a worldview. We all have one, and there are probably as many intricacies to worldviews as their are people in the world. Our worldview is highly determined by several factors:

Early, Initial Experiences. Language acquisition may be the best example of an early, initial experience. Our language system affects our concept of time. Our language (English) has past, present, and future, and we view time in this neatly sequenced mode. Languages that do not have these tenses may simply look at time as "now" or "not now." We wonder how they function, because the concept is not within our perceptual set.

Genetic and Biological Factors. A significant percentage of our temperaments are influenced by genetic and biological factors and are components of how we see the world. Parents who get angry generally produce children who get angry. Occasionally, they produce children who, so upset by anger, refuse to show their anger, which can manifest a different set of problems.

Cultural Values. These values also shape our worldview. Much of what we consider "proper" behavior is determined by the society in which we live. We have probably all heard of faux pas committed by unknowing diplomats—social blunders that have interfered with international relations.

Our worldview affects our "fact filter" perception. The work of Thomas Kuhn establishes that perceptions are so strong, even among those in the scientific community, that if evidence is presented that contradicts their perception, they will discount the evidence—or not even perceive it! We see this consistently. People who want to smoke can discount entirely the evidence that smoking causes a number of health-related problems. Racists or sexists do not register evidence that contradicts their strongly held beliefs.

Interpretation. The most telling element of an experience is our interpretation of it. For instance, we cannot

OUR FIELD OF AWARNESS

Field of Awareness Determines How We Think

How We Think Determines Our Motivation

Our Motivation Affects Our Behavior

Fact-Filtering Perception is Based on
Our Sphere of Influence

☜ ☜ ☜

OUR SPHERE OF INFLUENCE

We All Have a Worldview, Determined by:
•
Early Initial Experiences
•
Genetic and Biological Factors
•
Cultural Values
•
These Affect Our Fact-Filtering Perception

Worldview + Perception = Interpretation of Experience

Interpretation of Experience Determines Behavior

Reaction to Behavior
(the only point at which teachers can enter the cycle)

say that a neglected or abused child will always become a dysfunctional adult; nor can we swear that tragic events will always cause defeat.

It is our interpretation of an experience,
not the experience itself, that affects our behavior.

Perhaps we have all known families who have lost children to death. One family becomes disjointed and falls apart. Another family is drawn closer together and the experience strengthens the bond of those remaining. Experience is interpreted through perception and worldview.

Behavior. We finally come to the behavior itself. Our intent is to indicate that the behavior, although the most visible component, is really a relatively small part of the overall picture. Less than 10 percent of an iceberg shows above the surface; the majority is not readily apparent. The Titanic was sunk by what was not apparent on the surface. When disciplining students, we are usually intent upon changing the offending behavior. What we must remember is that the iceberg behavior is simply an overt manifestation of many underwater worldview components.

Feedback. The last factor to consider in this process is feedback—the reaction of others to the behavior in question. Feedback has the power to confirm or modify the other elements of the cycle. And this is the only point at which teachers can enter the cycle.

To put this worldview cycle into less theoretical terms, I'd like to relate two stories. One of a sociological event from an example I remember from an anthropology course during my undergraduate work, the other related by a teacher.

Humanitarians and Hindus

In the early 1950s, some humanitarians from England and the United States traveled to India where they observed the squalor and misery those of the untouchable class were experiencing. These people were sick, lived in unsanitary conditions, and had little opportunity to relieve their misery. Deciding to give an all-out effort to change things, the humanitarians went back to their respective countries and raised funds to establish medical clinics.

The plan was well thought out. The clinics would be free. They would be established in the heart of where people lived so transportation would not be necessary. And the clinics would be advertised. Great efforts were taken to ensure that all those who needed the service would be informed. When all was ready, the clinic doors opened. The humanitarians waited, but nobody showed up.

The question of why is answered simply by realizing that the humanitarians and the people they wanted to help were operating from different worldviews.

The humanitarians came from a Western European culture that basically had a Judeo-Christian perspective. Relevant components of this view are that the individual is highly regarded and anything that inflicts pain on the individual is regarded as an evil and is to be eradicated, if at all possible. And since we "only go around once" (a philosophy promoted by a beer commercial some years ago), quality of life issues are of high priority. This view also involves a linear view of history. That is, there is a past, a present, and a future.

What evidently wasn't realized by the humanitarians was that the people they were addressing had an entirely different worldview. Their orientation, from a Hindu perspective, was completely different. Whereas the humanitarians believed suffering was an evil to be eradicated, those they were trying to serve looked at suffering as a result of karma from previous lives. That is, pain and suffering in this life is a way to work out the bad karma built up over previous lives. In fact, if a person did not work out the karma in this life, the next would be even worse.

Given this worldview, do you suppose that those experiencing the suffering had a different perception of clinics designed to relieve their misery? Would this not, in turn, cause them to have a different interpretation of the experience of being treated? And would this not alter behavior?

In a class some years ago we were discussing this factor and a high school teacher of some emotionally disturbed students asked if I would role-play a situation with him. Always ready to participate in these opportunities, I agreed. He asked if I would play the role of the teacher, and he would be a student—a high school girl who had transferred into his class some weeks before. He said he would be fiddling with some makeup and that I should calmly walk up to him, gently touch his shoulder, and say, "I'd appreciate having you put that away and get out your work."

That seemed easy enough, but as I touched his shoulder, he jumped out of his seat, threw his chair across the room, and in a vulgar manner told me to keep my hands off him. Frankly, he took me by surprise. I had done nothing I could think of that would have caused that reaction. The teacher, afterward, said he had had the same thought. He was not aggressive toward the student, did nothing to publicly single her out, and had no anger. Why, then, the outburst?

The teacher put things into perspective. After this incident, the teacher found out that the girl had been sexually abused from the time she was a child by her father, brother, and uncle. Her early and initial experiences with men were less than wholesome. These men had caused her severe physical and emotional pain and her worldview of men was set.

As we travel around her cycle, it becomes easy to understand why her perception of men is that they are a source of pain; her interpretation of being touched by a male is understandably aversive. Her overt behavior is consistent with elements of her worldview.

The only opportunity for her teacher is at the feedback component, and the only feedback available at this time is via interaction dynamics—what this teacher says, how he says it, and when he says it. Isn't it easy to see how the teacher could confirm the previous components? If he had yelled at her, concentrating only on her behavior, he would have embarrassed her in front of the class. Further, the teacher's perception and interpretation of the experience would have served only to reinforce this student's negative view of males.

If the teacher had stepped back and been able to remain in control of himself, he might have said, "I don't know what I did, but I want you to know that I have no intention of offending you like that again. When we are both calm, I'd like to talk this through so I don't make the same mistake again." Such a response may impact the girl with the perception that not all men are bad, which would be a start in changing her behavior. The ultimate goal would be for her to believe that her brother, father, and uncle are the culprits—not all men.

Changing Behavior in the Classroom

We have extensively discussed perception and its relevance to discipline. The question is, however, since we seldom have the luxury of extensive one-on-one time with all students and we must focus on teaching skills and subjects, can teachers change perception within the parameters of the classroom?

To be effective in teaching change of perception, we must be aware of certain factors that are important to consider in the process:

Change Takes Time. We must be prepared to accept that a person's change could take about one month for every year the perception has been in place. The earlier we begin, the more quickly we can expect change.

Everyone's Experience Is Different. An individual's experience is the basis of his or her truth. We must be ever vigilant about setting ourselves as the standard and interpreting others' behavior through our own perception. We must attempt to understand a student's perception of events before we can effect real change.

A song lyric I recently heard said,
"If it feels so right, how can it be wrong?"
Even if we strongly believe that a certain perception
is wrong—in order for us to change a perception,
it is essential for us to first understand what it is
that feels so right.

Nonverbal Language Speaks Loudest. Tangentially, we must be aware of the power of nonverbal language in this process. We all respond much more to covert messages than to the overt, so we must develop this awareness. We can say one thing, and our eyes, our look, our bodies can say another. Nonverbal language often speaks louder than words.

Self-Worth Is to Be Encouraged. Any interaction that inflicts damage on a student's sense of self-worth will boomerang and probably set the offending perceptions even deeper. It is important to keep in mind that your intention is to boost self-worth, not diminish it.

Change Moves from the Inside Out

To make students change their minds is an impossibility. Our minds are changed from within, not from without.

A few years ago Diane and I were looking at some old photo albums with Aleshia, our daughter. We came across some pictures of Diane and me in, of all things, bell-bottoms. These were the real bell-bottoms—about three feet across at the extreme. Aleshia's comment was that she would not be caught dead in those. Diane's was even more revealing. She said she wouldn't either—now.

However, I remember when we bought those pants. I was in my first years of teaching and we were just scraping by. We wanted those pants so badly that we sacrificed for them. Now we would be embarrassed to even put them in a rummage sale. Our perceptions had changed about bell-bottoms, just as our perceptions have changed about a lot of things.

How did they change? A sure bet is that nobody *made* us. We chose to change. This is a critical observation when disciplining students and working for perception change.

The more we try to make someone change, the more likely we are to lock them into the offending behavior.

I recall a missionary telling a story of the church in North Korea when the Communists were attempting to purge the country of religion. They worked hard to make the people give up their faiths and severely persecuted those who didn't. The ironic result was that those professing religion became stronger in their convictions. As one underground church member said, "We were like nails being hammered into wood; the harder they pounded us, the deeper they drove us."

If I were a laundry detergent salesman, what would be the most effective way to increase the chances that you would change from what you are using to what I am selling? What if I would aggressively approach you with, "What you are using is stupid. Use my brand." Do you suppose you would throw away the old brand and hurry right out to the store and buy mine? Probably not. More likely I would get a negative reaction to my judgment of your buying habits, and you would use the old brand if, for no other reason, to show that I could not make these demands on you.

I would significantly increase my chances if I were to approach the situation by holding up two T-shirts and going into the following performance: "See this grungy, dingy T-shirt? This was washed in our competitor's brand. On the other hand, look at this bright, white T-shirt! This was washed in our brand. As a good parent, which one would you rather have your child wear?"

Sound familiar? Of course it does. Advertisement relies on getting people to *want to* change, not making them change. The formula has only three steps: (1) mutual agreement, (2) transition, and (3) change.

Let's analyze the laundry detergent scenario. In the first (where the customer is told what to do), it takes little insight to conclude that the behavior not only won't change but the customer will probably become locked in more strongly than ever to use the original soap. In the second, although there are no guarantees, it seems sure that there is an increased chance of change. Using the three-part formula, let's do a bit of analysis.

Mutual Agreement. The salesperson starts with two obviously different T-shirts: one dingy, one bright. There is mutual agreement concerning this. A question format achieves two purposes: (1) focuses the customer on the subject at hand and (2) gives the sales person feedback. If the customer's head starts nodding "yes," the sale is well on its way.

Transition. This is the most critical part of the process, because it must convey a covert message. Perhaps you have already identified the transition in this scenario: "As a good parent . . ." What a powerful ploy. All parents, even "bad" ones, want to be "good." Using the insight of "emotion precedes logic," the salesperson has further increased the chance of a sale.

Change. Although there are no guarantees, chances are great that the potential customer is at least thinking.

Chances are excellent that enough people will follow through to make the advertising campaign well worth its cost.

If this procedure is so powerful in advertising, could the same process be effective in the classroom, without being manipulative?

When dealing with problems, we often initiate conversation at a point of mutual *disagreement* and then wonder why the situation never gets resolved. Consider this typical conversation concerning a classroom disruption:

TEACHER:	Why are you always acting like some spoiled little brat in my class? Do you think you can just disrupt any time you feel like it? You're not that important! If you don't shape up, you're going to be sorry!
STUDENT:	Go ahead! Do anything you want. This is a stupid class and nobody likes you either!
TEACHER:	That does it! Get down to the office, now!
STUDENT:	I hate this class and I hope I never have to come back!

Does this sound familiar? Can we imagine how this conversation will progress? The power struggle will increase, the class will still be disrupted and emotions will flare. Negative perceptions will persist and there is little promise that the situation will get any better. Why? Largely because at the onset of the interaction, the teacher and student were not at a point of mutual agreement. When interaction begins at a point of mutual *dis*agreement, both parties are likely to prepare for battle.

Could this interaction have ended differently?
Let's see:

TEACHER: I've noticed that you're not too involved in the class. Do you think that you and I have a different view of what should be going on in here?

STUDENT: That's for sure. I don't like this subject. I wish I didn't have to be here.

TEACHER: I appreciate your honesty. Would you be willing to sit down with me soon to see if we can come up with an idea that would make this class better for both of us, and maybe for the other kids too?

STUDENT: Sure, but I may have some ideas you won't like.

TEACHER: Maybe so, but I'd still like to hear them. Can we meet about 3:10 today?

STUDENT: Yeah, I'll be there.

There are no guarantees, but I firmly believe that if the problem is *addressed*, a solution, rather than an increased power struggle, is more likely to unfold.

Most often, perceptions are changed when:

- Predictions don't come true.
- When we're allowed to think, and, as a result, we act instead of react.

✎ LOVE AND LOGIC TIP #5:
Guiding Students to Solve Their Own Problems

Step 1. Empathy
"How sad." "I'll bet that makes you unhappy."

Step 2. Send the "Power Message"
"What do you think you're going to do?
I'd like to hear your ideas."

Step 3. Offer choices
"Would you like to hear what other kids have tried?"

At this point, offer a variety of choices that range from bad to good. It's usually best to start out with the poor choices.

Each time a choice is offered, go on to step four, forcing the student to state the consequence in his or her own words. This means that you will be going back and forth between steps three and four.

Step 4. Have the student state the consequences
"And how will that work?"

Step 5. Give permission for the student to either solve the problem or not solve the problem
"Good luck. I hope it works out."

Have no fear. If the student is fortunate enough to make a poor choice, he/she may have a double learning lesson.

Changes in perception, rather than behavior, are a major theme in the chapters of this book. If this concept is new to you, give yourself time to absorb it, consider it and practice it. Keep in mind that your personal experience is the basis of your truth. Don't allow yourself to teach something with which you are not in agreement; your nonverbal language will give you away. Finally, your intention is to boost self-worth—in yourself as well as in your students. This is a process rather than a fix. Be patient. Changes do not happen overnight.

PEARL
▼
Oracles don't issue orders;
they share wisdom.

Love and Logic Experiment #8

STUDENT:

(Not following the rules during a game.)

Teacher:

There are two ways to enjoy the game.

One is by playing it and one is by watching it.

Which would you rather do?

STUDENT:

Well, I'm not the only one . . .

TEACHER:

Arguing was not one of the choices.

I'll see you on the bleachers for awhile. Thanks.

STUDENT:

It's not fair.

TEACHER:

I bet it looks that way,

and you may return to the game when

I don't have to worry about cheating or arguing.

CHAPTER SEVEN

Principles vs. Systems

I once viewed a videotape in which the presenter told of a time when he was giving a talk and a member of the audience clutched her chest and slumped to the floor in an apparent heart attack. He, trained in CPR, looked at the victim, then at the audience, then back at the victim. At this point he said, "I know CPR, but I simply do not have time to administer it to all of the people in the room, and to give this assistance to just one person, well, it just wouldn't be fair to the others."

Ridiculous, isn't it? Obviously, fairness being equated to equal treatment would be extremely unfair to the victim, if not downright immoral. And yet, we often are convinced that to maintain equal treatment is the only way to handle kids, even though we would never consider this in many of our adult relations.

Let's look at the idea of "fair." Just what does it mean? So much of the connotation of any word is in context. For instance, when speaking of equal pay for equal work, "fair" certainly means equal treatment.

However, in some instances, equal treatment may be completely unfair.

"Fair" is often not identical treatment,
but, rather, giving what is needed.

The Philosophy of Discipline

In one of Jim Fay's talks, he mentions two kinds of schools. Some are friendly and warm; others are cold and uncomfortable. Much of this atmosphere is established by the philosophy of discipline that thrives in that building.

Some schools are run according to a "system," in which rules are established and staff are expected to take action when there are any violations. Punishments are determined for given infractions and consistency is required, administering these rules and punishments equally to all, regardless of whether or not they effect positive change in an individual student. Expectations are imposed uniformly on all staff, regardless of their comfort level with any specific element of the system.

Other schools are run according to a collection of "principles," or values, that govern the behavior of students and staff. As in a systems approach, rules are developed and made known to those in the school. Likewise, staff are expected to take action when any of these rules are violated. Discipline situations, however, are handled within an accepted set of principles, on an individual basis. Consistency is maintained by adhering to the set of values rather than necessarily treating everyone the same.

Many teachers are initially cautious with the principles concept because they immediately recall some of the most uncomfortable words a student can say to an educator: "That's not fair."

THE TWO BASIC
PHILOSOPHIES OF DISCIPLINE

The Systems Approach:	The Principles Approach:
☞ Rules are developed and established.	☞ Rules are developed and established.
☞ Staff is expected to take action whenever a rule is violated.	☞ Staff is expected to take action whenever a rule is violated.
☞ Discipline is based on **specific punishments** for given infractions.	☞ Discipline is based on an accepted **set of principles.**
☞ Staff is encouraged to impose **uniform punishment,** regardless of comfort level with specific elements of the system.	☞ Staff is encouraged to apply **whatever discipline is necessary, on an individual basis,** based on established principles.
☞ Consistency is encouraged by **adhering to predetermined rules and punishments, administered equally to all,** with no individual consideration of differences.	☞ Consistency is encouraged by **adhering to a predetermined set of values** in administering consequences with regard for individual circumstances.

For instance, if I (David Funk) were enslaved by a strict systems approach to my interaction with people, I would have to treat everyone the same to maintain consistency. When talking about this concept in classes or workshops, I make eye contact with an audience member I don't know and begin the following discussion:

"You don't know me, other than what you have heard and seen so far, and I don't know you even that well. Given this level of relationship, would you expect me to treat you, in all aspects of life, the way you would expect your spouse to treat you?"

The answer is always no, as it should be. If I were to treat this person as I would my wife, our relationship would be stoic at one extreme or immoral at another. We simply don't expect or even want equal treatment in those kinds of situations.

Then I ask another question: "Would you like both your spouse and me to treat you with dignity and respect?" The answer is always yes. This demonstrates to me the difference between a systems approach and a principles approach and how they can both be consistent. A principles approach maintains consistency (a very important factor in human relations) by remaining true to a value.

I can treat everyone with
"dignity and respect" (values)
while not enslaving myself to treating
everyone "the same" (system).

This is not to say that we should throw out all programs built on a systems approach, however. A systems approach is definitely best when we are working with things. When getting into a commercial jet, for example, hopefully the pilot has a system of checking everything that needs attention. National fast-food chains take great pains to systematize their food preparation so their product is consistent from one city to another. A systems approach may be best when there are health, safety, or legal issues to consider. For instance, children may be prohibited from playing in dangerous places or be expected to follow specific fire drill regulations.

Science experiments, team player behavior, and preparation for and presentation of concerts normally come under system parameters to ensure anticipated outcome. When variables are limited—such as in standardized testing—a systems approach works best. Since determination of district levels is the goal, individualizing the tests would violate the purpose.

Although, even when dealing with people, there are times that a systems approach is efficient and appropriate, there are situations where being locked into a tight structure may not be best. For instance, when problem-solving is in order, a set of values most often works better than a prescribed checklist. When several options are available, or there are several variables to absorb, a set of principles, not a set of strict rules, will probably best determine the most appropriate choice.

Teaching Without a Thermostat

Whenever I think of a principles approach and its relationship to absorbing variables, my mind goes back to my Grandma's baking. Perhaps you have known people who cook by principle rather than recipe. That's the way Grandma cooked. I don't ever remember her using a cookbook or being overly concerned with how hot the oven was. She learned to cook in rural Iowa at the turn of the century, using a wood stove. There was no thermostat for her to worry about. She learned to cook by "feel."

One of Grandma's principles was that rising bread was ready to bake when it felt "like a baby's bottom." Pie crust was worked until it "felt right." She added spices and herbs to food until it "tasted good." We waited in great expectation for her meals because everything was always so good, although not always the same. I lived with her during my first two years of college. You can imagine the number of friends from campus I had!

The primary benefit of Grandma's style of cooking was that she could absorb variables. She lived in central Indiana for some time, where, in the summer, the weather was hot and humid. Winter was cold and dry. Grandma's house, partially because it used electric radiant heat, was extremely dry. But when Grandma made pie crust—no problem. Because she knew how it should "feel," she simply adjusted the ingredients. For those who cook by recipe, absorbing variables is anywhere from difficult to impossible.

The experience of most, if not all, teachers is that the classroom is full of variables. How many teachers can really plan what they will do that day on the way to work and follow their recipe faithfully? There are often interruptions we cannot anticipate, let alone write a lesson plan for. And how many of us have ever had two kids with the same experience, abilities, and interests?

Most classrooms run the gamut of abilities from disabled to gifted, and are full of students with different learning styles and home situations spanning a continuum from dangerously dysfunctional to stable and secure. A single set of prescribed reactions would be a great disservice to a majority of these kids. That is not to say, however, that we should allow lack of structure in the classroom. We need a pattern to maintain consistency, a structure to establish parameters for relationships, and a touchstone for measuring whether we are achieving our goals.

Consistent Reactions or Consistent Outcomes?

The best paradigm is one that allows for:

- Change in circumstances
- Opportunity to individualize
- A pattern that enables teachers to have a structure
- A process that treats students on a personal basis while maintaining the standard of "fair"

An important question at this point is: Are we interested in consistent reactions or consistent outcomes? That is, are we going to concentrate on ensuring that our students' and our own reactions are consistent with a prescribed list, or are we going to concern ourselves with interacting with students with a particular purpose or goal in mind?

The conclusion within Love and Logic, then, is that in most cases concerning student behavior and learning, a principles approach is preferred. There are three primary reasons:

1. A principles approach allows the absorption of both overt and hidden variables. Not only are there obvious factors to consider when dealing with students, such as age levels, but also the not-so-obvious variables as personality and experiences.

2. A principles approach assists in the process of internalization through the decision-making process. When engaged in making decisions and choices, students (and teachers) must do more thinking than reacting. In this process we are more likely to identify the connection between our behavior and the consequences and there-fore learn a valuable lesson. When we make good deci-sions, we feel good; when we make bad decisions, we feel bad. When we feel good, we act differently than when we feel bad.

3. A principles approach tends to reduce problems associated with being locked into a system. When there are hundreds of rules to live by, adhering to them all, on a consistent basis, becomes next to impossible.

In a course several years ago in a small community in west central Wisconsin, our class was discussing the development of school and classroom rules when a teacher raised her hand and said, "Until two weeks ago, we thought we had a rule for everything." As she was speaking I mulled over in my mind as many rules as I could think of, coming up with twelve or fifteen, such as "Keep hands and feet to yourself," "Bring your materials to class," and "Say please and thank you."

She went on to relate that in this elementary school, the handbook had 324 rules to govern student behavior. Then she told us that this week they realized they didn't have a rule that said, "Boys can't throw dead fish at girls." A boy had thrown this fish at a girl and, when he was repri-manded, looked innocently into the teacher's face (as most fourth graders can expertly do) and said, "But teacher, there's no rule against it." Can you imagine if this school were so locked into a systems approach that they thought only of developing rule #325, "Boys can't throw dead fish at girls"? Would that solve the real problem? Of course not. The next week the children would think of some other exemption, just like adults do for taxes.

Perhaps it would be better to have the class governed by a set of values that can apply in numerous situations, principles that consider personalities and experiences, and "rules" that leave adults with more opportunity to develop strategies that work with individual students.

The Only Rule You Need

In my own experience, before my training in Love and Logic, I was like every other teacher I knew. I unilaterally developed rules, posted them on the board, and made myself responsible for enforcing them. In one of my early encounters with Jim Fay, he indicated that he had but one rule in his school, and, once I heard it, it seemed so simple, concise, and applicable to so many situations:

> *You can solve a problem any way you want,*
> *provided it doesn't cause a problem for anyone else.*

I modified this slightly to "You can do anything you want in this class, provided it doesn't cause a problem for anyone else," but the effect was the same. This one principle was really all I needed for my classes. It absorbed all the variables I had to contend with in the classroom, and every student considered it fair.

We established this rule at the beginning of the year, with a scenario similar to the one that follows:

TEACHER: Kids, have you ever been in classes
            with a lot of rules?

STUDENTS: Yeah, Mrs. Smith had eighty-seven by
            the end of last year.

TEACHER: I used to have a lot of rules too, but my biggest problem was remembering all of them.

STUDENTS: Mrs. Smith had that problem, too.

TEACHER: I also discovered that kids were pretty creative about breaking the rules. I had a hard time fitting the rule to the infraction. Now I have only one rule. Can I tell you what it is?

STUDENTS: Sure, go ahead.

TEACHER: You can do anything in this class you want, provided it doesn't cause a problem for anyone else. How does that sound?

STUDENTS: Pretty good. Seems fair. What's the catch?

TEACHER: The only catch is that I'm a person in the class just like you, so we have to consider what would be a problem for me as well.

STUDENTS: Like what?

TEACHER: Well, if someone were disrupting my teaching, that would be a problem for me, just like if you had to study for a test and someone kept bugging you.

> We'll talk about this more as the year
> goes on, but do you have enough
> information for now?

This principle (rule) allowed the class to maintain a consistency, at the same time allowing individualization based on specific students and circumstances. With this rule, students were permitted a wide range of behaviors; still, parameters were established and enforceable.

A principles approach does not mean a lack of structure. Rather, a principles approach simply refers to conducting interactions with students based on a set of values. In essence, then, these principles form a paradigm, or pattern, by which we can assess interactions. Patterns are important because they give structure and consistency. The best patterns, however, are those that allow for change. This combination of allowing for change while maintaining a stable pattern helps teachers develop classrooms that maintain consistency and still meet differing needs.

The Love and Logic philosophy centers on four key principles developed from the early work of Jim Fay and Foster Cline. Briefly stated, they are:

1. A student's self-concept needs to be either maintained or enhanced. Under almost any condition, a student's sense of self-worth needs to be enhanced, even in—especially in—a "discipline" situation.

2. Control is a shared commodity. An adult takes only the amount of control needed and always leaves some for the student.

3. Consequences need to be served up with compassion, empathy, or understanding, rather than anger. To internalize the lessons of life, kids need to experience the consequences of their behavior. The application of consequences and empathy rather than anger tends to speed up the internalization.

4. Thinking needs to be shared. To the degree possible, students should do more thinking than the adult and be involved in making decisions that affect his or her life.

Each of the following four chapters will discuss, in detail, one of these key principles, which are the core of Love and Logic philosophy. These principles are valuable because of their applicability to so many situations teachers face in dealing with student performance and because they provide a balanced structure for interacting with students on an individual basis. This, after all, is what good education is all about.

PEARL

▼

Shift your thinking from, "What do I say?"
to, "What do I ask?"

Love and Logic Experiment #9

STUDENT:

I don't have my homework. I lost it.

TEACHER:

Not to worry.

I'll accept it tomorrow for reduced credit.

▼

CHAPTER EIGHT

The Enhancement of Self-Concept

KEY PRINCIPLE NUMBER ONE

*W*hen Jim Fay was fourteen, he was arrested for fishing in an old quarry. As he was leaving for his court appearance, his father gave him the following advice: "Ride the right trolley. Don't be late. Stand tall. And say 'sir.'" Jim's dad stayed home that day, while Jim went off to face the consequences of his behavior.

Nobody thought Jim's dad was a bad parent for not accompanying Jim to court. Today, in the same situation, lawyers would be retained, the quarry owner would be on trial, and Jim's entire family and circle of friends would come to court.

Some may look at Jim's dad's handling of the situation as cold and uncaring, but Jim doesn't think so. This incident strengthened Jim's self-concept because it gave him the opportunity to demonstrate his capability.

Why is Self-Concept at an All-Time Low?

Self-concept has become a key factor in today's education because so many kids have a poor one. There have been innumerable teacher-training programs and student curricula developed in the recent past to deal with this educational malady. They were developed in response to a need—a severe need. An understanding of how we arrived at this point may give us, as parents and educators, insight into effectively dealing with the problem.

A large part of the dilemma relates to the loss of the extended family. It takes a community to raise a child, and we, in large part, have lost that. Before, if young parents were having a problem, the normal procedure was to talk to Grandma, who had built up years of wisdom through experience. More often than not, a comment like, "Your father was like that . . ." gave not only comfort, but also a strategy. This strategy was especially effective because it considered many individual aspects about a child in terms of family values, (sub)cultural mores, and societal expectations. In essence, Grandma was able to help young parents devise effective individual behavior plans for their children.

In Chapters eight through eleven, Dave Funk's in-depth look at the Four Basic Principles of Love and Logic clarifies their wide-reaching applicability and provision of a basic structure for dealing with students on a personal level.

Society had expectations of the extended family. Kids were to watch adults and learn from them how to solve problems. Adults were expected to give good advice and be examples for kids to follow. Most certainly there were exceptions, but, for the most part, a kid's self-concept was not an issue, because kids were developing their own self-concepts through struggle.

Too often today, the situation is far different. We have largely disregarded the experience of Grandma—perhaps because of inaccessibility, or less regard for its worth—and come to rely on "experts" who are giving specific advice based on general experiments for kids whom they've barely seen. The real variables that affect kids' behavior—such as interpersonal family dynamics, religious views, and economic pressures—which would be well known by Grandma, may be totally unknown by the expert.

To know what to do for a kid
without a knowledge of that kid's intimate variables
is often little more than a hopeful shot in the dark.

As teachers, does that mean that we can or should do nothing? Not at all. It is well documented that achievement and behavior are highly related to self-concept. For us, as educators, to do nothing is simply to exacerbate the problem. However, to approach this problem with faulty or inadequate strategies only continues the spiral. To get an idea of some foundation ideas for working with self-concept, let's look at a time when children developed positive self-concepts naturally, when it was not of particular concern to society.

I got some inkling of what this past time was like while observing some Amish families in central Wisconsin. There, children are considered a "gift of the Lord" and each has his or her worth as part of the family and community. There is no such thing as an unwanted child. Further, from the time they are able, each child has a job and this job is vitally important to the functioning of the family. Finally, every adult in the community has some responsibility for the others, and each is to be an example to the children. Experience and wisdom are highly prized. Self-concept is not an issue, because they have positive ones. They are developed early.

*The Amish live by a concept that our society was once
based on but which most of us have long lost:
A positive self-concept comes from feeling capable.*

Many experts in education have indicated something
else. They have conclusively shown that resourceful, well-
adjusted kids have a good self-concept; and unresource-
ful, poorly adjusted kids do not. Their conclusion was
that by infusing a positive self-concept into children they
automatically would become good students. So, positive
self-concept came from being told how good they were.
The result, however, was the creation of passive kids waiting for adults to install this attribute.

Another shift has been what "good-self-concept" kids
look like. We have been given the picture that these kids
are happy all the time. In the past, "happy" was not a
requirement; it was expected that children would occasionally feel bad as they were learning to grow into adulthood. Experts convinced us, however, that unhappiness in
children was to be avoided at all costs, because it could
disrupt their development.

As a result, over time, parents and teachers have
become afraid to say no, to set limits, or to hold kids
accountable for bad decisions, because to do so might
make them feel "unhappy." The adults' job is to make kids
feel good. But this orientation can boomerang with far-
reaching results.

The work of family psychologist John Rosemond,
author of John Rosemond's Six-Point Plan for Raising
Happy, Healthy Children, addresses this issue. In the
course of over more than twenty years counseling families he has made these important discoveries:

☞ *Parents who work hard to make their children happy are likely to raise children who are unable to make themselves happy.*

☞ *Parents who try to shelter their children from any and all frustration are likely to raise children who cannot handle frustration and, as a consequence, respond with destructive, even self-destructive behaviors when frustrated.*

☞ *Parents who solve problems their children could have solved for themselves (albeit with guidance) are likely to raise children who give up early.*

Classrooms inherit these kids who give up easily and hate to struggle. Teachers are often locked in to the same precept of making learning fun. They do the struggling for the students, trying to find new ways of delivering instruction that will be acceptable to the kids and their parents. The end result is often that teachers are exhausted and kids continue to wait for the teacher to install an education in them.

Still, we need to address self-concept in school because of its importance to student performance. However, we also want to be effective in the long haul. Within the Love and Logic approach, self-concept is developed, not from a workbook, but from the influence of people who matter in a kid's life—the "magic" people who model appropriate behavior and, by the very way they think, speak, and act, affect who that child turns out to be.

Who We Believe We Are

It may well be that self-concept is a misnomer because there is so little "self" in it. What I think about myself is highly determined by what I think other people think about me. Contemplate, for a moment, how dependent the fashion and cosmetic industries are on maintaining this concept. What has constantly intrigued me is that we are so sure we know what others are thinking without asking them or further verifying our perceptions. It is so easy to attribute someone's behavior to "being mean," "not liking me," being "unscrupulous," or any number of other characteristics that, frankly, get us off the moral hook.

Once we have convinced ourselves that someone has less than positive motives, we alleviate any guilt that might invade our minds were we to think the error was with us personally. It is of further interest that we seldom investigate whether or not our own perceptions are correct.

Strong-Willed Errol Cares What Others Think

I can recall several instances in my (David Funk) own experience, but one in particular involves a family story that happened some years ago. My brother's family and ours were eating at a restaurant after church one Sunday. Jaben, our son, was five years old, and Aleshia was seven. My brother Errol and his wife, Sheryl, at that time had two daughters: Becky was just an infant; Janelle was about two and getting really good at going "potty" by herself. To experience the full benefit of this story, the reader must visualize my brother.

Errol is not overly tall, but extremely strong physically. Even though I was three years older, I

✎ **LOVE AND LOGIC TIP #6A:**
Using Negative Assertion

It is difficult for a student to continue a power struggle when the teacher won't play his or her game. Negative assertion is a tool used to diffuse the power play.

TEACHER:	*(Calmly)* I'm going to change your assigned seat, Connie. There's too much visiting going on. I can't teach with the distraction.
CONNIE:	Geeze! You can't even teach with little distractions! If you understood, it wouldn't bother you.
TEACHER:	There's probably a lot of truth to that. Connie, I want you to sit in this seat right here.
CONNIE:	That's not fair!
TEACHER:	That's a real possibility, Connie.

---

never remember being able to beat him at wrestling when we were growing up. At the time he was a carpenter, used to hard physical labor, and a part-time custodian at the school I taught at. In addition to being physically strong, he was strong-willed. It was not likely that a person like this would choose to make a fool of himself in a public place.

We had been seated in a far corner, as far distant from the rest rooms as possible. Soon into our conversation, Janelle announced that she had to use the rest room. Her mother offered assistance, only to be confronted with a resounding "No, Mommy. I can do it myself!" She did allow her mother to show her the right door, but insisted on completing the job independently.

✎ LOVE AND LOGIC TIP #6B:
Using Negative Assertion and Broken Record

It is difficult for a student to continue a power struggle when the teacher won't play his or her game. Negative assertion is a tool used to diffuse the power play.

TEACHER:	*(Calmly)* I'm going to change your assigned seat, Connie. There's too much visiting going on. I can't teach with the distraction.
CONNIE:	Geeze! You can't even teach with little distractions! If you understood, it wouldn't bother you.
TEACHER:	I can understand how you might feel that way, and I expect you to move to this seat.
CONNIE:	That's not fair!
TEACHER:	I can understand how you might feel that way, and I expect you to move to this seat.
CONNIE:	But you should be making the other kids move instead!
TEACHER:	I can understand how you might feel that way, and I expect you to move to this seat.
CONNIE:	Oh, all right! What's the big deal anyway?

Sheryl returned to our table and we continued our conversation. It did seem that Janelle was taking quite a long time, but, after all, she was new at this. After awhile, though, we heard some tittering and giggling. You may have guessed, Janelle was walking (actually hobbling) to our table. She had pulled her dress up to her chest, her pants were around her ankles and she was not shy about her request: "Mommy, come and wipe me!" At this point, my strong-willed, able-bodied brother crawled under the table and pleaded, "Sheryl, do something."

The next day I had a chance to talk to Errol. I asked him about the episode of the previous day. I told him his reaction was interesting to me because I had never seen that behavior before. There was no way that anyone could have physically stuffed him under the table, and I don't think any argument could have convinced him otherwise. In short, he had to choose to get under that table. Visibly uncomfortable, he said he felt embarrassed because he just knew everyone in the restaurant thought he was a bad parent.

Imagine! His behavior was dictated by what he thought other people thought about him. What a powerful force. What interests me in retrospect is that I remember comments of the people there. Some were saying, "Isn't she cute?" Most were saying, "Glad that's not my kid!" I highly doubt if any were thinking Errol was a bad parent, but that's what *he* thought. Therefore, he behaved accordingly.

In the classroom, and with regard to discipline in particular, the principle of self-concept is extremely important because we tend to act out who we believe we are. I recall a woman who attended one of my classes several years ago. We were heavily into a discussion of this topic, emphasizing that we tend to conform to what we think other people think about us. She related the story of her own upbringing with a verbally abusive father and told some of her school experiences. She indicated that her father made her feel "like dirt." As a result, that's what she felt like inside herself. She had, at best, a mediocre school experience and, not unpredictably, got into a physically abusive marriage. Always feeling the abuse was her fault, she remained in that situation until, literally, it became life-threatening.

Sometime later, she remarried, in her words, a "wonderful man." For the first time in her life, she felt loved for who she was, unconditionally. As her esteem rose, she decided to go back to school. In one of her first classes, she received an A on one of her papers. Because of her past experiences, she did not believe she was capable of receiving this high a grade. She spoke with her instructor at the next class and indicated to him that he must have made a mistake, perhaps transposing someone else's grade to her paper. The instructor assured her that she had, indeed, written a paper of A quality and that the grade was hers, not someone else's.

That situation was a turning point for this teacher and was another step in healing wounds inflicted so long ago. She wept after telling that story (as others in the class did) and emphasized the desperate need children have to develop healthy self-concepts.

The Role of Implied Messages

We cannot discuss self-concept without acknowledging the fact that our behavior is influenced by what we think other people think about us. What are the dynamics of this phenomenon? A substantial part of the answer lies in a study of implied messages.

Albert Mehrabian (1972) indicates that the majority of communication meaning comes from nonverbal aspects of language. We briefly discussed this in Chapter Six, Perception and Behavior, but carry it a step further here. Mehrabian divided communication into three parts and indicated that only 7 percent of meaning derived from any communication comes from verbal expression. Seven percent!

Part of nonverbal communication involves such factors as vocal stress and intonation. We can all change the meaning of a simple sentence by merely changing these aspects. I can say "I love you" with dripping sweetness or with a caustic sarcasm. We have probably all had our parents tell us to apologize to a sibling "like you mean it." But, there is more to the nonverbal that is even more powerful: the presuppositions of language.

When I am speaking to groups on this subject, I often single out a female member of the audience who appears to be somewhat assertive and I make the statement: "You know, this Love and Logic stuff is so simple even a woman should be able to understand it." Then I step back about three feet so I don't get hit.

The effect of this statement is predictable. Not only does the person I am speaking to become, at least, annoyed, but I hear threats of bodily harm throughout the audience. Then, together, we analyze the statement. Many times we become upset at what people tell us because a vulgarity is used. Sometimes double entendres can do the same thing. However, neither of those were used in this case. Something more subtle was in force. In this situation it was the coded word "even" (accompanied by sarcastic or snide intonations) applied to the word "woman." Sometimes these presuppositions of language are identifiable as separate entities, as is the case with coded words. Sometimes the context determines the ulterior meaning.

I recall a situation at a recent in-service program. It was break time and we were lining up for donuts. A male teacher, who may well have had an elevated opinion of himself, bowed deeply to a group of female teachers and said, "You girls go right ahead." The response of one of the women was very clear when she said, "I am *not* a girl," and her opinion of the male teacher became evident. Of course, there is nothing wrong with the word "girl" except in certain contexts. In this case, it was an implied put-down.

We respond to covert messages
much more than we ever do to the overt.

Imagine the following scenario involving a teacher who had had a hard day. Three kids got sick in the classroom, the specials teacher could not take the class, and the whole test had to be written on the board because the copy machine had broken down. On his way home, the teacher ruminated over the day but comforted himself that at least he would have a good meal when he got home. His wife, however, having had an equally bad day, just wanted to put her feet up and have something cold to drink. That home-cooked meal dropped out of the picture.

This man sat down at the table and saw before him a TV dinner—and not even a brand-name one at that. He looked at his wife and in a sweet tone of voice said, "Honey, when I was growing up, my dear mother always had time to make me a good meal." The wife's reaction was predictable and I need not go into detail about what she said. But, let's look at the husband's comment. He used a term of endearment, spoke in a "sweet" voice, and was, at the verbal level, giving a compliment to his mother. Why did his wife get upset? Because the real message was about the expectations he had of her. It was an implied put-down, and there was no mistaking it for anything else.

Implied messages give meaning and many children have great expertise at picking them up. I remember testing a first-grader some years ago. I was asking preliminary questions about her grade, teacher's name, and how many brothers and sisters she had. Then I asked her age. "Six and one-fourth," was her quick response.

There are several components of our personhood. Self-concept seeks to protect itself and, when attacked, tends to assume a "fight or flight" mode. That is, when we face something threatening us, we will either fight against it or run away. Obviously this young girl's age is important to her. Imagine how we could inflict pain on her developing ego by reprimanding her with, "Even a four-year-old knows better than to count fractions as part of your age."

Our self-concept has two main characteristics:

- ☛ It is fragile and easily broken.
- ☛ It is conservative and resistant to change.

This combination results in our creation of defense mechanisms to protect our self from the necessity to change. To say my behavior is wrong is bad enough. To say that "I" am wrong is often intolerably painful. We seek to maintain our view of ourselves and often will go so far as to reject clear evidence to the contrary.

Because of this factor, we need to interact in particular ways with students who have shaky self-concepts. We want to apply what works effectively on a student's perception rather than on behavior. Discipline situations are ripe for this type of interaction.

The Role of Achievement

Another aspect of self-concept that especially applies to the school situation is the connection between self-concept and achievement. As we've already learned, the desire to achieve is a universal human characteristic. It can validate us and demonstrate that we are capable. It can make us feel good, whether we are a toddler balancing blocks or an adult making that last car payment. But sometimes achievement takes a nasty turn in the educational system that negatively affects self-concept.

As long as achievement is an extension of self, there are usually few negative effects. However, when achievement becomes a measure of self-worth, student performance can take a turn for the worse. Unfortunately, our educational system has innumerable opportunities for destroying self-concepts. The Love and Logic approach, however, seeks to remedy this by focusing on natural interaction between people.

The Three-Legged Table

For us to work on self-concept, it will serve us well to have a paradigm. Jim Fay's classic is the visual analogy of the "three-legged table":

1. I'm loved by the "magic" people in my life.
2. I know more about my strengths than my weaknesses.
3. I can handle the consequences of my own behavior.

I'm Loved by the "Magic" People in My Life. One of our strongest desires is to be loved for who we are, not for how we perform. The most influential love is unconditional. If we have the sense that our magic people—those involved in our caretaking and learning—love us unconditionally, we feel established as being worthy in our own right, regardless of our abilities, behavior, or other characteristics. People who do not have this unconditional love in their natural environment will often pay a thera-pist to obtain the closest substitute.

Teachers who establish a relationship of unconditional acceptance and respect with students are at a great advantage. Students in the presence of teachers who fill this basic need (i.e., validation of worth) tend to put forth extra effort to maintain their expectations, as well as their relationship with the teacher.

How do you demonstrate acceptance in an unconditional manner? The key is to give positive relationship messages whenever a negative content message is sent. For example, if, in a tone of respect, I say to a student who has just committed an infraction, "Just because I like you, do you think I should let you get away with that?" I have tangibly demonstrated acceptance.

The basic rule is:
Unconditionally accept the worthy person,
even while rejecting the questionable behavior.

I Know More About My Strengths Than My Weaknesses. To a large degree, schools are designed to remedy deficits. Therefore, in school, kids can be reminded of their weaknesses on a daily basis. This constant reminder can have detrimental effects on a kid's self-concept. It is little wonder that performance deteriorates as children move through school.

In my elementary school years, I (David Funk) was a basic motor klutz and a kid who hated recess, the time my weaknesses were especially evident. In our school, team sports were popular and it was the habit of classroom teachers to have the most able athletes pick sides. I vividly recall being among the last kids chosen—me and a girl I got to know quite well. It's a wonder we didn't get married after spending so much time together waiting to be picked.

The pain of this public exposure influenced my behavior. By fourth grade, I was an expert at behaving badly enough in class to be kept in from recess. That year I think I copied the entire dictionary (the punishment of choice). I didn't like copying the dictionary, but it beat the feeling of humiliation I experienced on the playground.

As adults, how many of us regularly invite several of our friends over to watch us do something we aren't very good at? Never! As adults we fly on our strengths. Those who constantly remind us of our weaknesses are people we avoid.

We do not want kids to ignore what they need to work on, but if they do not learn what their strengths are, their weaknesses become defeats.

Part of the responsibility of the magic people in a kid's life is to provide opportunities for the kid to demonstrate what she or he is good at.

I Can Handle the Consequences of My Own Behavior. Consequences are probably the best tool to use in our quest to internalize controls. We will talk more about consequences in Chapter Ten, Consequences with Empathy. In the meantime, suffice it to say that when kids actually see the connection between their behavior and what happened as a result of that behavior, they learn.

A significant problem in our society is that we tend to rescue kids from consequences far too frequently.

Learning from consequences is a struggle that can cause pain, but surviving the struggle is a great self-concept builder. We learn that we are capable.

Consequences are important in another way. It is evident that pain is often necessary to change behavior. Psychologists have pointed this out for years and it certainly conforms to our experience. It is less seldom pointed out that in dealing with student performance, we need to consider two kinds of pain: outside pain (such as being hit, yelled at, or teased) and inside pain (such as guilt, regret, or remorse).

Outside Pain. When reacting to outside pain, we identify the source and usually make one of two determinations: to fight or run away.

Inside Pain. Pain inside us is more complicated. Since there is no external object to react to, we must make more internal decisions. Inside pain can contribute much to our self-concept because of the decisions it requires. We will learn more about this in the following chapters.

Changing Self-Concepts

We have reviewed self-concept in terms of how it is established and maintained. Changing it takes time, patience, and a new way of thinking. Let the following be your guide:

1. Use eye contact, smiles, and appropriate touch. These are primary bonding mechanisms that have worked throughout human history.
2. Allow kids to own their feelings. We often rob them of both pleasure and disappointment by phrases such as, "I'm so proud of (or disappointed in) you."

Instead, saying "You can be proud of that" allows the feeling to reside in the child instead of orienting him to make his feelings and, subsequently, his worth dependent on how somebody else feels about him.

3. Let kids learn from the consequences of their behavior. Consequences produce pain from the inside out and enhance internalized learning—the most permanent kind.

4. Find something unique about each child and share it with him/her.

Be sure to use positive descriptive statements rather than statements of judgment or value.

In the chapter that follows, we move from the principle of self-concept enhancement to the principle of shared control. More new thinking is required on your part, but we feel confident that the consequences will result in a more effective classroom for you.

PEARL

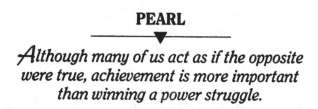

Although many of us act as if the opposite were true, achievement is more important than winning a power struggle.

Love and Logic Experiment #10

STUDENT:

Those boys were spitting on the playground.

TEACHER:

Don't you hate it when that happens?

CHAPTER NINE

▼

Shared Control

KEY PRINCIPLE NUMBER TWO

*W*ithin two weeks of teaching my first class, I (David Funk) realized that in my four years of preparation, I had never been taught to teach. One of my first students, a kid named John, taught me that lesson. He caused me to realize that I had learned how to do research and collect and disseminate information, but, other than what I had learned from my dad, I didn't know what to do when kids didn't want to learn what I had to teach.

One day during those first two weeks, when I was teaching the difference between transitive and intransitive verbs, John and a fellow student got into a fight. Frankly, this took me by surprise, and I had a knee-jerk reaction: I sent them both to the principal's office. For the rest of the day I wallowed in the throes of agony wondering if I had just invalidated myself as a teacher. Here I was, a new teacher who couldn't control his class. I made a decision that day: I would never kick a kid out of my class again. I would deal with misbehavior within my classroom, or I would get out of teaching.

This was not the wisest decision, because I had no idea how to effectively discipline and there were times when removing a kid would have been best for the kid, for the class, and for me. I had had no discipline courses, not one unit I could remember in my teacher-training experience. Due to this lack in my education, I locked into a mind-set: My primary goal in my classroom would be to control kids.

From Intimidation to Manipulation

Because I had received no training, I could only reflect on others in my past experience whom I had seen control kids. This pretty much limited me to my dad and a few teachers. As I reflected on their approaches, it seemed there were two factors I needed to remember: My main technique would be basically to overpower my students. My immediate goal was to make kids do things they didn't want to do. I refined this technique and actually got pretty good at overpowering through the use of intimidation, threats, and anger. These held me in good stead for several years.

I had begun my career as an English and social studies teacher. After a few years I gravitated toward special education. For the first five years of being a teacher of the learning disabled, I had only boys, and my discipline strategies, which were based on overpowering the students, worked reasonably well.

In spite of my manner of discipline, I got along well with my students. Then I got my first female student—Donna. Donna was different. She was a kid I didn't want to like. My overpowering techniques didn't make a dent in her behavior, and I felt impotent. For instance, she would tell me eight or ten times a month that she thought her period was starting and would ask to go to the rest room. Then she would never come back. I felt I couldn't tell her she couldn't go, and I couldn't go down after her. I didn't want to involve any of my teaching peers for fear that I would be considered ineffective. I was in a bind.

One day I became so angry with Donna that I hit her. I'm certainly not proud of this. I envy any teacher who has had the fortitude to never become frustrated with a student. However, I had exhausted all of the resources I had, and the power struggle had escalated to such a point that I reacted with no restraint.

Donna was a kid who didn't suffer in silence. About 3:30 that day there was a call over the school speakers: "Mr. Funk, please report to the office." Donna had told her mother, who called the principal. My principal was fair and balanced and let me tell my side of the story, weak as it was. Then I was told that this school did not handle discipline problems that way and that I would have to devise different methods.

I found and locked in to a new concept that was becoming established in education at that time: behavior modification. My thought was that if I could no longer overpower kids into behaving, maybe I could manage their behavior through manipulation. I bought a small library of books on the subject, actually got pretty good at the techniques, and began in-service programs for teachers. My one fear plagued me every day: I was afraid that the kids would discover what I was doing. Behavior modification works best on people when they are unaware of what is being done to them.

I vividly remember one incident regarding a student named Ken. I was sitting next to him, teaching him reading, and he was misbehaving. I was using all the behavior modification techniques I knew, including a heavy infusion of ignoring the inappropriate behavior and reinforcing the appropriate behavior. Sounds great in theory, but it was not working. What do we often do when the new stuff isn't effective? That's right, we go back to the old.

I didn't mean to hit him that hard, just enough to get his attention, but my aim was off and I connected with his solar plexus. Ken was another kid who did not suffer in silence. At 3:30 there was another speaker call: "Mr. Funk, please report to the office." This was three years after the Donna incident. Different student, but the same principal. He remembered the previous hit and said something about "strike two." I don't know much about sports, but I did know about "strike three and you're out."

From Control to Cooperation

My concern was heightened. I had a wife, two kids, and a mortgage, and didn't want to lose this job. After all, I enjoyed my work and, most of the time, I was pretty good. I had even won a good teacher award. My quest for how to control kids continued.

In this search, I discovered an audiotape called *The Science of Control* by Jim Fay and Foster Cline. I still lived by the paradigm of controlling kids and the reference to "science" attracted me, since I was searching for something that was organized and proven. Rather than recommending a warm, fuzzy, touchy-feely approach, the tape seemed chock-full of information I could use without affecting my manhood.

I listened to it the first time and was a bit irritated. On that tape Jim said that control is like love. The more you give away, the more you get in return. This seemed stupid to me at the time; the same mentality that says, "If you lean into a punch it won't hurt as much." I had paid six dollars for that tape, but after hearing the control-is-like-love part, I thought it wasn't worth more than a dollar to me. I would have felt ridiculous returning the tape just because I didn't like what it said.

Because the tape was worth only a dollar to me, I decided I would listen to it six times. That way, each time would only be a dollar's worth. This was perhaps not the most logical thinking, but, nevertheless, a way to justify this expenditure to myself.

The next time I listened and got past the control-is-like-love part, I heard:

We either give control on our terms,
or the kids will take it on theirs.

That thought made sense to me. As I listened to the tape four more times, I thought back to John, Donna, Ken, and a lot of other kids I had tried to control. I had long been aware that fighting kids for control was not fun, but I had been locked in to a mind-set—a paradigm—that conditioned me to believe that in order to be an effective teacher, I had to control my kids.

By the end of the six "training sessions," I realized I had never asked myself a fundamental question:

Do I want to control kids
or do I want to obtain their cooperation?

I was to discover that obtaining cooperation is not only more pleasant but is far easier because it involves much less stress for the teacher.

Shared control may, at first, appear to be an oxymoron. However, when considered in view of basic psychological needs and human interaction dynamics, it makes perfect sense. Is there anyone you know who likes to be forced to do things? None of us does, not even when it is in our own best interest. When people make us do things, we feel a loss of autonomy; yet, something within the human psyche seems to push us to get power and control. My suspicion is:

We need control over our own lives.
When we don't get it, we go after control over others.

This phenomenon is often evident in interactions between children and their parents and teachers. When these control issues emerge, we often see power struggles escalate into win-lose situations. And who usually loses? The adult. Sometimes the power struggles are blatant; sometimes they are rather sophisticated. Sometimes there is yelling and screaming; at other times, kids simply engage in a game that eventually exhausts the adult. That game is called "Brain Drain."

I recall an incident that happened some years ago when I was getting my hair cut. A teenage boy with shoulder-length hair had obviously been coerced by his mother into coming into the shop. He was clearly being made to do something he didn't want to do; the Brain Drain game between them went something like this:

MOTHER: I don't know why you have to be so stubborn about this. There are no other boys who have their hair as long as yours.

SON: Yes, there are.

MOTHER: Well, I've never seen them. And
            besides, when your hair is that long
            it looks greasy and scraggly.

SON: No, it doesn't.

MOTHER: And besides, it's not normal for boys
            to have long hair; you're just being
            rebellious. If you had any respect for
            our family, you would get your hair cut.

SON: Mom, Jesus had long hair.

With this last statement, the son had just won this session of Brain Drain. Every time the mother wound down, the son simply made some low-effort statement that wound her up again. She was focusing all of her mental energies on trying to make the kid do something he didn't want to do by moralizing, cajoling, and arguing, all of which take tremendous mental energy. It didn't work. They eventually left without any hair being cut. I suspect this was not the first, or last, incident in which the mother had engaged in a win-lose situation—and lost.

How many times have we seen a similar situation in school? Throughout the history of education, teachers have worked hard to make kids learn, do their homework, study for tests, and engage in behaviors that serve only to sap the energy of teachers and divert their efforts. Teachers and students who engage in classroom combat end up with a zero-sum power base. That is, for every gain by one party, there is a loss by the other party. Kids tattle on the "good" kid, who is, therefore, taken down a notch. Students hand in their homework as the teacher demanded, but it is of low quality or messy. Kids laugh at the mistakes of others so they themselves don't look so bad. Some kids actually strive for rewards only to forfeit them, for no other reason than to deprive others. And some will disrupt the classroom so no one can have free time or go on a long-anticipated field trip.

Choices Within Limits

Control battles are destructive. They create stress in the classroom, hinder achievement, and result in dysfunctional behaviors. But, can teachers eliminate these power struggles in the classroom without giving up their authority?

Within the Love and Logic philosophy, there is a resounding yes. A majority of control battles in which teachers find themselves can be avoided by sharing control with a simple technique called "choices within limits."

Let's first look at the concept of limits. Limits are important because they determine the boundary of our security. Without certain limits we feel anxious. Imagine getting a contract with no numbers on the line designated for salary. If we were to get such a contract and be told to not worry, we would still worry. We need boundaries like this one. How they are set is what is important in relationships.

The key is to set limits without waging war. As teachers, we can make a conscious decision about setting limits by using either fighting words or thinking words. Fighting words (FW) tell kids what the adult is going to *make them do*. Thinking words (TW) tell the kid what the *adult will do*. Notice how the same limits can be set using fighting words and thinking words, but the reaction each inspires is very different.

✎ **LOVE AND LOGIC TIP #7:**
Gaining Control by Giving Some Away

Magically, giving a child choices and ownership of his or her decisions actually gives an adult more control. Why? Because a child who has no control over his life is a child who will spend nearly 100 percent of his time trying to get it. These are the kids who work to manipulate teachers and the system as well.

A child with some control over his or her life will spend little time trying to gain more. That's why this paradox is true:

Teachers gain control by giving some of it away!

Imagine walking onto a used-car lot and having the salesperson say to you, "Look, either buy a car or get off the lot." Our response, and that of most other people, would be to get angry and leave. This salesperson has limits, but they are so confining that we, as customers, would have no opportunity for control. When we have all control taken away from us, we will fight to get some back.

When there is shared control, however, everyone has some and there is no reason to fight. Here's another scenario that takes place at another car lot down the street:

SALESPERSON: Hello. Interested in a car?

CUSTOMER: Uh-huh.

SALESPERSON: Are you more interested in a family car or sporty car?

CUSTOMER: Oh, I guess a family car.

SALESPERSON: Would a station wagon or sedan be what you're looking for?

CUSTOMER: Well, we have three kids and a dog. Guess a station wagon would be best.

SALESPERSON: And about the engine, would you prefer one designed for performance or economy?

CUSTOMER: I'm a teacher—economy.

Salesperson: And about the interior. Would cloth or vinyl be best?

Customer: I think vinyl. It cleans up better.

Now, this dealer can't guarantee a sale, but would you guess that there is a greater chance of making one at this lot than at the previous one? Both salespeople had the same limit: buy a car or get off the lot. The first gave it overtly, with no opportunity for the customer to have any control. The second gave the limit covertly, with opportunity for some customer control. And the control was in the form of simple choices, made by the posing of questions.

When we give choices in the proper manner, we give away some control. Then, the other person has no need to fight us for it. Choices are extremely effective ways to share control, but the act of giving them requires some limits of their own:

1. Choices must be legitimate. We usually are not fooled by choices that are given for ulterior motives.

The choice "Would you rather embarrass yourself in public or have me do it for you?" doesn't offer much shared control.

2. Choices need to be equally acceptable to the person giving them. Given the choice to "do your work or sit here until you do," a resistant kid will probably sit there until the teacher gives up. Never give one choice you like and one you don't, or the child will go for the one you don't.

3. Choices need to be given with equal "pizzazz." If we stress one choice (i.e., the one we want a person to choose), we give the impression that we are manipulating that person, and a control battle is likely to ensue.

High on Control

Whenever I think of choices, I remember an incident that happened at a local restaurant. After an especially hard day, I was comforting myself with some coffee and a piece of banana creme pie when I noticed two women and a little boy enter. They were seated in the booth across the room from me, and I heard the mother say to the boy, "Pick out something to eat." I paid little attention beyond that, other than to note that they looked like a happy threesome.

Soon, the waitress came over and I overheard her ask the boy what he wanted. As soon as the question was asked, he said, "Sketty." As soon as he said that, his mother said, "You're not getting spaghetti. You're getting a hot dog." She said this statement with such firmness that it caught my attention. My curiosity was peaked to see what would happen. What I saw was a lesson in human interaction dynamics.

✎ LOVE AND LOGIC TIP #8:
Thinking Words and Fighting Words

In many classrooms, setting limits means issuing commands. Love and Logic teachers ask questions and offer choices instead, which places the responsibility for decision-making on the students.

Love and Logic schools help kids do exactly what we want them to do: think—as much as possible. When children choose an option, *they* do the thinking. This makes the choice stick with them. Note the difference between fighting and thinking words in the examples that follow. Say them out loud; practice them at home or with fellow teachers to hear what your students will hear.

Fighting Words:	You're going to have to clean this desk, or I'm not letting you go to recess.
Thinking Words:	I'll be happy to let you go to recess, just as soon as that desk is cleaned.

✏ ✏ ✏

Fighting Words:	I'm not letting you go out for sports with grades like that.
Thinking Words:	Feel free to stay in sports as long as your grades are okay.

✏ ✏ ✏

Fighting Words:	I smell alcohol. You're not driving the car from now on!
Thinking Words:	The car is available to you whenever I don't have to worry about alcohol.

The mother had first given the boy some control with her suggestion that he "pick out something to eat." The boy complied. He was given a kid's menu and was happy with those limits. He did not insist, for instance, to pick from the adult menu. He was happy while making his choice, within the limits of the kid's menu—a choice that would affect him (i.e., what he would be eating). Then, the mother narrowed the limits to zero choices. In essence, whether she was aware of this or not, she was saying, "Let the battle for control begin."

My focus was the boy. Up to this time, he seemed to be happy, content to be engaged in making decisions. Now the decision had been made for him and his focus changed. If we can't or don't have control over those things that affect ourselves, we are more than willing to exert whatever control we can over others.

The first thing I noticed was the boy began controlling the direction of the adult conversation. Before, the two women had been engaged in pleasant talk; now they were both looking at the kid. The second thing the kid began to control was the color of his mother's face. It was interesting to see that change, even through her heavy makeup.

I think the kid started to get high on this control, because he continued the offensive and found he was able to control the volume of his mother's voice. Actually, I did not know what the kid's name was until this time, but now it came through loud and clear: "Danny, quit that." "Danny, eat your food." "Danny, wait until we get home!"

Then came the coup de grâce. I knew Danny

had won when there was clear evidence that he had finally controlled his mother's very intellect. She said, "Danny, if you don't eat, I'm going to call the manager!"

I thought, "Oh yeah, lady. What are you going to say to the manager? My little boy is not eating, do something?" The mother lost a battle that never had to occur in the first place.

Let's analyze the situation. Why didn't the mother want Danny to have spaghetti in a public place? Maybe it's too messy. Or maybe she wanted to spend less money.

> *To be given control and then have it taken away produces predictable results, whether with a kid at a restaurant, students in a school, or citizens of a country. Once we have it and lose it— we will fight to get it back.*

Danny was about four years old and didn't have the same prerogative as the customer at the car lot. He couldn't just leave, but he could get control in other ways. It appeared that he had already had ample practice.

From the experience I have had with choices and from what others have told me, I think Danny would have been just as engaged in decision-making if he had been give the choices of a hamburger, chicken leg, or hot dog. Three legitimate choices, equally acceptable to the mother, and given with equal pizzazz. In the same way, there are numerous choices that don't disrupt the classroom or compromise the curriculum available to teachers:

- Would you rather study with a friend or by yourself?

- Should we do reading first or social studies?

- Do as many homework problems as you need to be sure you know the concept.

- Do you want to trade your extra points for a homework pass or for some free time?

Jim tells the story of visiting a class where the teacher gave choices as a primary classroom management technique. She taught kids with behavioral disabilities and knew that to fight kids for total control would guarantee a power struggle. She gave the kids control on her terms, control that would facilitate their learning and not interfere with her overall teaching goals.

For instance, when she gave out math homework, she might say, "Kids, don't worry about doing all of those problems. You decide whether to do the even ones or odd ones." At other times she might tell the kids to do the easiest half and pick out one of the hard ones for her to do on the board. Later she explained to me that she always gave twice as many problems as she wanted the kids to do. She was not lowering her standards in any way.

Her kids were so engaged in deciding which problems to do, they forgot they didn't want to do any.

On one visit, the teacher said to Jim, "Watch this." She gave the following instruction: "Kids, today you have to do all of the math problems." This was not well accepted and one student said, "Hey, no choices! We want some choices."

"Okay," she said, "This time you have to decide if you're going to put the answers on the front of the paper or the back."

Jim thought that no kid would fall for that, but as he looked over the group, several were turning their papers from front to back, deciding which side to put their answers on.

Allowing students to have some control over their learning is a primary factor in sustained achievement.

In his research decades ago, Ferdinand Hoppe established that when we are allowed to set our own goals (i.e., have some control over our learning), we will inevitably perform between a level that is too easy to be satisfying and another too difficult to be accomplished.

When students are involved in their goal-setting, previous accomplishments become the "lower end" and, therefore, are too easy to be satisfying. Typically, the student will engage in a goal at a higher level, and achievement progresses.

Avoiding the Cycle of Defiance

As wonderful as choices are, there are times when the adult must make a unilateral decision. At these times, it is vitally important that a "control account" has already been established. Without this account, kids can sabotage teachers at crucial times.

Imagine a classroom where the kids have had all control taken from them by their teacher. As long as they are "contained," the teacher might be fairly successful. But what happens on a field trip, or at an assembly, or when a substitute comes in? These are ripe opportunities for the

✎ **LOVE AND LOGIC TIP #9:**
Choices vs. Threats

Threats work for some kids, but for many they fail. Why? When someone threatens Sandy, the first thing Sandy thinks is, "She can't make me do that." Her second thought is, "But maybe she can." An internal dialogue begins. "No, she can't." "Yes, she can." Soon the dialogue becomes an internal argument. Sandy gets angry and resentful. She becomes either passive-aggressive or passive-resistive.

If she becomes passive-aggressive, she hurts you back, sometimes so subtly, you don't even know it's revenge. When her teacher refuses to answer Sandy's tenth unnecessary question about an assignment she was made to do, Sandy says, "My mom says good teachers make sure a kid knows what she's doing before doing an assignment." Or Sandy "accidentally" breaks one of her grandmother's dishes to get back at Grandma for threats made to get Sandy to wash them.

If Sandy responds to threats in a passive-resistive way, she resists without letting you know she's resisting. When Sandy's teacher tells her to come into the classroom, her body may move in low gear.

At home she might wash the dishes but leave the sink full of dirty water and the counters unwashed.

These kids are saying, "You might be able to make me do it, but you can't make me do it *your way.*

**This cycle is easily avoided
by offering choices instead of making demands.**

kids to exercise control by embarrassing and/or frustrating the teacher.

A much easier scenario occurs with the teacher who has customarily given bits of control on a daily basis. When the time comes to make unilateral decisions, this teacher can say to the class, "Am I usually reasonable in giving you choices? Well, we are going to be in a situation next week (field trip, assembly, substitute) where I'm going to ask you to act in a certain way and I can't give you choices. I'm sure you will understand."

Because there has been shared control in the past, it is highly likely that teachers and students will work out actions that do not pull them into the cycle of defiance. This is a subtle relationship; but once you, as an educator, are aware of it, you don't have to fall victim to it again.

To review the cycle of defiance:

Intimidation. At the top of the cycle is intimidation, which occurs in several different forms, such as threats, warnings, and restrictions. This intimidation is a message from teacher to student that "I can make you do things you don't want to do." (You have no control.)

Psychological Reaction. Whenever we are made to do things we don't want to do, we feel an immediate loss of autonomy and an accompanying desire to regain some of what we feel we have lost. Sometimes kids openly rebel and become aggressive, but more often than not, the kids will engage in a more sophisticated response: passive-aggressive and passive-resistive behavior. School examples are: When kids hand in messy work they were *made to do*. Kids will embarrass the teacher when a parent is in the room or refuse to participate in a class activity. And much of this is an attempt to regain some control. (Oh, yes, I do have control.)

Stronger Threat. This results in the teacher issuing a stronger threat. The result? The cycle spins in full force. Teachers who recognize it try to avoid this cycle, but some kids are so good at spinning it that we can get involved without realizing it. At these times, the teacher often has to

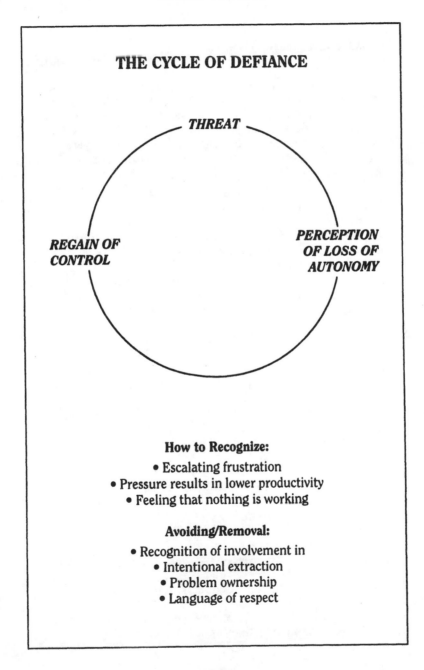

THE CYCLE OF DEFIANCE

THREAT

*REGAIN OF
CONTROL*

*PERCEPTION
OF LOSS OF
AUTONOMY*

How to Recognize:
- Escalating frustration
- Pressure results in lower productivity
- Feeling that nothing is working

Avoiding/Removal:
- Recognition of involvement in
- Intentional extraction
- Problem ownership
- Language of respect

✎ **LOVE AND LOGIC TIP #10:**
Possible Choices in the Classroom

The following is a list of choices teachers can offer their students as a way of sharing control. Remember to offer only those choices that agree with *your* value system. Any that do not can be used to stimulate your creativity to develop choices you prefer. Offering many tiny choices to students sets up an environment in which students feel a sense of healthy control, which makes them less likely to be defiant or resistive.

Have it your way! Do you want to:
1. Put your desks in a circle or in rows?
2. Whisper or talk quietly?
3. Choose your own partner? Have teacher choose your partner?
4. Edit your own paper or have a partner do it?
5. Have lights on or off? Have music on or off?
6. Turn in your assignment at the beginning of class or at the end?
7. Call your own parent or have your teacher call your parent?
8. Walk to time-out room alone or be escorted by the principal?
9. Answer the questions on paper or out loud?
10. Use crayons or colored pencils?
11. Choose topic one, two, or three for your written assignment?
12. Choose to eliminate one problem from this math assignment?
13. Find a way to solve your problem without creating a problem for others?
14. Read your book on the floor or in your seat?
15. Play a group game or an individual game?
16. Do the assignment by acting it out, reading it or writing it?
17. Use your coupons for drinks, trips to the rest room, or an official excuse from today's assignment?
18. Choose the order in which to do the lesson?
19. Choose a topic to study from the several on the board?
20. Have a.m. recess or p.m. recess?
21. Have read-aloud time or study time?
22. Pass your papers forward or backward?
23. Have homework Monday through Wednesday or Wednesday through Friday?
24. Get your current events assignment from a newspaper, magazine, or television?
25. Go to the library with the Monday group or the Friday group?
26. Turn your work in on time, or later for a lower grade?

take the initiative to stop the process, even if it necessitates the extreme measure of admitting responsibility.

Imagine a defiance cycle scenario. What do you think the kids' response would be to the teacher who says, "I think I may have just blown it. I just realized that I'm trying to make you work, and you keep telling me I can't make you. I'm not feeling good about what I'm doing now. Would you give me some time to think this through?"

Most kids would be willing to give the teacher all the time that was needed. The cycle has stopped and the teacher has provided an opportunity for a new start to their relationship.

Shared control, the second key principle of Love and Logic, meets a basic need we all seem to have for feeling some power and autonomy. Teachers who recognize this can learn to give kids what they need in ways that do not violate the teaching process. Classrooms with shared control are more than just happier places than classrooms that involve daily power struggles. They provide an environment in which learning can more readily take place and teachers have less stress.

As you move forward on this path from enhancement of self-concept to shared control, you will discover that the next principle, consequences with empathy, is a natural outcome of what has gone before. This involves more new thinking, but it's the kind that makes old-fashioned good sense.

PEARL
▼

Students base their behavior on the examples set by the adults in their lives.

Love and Logic Experiment #11

STUDENT:

I can't do the assignment.

I forgot my book at home.

TEACHER:

Nice try, Jeremy.

☞ ☞ ☞

Love and Logic Experiment #12

STUDENTS:

(Two students deny responsibility for a misdeed.
The teacher knows that one of them is lying,
but doesn't know which one.)

TEACHER:

What do you think I think?

(This does not produce proof positive.
However, the one that is lying usually says,
in a loud voice, "You think I'm lying!")

TEACHER:

And why do *you* think I think that?

CHAPTER TEN

▼

Consequences
with Empathy

KEY PRINCIPLE NUMBER THREE

One of the great psychological truths is that we often
have to be subjected to deep hurt before we will
make changes in our lives. Pain is not always bad. In a
sense, it is a way of saying something is wrong. People
who have no physical pain sensors live in a dangerous
world. Imagine not hurting when we touch a hot stove.
Likewise, it would be a cold, robotic world if there were no
emotional pain. Imagine what might happen if no one
ever felt remorse for doing wrong.

Many educators have recognized for some time that
pain must come before change occurs. Within the framework of Love and Logic, we recognize that pain comes in
two ways: from the outside in and from the inside out.

Those who make kids hurt, and do so by yelling, embarrassing, and imposing various restrictions, induce pain from
the outside in. People who are hurt in this way, by something outside themselves, tend to react in a "fight or flight"
manner. That is, they either try to attack the source of pain
or run away from it. In the classroom, this can be overt

(yelling back at the teacher or vandalizing the building) or subtle (becoming extremely passive or avoiding class).

People who hurt from the inside and recognize that they have caused their own pain tend to react differently from people who feel something or someone else has caused their pain. The best discovery that we who hurt from the inside can make is that we are the ones who are responsible for that pain. When that happens, we are on the road to recognizing that there are only two ways to get rid of our hurt:

- Wait until the pain goes away.
- Make a decision to change whatever caused the pain.

Making the Decision to Change

Love and Logic recognizes the value of some types of hurting, because it can create actions and lessons that are beneficial to us. Most of us have experienced the loss of a loved one and realized that only time can heal the hurt. In those cases, waiting is part of the process of healing the pain. But with other kinds of inside pain, to wait only exacerbates the problem. Tough as it may seem, the best way to quit hurting is to make a decision to change our behavior.

Several years ago, a decision was made to paint the outside of our house. Painting is not my (David Funk) all-time favorite activity, and I started the job with a less-than-positive attitude. Near the end of the job, I realized I had not purchased enough paint and was going to be about a gallon short. This intensified my negative attitude. Convincing myself that, with the right timing, I could finish painting that evening, I called the store to check on their closing time. To my dismay, the clerk said they were closing in a few minutes, far too soon for me to get there in time. "But," the clerk said, "I live just about ten minutes from you. I can mix the paint, bring it home, and you can pick it up there."

At the designated time I picked up the paint and was deliriously happy that the end was in sight. I rushed home, ignoring the speed limit, and, as I was coming around one curve, my eye caught the glare of a white car with lots of lights and decals parked in a secluded turn-off. My religious fervor was immediately aroused. I started hoping for a miracle. I prayed that this officer of the law was asleep, that the radar was locked, and that my car was really a stealth vehicle.

None of that happened. As I looked into my rearview mirror, all I could see were flashing lights. Realizing the inevitable, I now could only hope this process would not take too long. After a dramatic pause, the officer walked calmly to my car and said, "Sorry I have to do this, but the chief says that anytime we clock someone doing more than twenty miles over the limit we have to issue a citation." He never accused me of anything; he simply asked if I realized how fast my car was going. He then showed me several options I had and encouraged me to do what would be the most convenient. I could pay the fine within twenty-four hours at the local police station or at the county courthouse after that. He even indicated how I could contest the ticket and reviewed all of the steps with me. He wished me well.

I realized I had made a mistake. Whenever we come to this realization, we hurt.

Our brains are equipped with wonderful defense mechanisms. We desperately don't want to be wrong; and when we realize we have made a mistake, we will go to any length to transfer responsibility for the mistake to something outside ourselves. That way, it's not our fault and we don't have to feel responsible. I can blame someone or something else rather than admit that I have to change. I couldn't blame the officer. After all, he didn't even want to give me the ticket. So, being the red-blooded American husband I am, I decided to blame my wife.

I knew I wouldn't get very far by just walking in the door and saying, "Diane, it's your fault I got a ticket!" I had to devise a plan. It didn't take me long to come up with a good one. It had been Diane's idea to paint the house in the first place. If she hadn't insisted on this being done, I never would have gotten the ticket. I also had a backup, just in case the first plan didn't work. It had been Diane's idea to move in the first place. For me, the old house had been just fine.

Obviously, this thinking process was not logical, but emotions precede logic, and I was in an emotional state. All I needed now to transfer the pain I was carrying was something to react to. If Diane would get angry, I would have my high emotional trigger to complete the transfer.

She never gave me the chance. When I told her, she simply looked concerned for me and asked where I was going to get the $90 for the fine. The pain stayed inside.

This was not the end of the story. You see, this was my third moving violation in eighteen months. Within a couple of weeks, I got a letter from my insurance company. It started out with "We regret . . ." and then went on to indicate that they could no longer take a chance on me. However, they were still concerned for me and gave several suggestions as to where people like me might find other coverage.

I started to hurt all over again. I tried to blame the

insurance company, but that was hard. After all, they regretted dropping me and they demonstrated their concern by offering help. I took one of their suggestions and contacted an independent insurance agent. I told her my predicament and she encouraged me by saying she was there to help. "I'll look around," she said, "and get back to you in a couple of days."

When she called her first words were, "Dave, I'm sorry to have to tell you this . . ." By this time, I was getting tired of people feeling sad that I had a problem, because that usually meant a little more pain was coming. She told me that she could get insurance, but that I would be paying about six times what I had been paying before. I tried to get mad at this agent, but she was so concerned for my condition that I couldn't. The pain stayed inside.

I realized that if I waited for the pain to go away, I was in for a long session. I made a decision to change my behavior: to drive within the speed limit. It took three years to get off high-risk insurance, but I no longer have pain about my driving. Now, I look back and realize that I learned a valuable lesson.

I also realized that if this process could be broken down into identifiable components, the lesson I learned could be used in my classroom. Here is the breakdown:

1. There is a problem. When the officer gave me the ticket, all parties involved agreed there was a problem. This is vitally important because nobody is going to spend much time and effort working on a non-problem. The officer's flashing lights were my cue. When you've passed flashing lights on the highway, don't you automatically say to yourself, "Looks like somebody's having a problem"?

2. Identify whose problem it is. This is vitally important, because people often get suckered into working on a problem that is really not theirs. Parents get churned up over their kids' low grades; teachers become upset when their students act up for a sub. The officer did a wonderful job of demonstrating whose problem this situation was by his manner. He was calm, polite, and smiled sincerely. Diane and the insurance people were concerned about what *I* was going to do about the situation. They let me know the problem was mine, not theirs.

3. Show empathy. Empathy is powerful in terms of problem ownership because it is virtually impossible to transfer blame to someone who legitimately feels sad for you. Everyone's empathy made it impossible for me to transfer my inside pain. I was forced to make a decision about *my* behavior.

4. Offer a positive relationship message. Everyone who gave me a negative content message ("You are getting a ticket.") ("We are dropping your insurance.") ("You are going to pay more.") always balanced it with a respectful response. Each person who spoke of my problem and my consequences did so with compassion. Even though my behavior was unacceptable, I still felt everyone's regard. The police officer always called me Mr. Funk, insurance people gave me options, and Diane was sad because the money spent on the fine could have bought at least a couple of power tools. Their messages to me helped demonstrate that this situation was my problem, which made me more and more anxious to get it solved.

Imagine my attitude if the officer had been belligerent. I would have spent time and energy putting down the police department. If Diane had been sarcastic, I would have concentrated on her faults. If the insurance company had been rude, I would have written letters giving them a "piece of my mind." Instead, I had no way of alleviating my pain other than to make a conscious, volitional decision to change my behavior.

The Difference Between Consequences and Punishment

One of the major goals of Love and Logic is to help kids become wise. We need to realize that when kids make mistakes, they hurt. Where they interpret the hurt coming from (i.e., the inside or the outside) depends largely on circumstances and how adults react.

When we hurt, we consciously or unconsciously ask ourselves a question: "I'm hurting. Who caused all this pain?" The answer is vitally important. If the answer is—my teacher, my parent, the police officer—I will focus my attention on something other than my own behavior.

Jim Fay tells this story from his elementary school years:

The Writing on the Wall

I had a teacher I didn't like, and one day I told her so. She promptly sent me to the principal's office. The principal at that school was an impressive man, aware of the psychological principle that kids have to hurt if their behavior is going to change. He had me scrub black marks off the floor for a week. As I scrubbed, all I could think about was how unfair the teacher and principal were to me and how I could get revenge.

I came up with an idea: I would express my views on the walls of the rest room with my crayons. I felt extreme pleasure when the principal walked into each classroom trying to get the guilty party to confess. He never found out who wrote on the walls—that was my reward!

I was hurting and, as I scrubbed, I asked myself who had caused the pain I was feeling. It was easy for me to answer, "the principal did." The continuation of my inappropriate behavior was predictable.

Imagine the difference if the answer had been, "I did." If I had felt remorse for my behavior rather than the need for revenge, the disciplining process would have been far different. If I had felt inside pain, I would have done my own disciplining.

The difference between consequences and punishment is where we interpret the pain emanating from. Consequences result in pain coming from the inside; punishment results in pain coming from the outside.

We might immediately think that the solution is to make up two neat lists of what makes up punishment and what makes up consequences, and then only use consequences in the classroom. Such a determination, however, is largely in the eye of the beholder. Each particular experience is relatively neutral. How we interpret that experience is the vital factor.

The difference between consequences and punishment is not so much the particular action resulting from the behavior but, rather, how that action is interpreted.

Kids will respond positively to a penalty when they see a logical connection between their behavior and what happens to them as a result of that behavior.

This may well explain why penalties such as detentions, writing names on the board, and calling home will work for some kids and not for others.

How, then, can we increase the chances that kids will feel they are being consequenced rather than punished? Consider the following:

- The teacher can develop consequences for infractions.
- The kids can suggest ways to solve the problems they create.

Remember the story of Parley Jacobs, the principal? The student he was dealing with was consequenced, not punished. He was given the opportunity to come up with his own solution, one that would work for him. The answer was inside the child, and the way Parley interacted with him gave the child the opportunity to identify that solution, which in turn became the consequence.

When I (David Funk) was dealing with kids, I often didn't know what would work for them, but the kids usually did. In fact, given the opportunity to do so, most of the time they could give me a list that would work for them. When a student had a problem, and I wasn't sure what would work, my standard question was, "What do you think might happen if you keep doing that?" Here's an example:

TEACHER: Tom, seems hard for you to work on your project today. What do you think might happen if you keep talking instead of working?

STUDENT: I might get a pretty low grade.

TEACHER: That's a possibility. Anything else?

STUDENT: You might keep me after school.

TEACHER: That's another possibility. Anything else?

STUDENT: You might not let me sit next to my friends.

TEACHER: That's another possibility. Tell you what. I'll come back in a couple of minutes. If it seems you're still having trouble concentrating, I'll pick one of those suggestions.

Usually, the kid goes back to work. However, I now have three "consequences" I can put in my bag of tricks for this particular student. The student has identified to me that grades, staying in after school, and sitting by his friends "connect" with his behavior. For other kids, these might be punishments rather than consequences and would increase antagonism or inappropriate behavior, which would render them totally ineffective.

I listened to a story on one of Jim Fay's tapes in which two first-grade boys had been hitting, kicking, and bending the arms of other students on the playground. Jim spends less than fifteen minutes with these kids, has them identify their misdeeds, and arrives at the conclusion that the kids will solve this particular problem themselves. Their assignment, before being allowed back on the playground, is to develop a written plan identifying what they will do the next time they feel like fighting.

Although the tape itself does not identify the boys' solutions, Jim completed the story in a subsequent conversation I had with him:

"The next day one of the boys came in with his plan written on a piece of paper. I can imagine he asked his mother really nicely if she would help him that night. His plan stated that the next time he felt like fighting, he would stand by the playground aide. I would never have thought that would be right for this kid, but that was the plan he devised. Since he had fulfilled the requirements, he was back out on the playground that day.

"The other boy had more difficulty. He had heard that the first plan was successful; so, he decided he would try it for himself. He, too, came into my office with a plan to stand by the playground aide whenever he felt like fighting.

"When I asked if that was his own plan or the plan of the other boy, he replied, 'Oh, it's Wayne's plan.' In that moment, he realized he was going to have to come up with his own. He came up with the plan that the next time he felt like fighting, he would 'sit on the orange bench.' This plan fulfilled the criteria, and he was out on the playground in short order."

A couple of weeks after this incident, Jim was on the playground talking to the aide. He pointed to the two boys and asked about their behavior. The aide said she had not caught them fighting since they had seen Jim, but that one kept following her around a lot, and the other was often on the orange bench. I doubt if Jim would have thought of either one of these solutions. They don't strike me as the kind of solutions teachers would think are effective. But they worked for these kids because they were consequences and solutions, not punishments.

Guidelines for Administering Consequences

There will always be students who will refuse to come up with a consequence, list only those consequences that are totally inadequate, or not be able to come up with any at all. At these times, we as teachers need to make some decisions about what consequences are going to be administered.

These times should be anticipated and prepared for. Some guidelines would include the following:

1. Make the consequence as close to the time and place of the infraction as possible. If there is a lunchroom problem (e.g., throwing food), the consequence should revolve around lunchtime and the lunchroom.

2. Give the child the opportunity to be involved in the solution/decision-making. If the student cannot or will not come up with a suggestion, develop a menu of items with the student.

3. Administer consequences with calm interest. Administering consequences with anger, retaliation, or threats defeats the purpose. Since consequences leave students with no opportunity to displace any anger or pain resulting from the misbehavior, administering them with "calm interest" works best.

4. Give students the opportunity to develop a new plan of behavior. Consequences orient students to the future. Given the chance to look forward, they almost invariably plan with positive intentions.

5. Let students make their own value judgments. Consequences will allow students to make their own judgments rather than have them imposed by adults.

6. Demonstrate problem-solving techniques. Kids benefit from being given the opportunity to see a demonstration (by an adult) of problem-solving techniques. Be constantly aware that modeling is the highest form of teaching.

7. Allow students to feel empowered. Students need to resolve their problems and be left with a feeling of positive self-control, not a feeling that power has been imposed on them by an adult.

Consequences in and of themselves are important, but it is simple to cancel out their effectiveness by coupling them with anger, moralizing, unsolicited advice, or sarcasm. When people tell us what we should be learning, or how wrong we are when they are right about a situation—and their advice is correct—we tend to reject their opinions, even when it is to our own detriment to do so.

Empathy enhances the power of consequences—
that is, a legitimate feeling of understanding
for another person's circumstance.

✎ **LOVE AND LOGIC TIP #11:**
Punishment vs. Discipline

When a child misbehaves, an adult can decide to either punish or discipline. The purposes of these two actions are different and so they produce different results.

	Punishment	**Discipline**
Purpose:	Punish the child's past behavior.	Shape the child's future decisions.
Techniques:	Isolation, time-out, withdrawal of privilege.	Isolation, time-out, withdrawal of privilege.
Emotions:	Tension, frustration, rage, raised voices.	Disappointment, love and concern.
Results:	Child feels angry, out of control; feels loss of self-esteem; focuses on revenge, regaining control.	Child feels adult's disappointment, concern; can focus on second-chance opportunities.

We punish a child for past choices; we discipline to shape future ones. Whereas punishment comes out of frustration and rage; discipline comes from love and concern. Although both actions may use similar techniques—isolation, time-out, or withdrawal of a privilege—the emotional atmosphere of the two is different. The results? Find out for yourself. We find that discipline is the more effective choice every time.

The powerful aspect of empathy stems from the fact that we don't so much want to be agreed with as to be understood. Empathy can validate the person without necessarily condoning the behavior or feeling. I can feel sad for someone who makes a particular mistake without saying the behavior was all right. One of the phrases I recall from my early training in Love and Logic is: "Consequences will do the teaching; empathy will lock in the learning."

Jim's favorite saying is:

Empathy drives the pain of the consequence down into their little hearts, where it can be converted into wisdom.

We have discussed at length the relationship between consequences and punishment and how consequences are involved in the internalization process. Locking in this learning at emotional and subconscious levels is vitally important.

PEARL
▼

No behavior technique will have a lasting, positive result if it is not delivered with compassion, empathy, or understanding.

This Love and Logic Pearl is the most significant difference between Discipline with Love and Logic and other traditional discipline programs. Internalize this belief, use it in all of your interactions, and it will be a friend forever.

Love and Logic Experiment #13

STUDENT:

I don't have any friends.

TEACHER:

That's really sad. What do you think you're going to do?

STUDENT:

I don't know.

TEACHER:

That's even sadder. Would you like to hear what some other kids have tried before?

❋ ❋ ❋

Love and Logic Experiment #14

STUDENT:

(Student is visiting when she should be working.)

TEACHER:

(Whisper in her ear)

Could you save that for Mr. Thompson's class? He handles that better than I do. Thanks.

(Turn your back and walk away without waiting for an answer.)

CHAPTER ELEVEN

▼

Shared
Thinking

KEY PRINCIPLE NUMBER FOUR

*H*ave you ever noticed, at the end of a school day, how kids explode from school with energy to spare, and teachers drag themselves to their cars in complete exhaustion? I'm convinced the reason for this is that teachers use massive amounts of mental energy doing much of the thinking kids could do for themselves.

In too many cases, schools give kids the opportunity to use their creative energies only to buck the system. Remember the elementary school that had 324 rules? Did that stop kids from thinking up new and innovative ways of confusing the teacher? Not at all. Systems that restrict autonomy, attack self-concept, and rely on punishment make the situation ripe for kids to focus their energies on making the classroom more interesting for them. Consider for the moment what it would be like in school if kids focused all their energy on learning, developing their skills, and exercising self-control.

Thinking: Who Does All the Work?

Teachers are often confronted with students, parents, and other interested parties who are in emotional states. Perhaps a student just failed a test or got caught in a fight. Maybe an irate parent came to school ready for battle, or a teacher at your school had just "had it."

What is the likelihood that an effective solution will be developed while one of these people is primarily running on emotions? Probably none, because it is as difficult to reason with people drunk on emotions as it is to deal with people drunk on alcohol. To solve a problem, or even get an adequate perspective on a situation, we must be engaged in clear thinking that is not distorted by the faulty perception that comes with being in an emotional state.

How do we get ourselves and others into a "thinking" state instead? The answer is contained in a reexamination of the first three key principles. Let's briefly review them.

Enhancement of Self-Concept. Our self-concept is easily broken and resistant to change, two factors that cause us to use defense mechanisms to protect who we believe we are. Situations that we feel attack our personhood invoke the "fight or flight" response. We feel we must protect our self-worth, and emotions precede reason. A person in an emotional state needs interaction that enhances that person's self-worth. Then, he or she can begin to think clearly. Experienced teachers learn that emotional parents often enter the "thinking state" after the teacher has done an expert job of listening. The parents' need to be understood has been satisfied.

Shared Control. Autonomy is one of the most valuable commodities. It is cheap to distribute but sometimes hard to recover once it's lost. People who feel control is either being taken away or unjustly imposed will fight to get it back. When we are fighting for control, emotions, once again, precede reason. Fighting any person who is in an emotional state for control usually does nothing more than escalate the power struggle. We need to remember to share control through choices, whenever possible.

Consequences with Empathy. Most negative feelings develop from an expectation that has not been met—our sense of what *should be* is violated. Empathy tells us that someone is, at least, trying to understand our position. Our personhood is validated, even if our behavior is not condoned. Consequences with empathy work well, because they satisfy our need for order and create a situation that does not disrupt our thinking process. One of Jim's favorite sayings is:

> *Consequences with empathy allow the teacher*
> *to be the "good guy" while the questionable decision*
> *becomes the "bad guy."*

Ensuring that people are in the thinking state is vital if performance is to be optimal. How to orient students to this state is the challenge. Proper utilization of the first three key principles allows people to think, but there are times when we may have to force thinking.

The Power of Induced Thinking

Our most powerful tool is interaction dynamics, made up of two equally important parts: asking questions and modeling.

Asking Questions

I remember reading, some years ago, that the use of questions is a tool teachers often overlook. Many do ask questions in class, but are unaware of two essential aspects: (1) how we process questions and (2) the level of questions asked.

How We Process Questions. Our brains are marvelous computers. Even with our current technology, a computer the size of a state would be necessary to perform as many functions as fast as the human brain. However, there are some drawbacks to this complex machine we carry around in our heads. The brain can process only one cognitive function at a time. Further, there are times we don't have total control over our thinking.

For instance, if you were told to not think about what you had for breakfast, you would immediately think about what you had for breakfast. Similarly, it is impossible for us to not, at least mentally, process a question that we have listened to. This processing is a cognitive function, and, as mentioned before, we can only do one of these at a time.

As teachers, we can use these phenomena in our classrooms. Questions, when asked with calm interest, without high emotional overlay to react to, are powerful tools for working with kids.

The Level of Questions Asked. Equally vital is the level of the question we ask. An examination of Bloom's Taxonomy (Bloom 1956) gives us some guidelines for this type of interaction. As you may recall, this system of classification has a hierarchy, from simple to complex:

This is important in the classroom, not only in discipline situations, but in overall involvement in the learning process. What we can verify through observation is that the level of a response (and, therefore, the amount of effort involved) is directly related to the level of the question asked.

For example, if I were to ask you the first digit of your address (Knowledge Level), you would probably give me only that number (Knowledge Level). You would probably not elaborate any further or think any further. This answer, at such a low level, could be labeled a reaction.

However, if I were to ask how your current residence compares with where you lived previously (Synthesis Level), it is highly predictable that much more thinking energy on your part would be involved. This is the important factor in the classroom when dealing with student performance. And the happy truth is:

It takes no more energy on my part to ask a "knowledge" question than to ask a "synthesis" question. However, a synthesis question takes much more thinking for the listener to process.

If a teacher asks a question in such a way that a student focuses on the question rather than on the teacher's emotional overlay, the student's thinking process is more likely engaged than his or her emotional reaction. Thinking increases the chances that a problem will be addressed. An emotional reaction ensures that a student will be distracted from solving the issue at hand.

There is another factor to consider—an overall feeling of satisfaction on the part of a student. There seems to be a settling effect when we have an opportunity to think through a situation.

BLOOM'S TAXONOMY

Knowledge: Recalling or recognizing information as it was learned.

Comprehension: Understanding the material communicated without relating it to anything else.

Application: Using this information to solve a problem with a single correct answer.

Analysis: Breaking information down into its component parts.

Synthesis: Creating something new from parts not previously related.

Evaluation: Making judgments, putting opinions in order, and applying standards.

There is ample evidence that how we ask a question and the level of question asked (relative to the taxonomy) can predict how much mental energy the listener will exert in response.

| How we ask a question | + | Level of question asked | = | Amount of mental energy exerted |

When we engage in thinking,
we demonstrate to ourselves that we are capable.

As we already know, feeling capable is a powerful issue in developing and maintaining self-concept.

When we as teachers allow this process to progress in our classrooms, whether dealing with achievement, behavior, or other student performance issues, we give kids the opportunity to experience what they need without reliance on substitutes for these needs—such as arguing, defiance, and passive-resistive behaviors. Thinking is a natural high.

Earlier in this chapter, it was mentioned that there are times when we need to force thinking with questions. We discussed how these questions need to be asked to be most effective (with calm interest) and that the questions need to be legitimate, as opposed to rhetorical or phrased as put-downs.

Although within Love and Logic, we tend to stay away from lists of what teachers should do, in the case of initiating thinking, it may be helpful to have examples. Some rehearsed phrases may serve us well in situations where there are emotional issues involved (e.g., classroom disruptions, irate parents, or an angry student). In one of Jim's programs, he offered this list for consideration:

Magic Words and Phrases.
- What would you like to happen?
- Would you like my thinking on that?
- Is it possible that . . .?
- How do you feel about . . .?
- Is there any chance that . . .?
- How do you suppose that might work out?
- What do you think I think?
- On a scale of 1–10, how good a decision do you think that is?
- Would you like to hear what others have tried?

These are "magic" because of the enchanting predictability of the other person's behavior when they are used. On one level, they are effective because of what we have recently discussed concerning questions and psychological principles. On another level, they work because, since they are stated in an attentive way, there is an undeniable demonstration that the person is cared about. This is the power of empathy.

Jim Fay tells a story about a teacher who managed most behavior situations with questions. Consider the positive power of this middle-school teacher.

One of her troublemakers entered the classroom with his hat on. She looked at him with curiosity, pointed at his hat, and in an unbelieving way asked:

TEACHER: What's that?

STUDENT: Hat.

TEACHER: Why?

STUDENT: 'Cause I like wearing it, and it doesn't hurt nothin'.

TEACHER: *(Smiling:)* On a scale of 1–10, how good a decision do you think it would be to keep it on your head? Thanks for giving it some thought.

The teacher turned her back and walked away, leaving the student's self-concept in place by giving him time and space to make his decision. A few minutes later, he stuffed his hat into his pocket.

Jim approached the boy later and asked why he decided to take the hat off. The answer he got from the youngster was:

STUDENT: Oh, might as well take it off.
            She'd probably make it a federal
            case after school if I didn't.

This teacher knows the power of "induced thinking."

Trials over Time

When allowing people to think, there is another critical factor to consider: time. In our busy world, time is almost a luxury, but it becomes a necessity when working with people who are solving problems, learning new skills, or internalizing values or behavior.

The best way for the brain to learn new things is via repeated trials over time. We need to mull over ideas, contemplate, and weigh the alternatives before we can come to the best conclusions. And all of this simply takes time. Just because kids have more energy doesn't mean they need less time.

If we give them sufficient time, kids will often come to the same conclusion an adult would.

Earlier in this book we mentioned an interview Jim had with two "First-Grade Terrorists" who had gotten into trouble for fighting on the playground. During that interview, Jim mentioned that if there had been no rule against fighting, the boys would not have been in trouble. They concurred. Then Jim asked them if they would like to get rid of the "no fighting" rule and gave them time to think this through.

The boys' conclusion: Keep the rule. Their rationale was that there were only two of them and fifty other kids. They came to their very reasonable conclusion—the same as the adults who had originally made the rule—because they were not forced into defending themselves or feeling they had to defy authority to prove their own worth. But another reason for their conclusion is that Jim gave them the opportunity and the time to think through the alternatives.

I recall a conversation several years ago with Bill, a student who was disrupting my class:

TEACHER: Bill, I've noticed that you've been doing lots of things in class today besides working on the assignment.

BILL: Yeah.

TEACHER: I'd like to know where the best place for you to concentrate on your work would be, here in class or in the IMC?

BILL: Here. I don't want to go to the IMC today. I'd rather stay here.

TEACHER: Bill, are we talking about what you want, or where the best place for you to concentrate is?

BILL: Concentrate.

TEACHER: What do you think?

BILL: Here.

TEACHER: That sounds fine. How will I know this is the best place?

BILL:	If I do my work and don't talk.

At this point, Bill had come to the same conclusion I was hoping he would come to. This new behavior, however, was not fully internalized and, you guessed it, Bill started talking and not working again. Notice his reaction to the next questions.

TEACHER:	Bill, guess what?
BILL:	I'm talking again.
TEACHER:	That's right. What was the decision we talked about earlier?
BILL:	That if I talked, I'd have to go to the IMC.
TEACHER:	That's what I remember. When can you come back to the room?
BILL:	When I can do my work and not talk.

At this point Bill shuffled off to the IMC. He really didn't want to but he was obligated by his decision. I especially noted that he said he would "have to go to the IMC," which is not part of the original conversation.

Bill conformed to the rules largely because he was treated with dignity and allowed to think. Like many kids, he was considered a discipline problem and unmotivated to do school work. This one interaction may not have changed him completely, but with repeated trials, over time, new behaviors can lock in.

Anchoring and the Bias Effect

There is another aspect of induced thinking to look at. As you are no doubt aware, what we do is often much more powerful than what we say, and part of this is involved in the psychological phenomenon called "anchoring," or "bias effect."

When someone wants to sell us something, this practice is used extensively. To think we have gotten a bargain, a price may be listed as $299.99. We focus, or anchor, on the "2" even though this is really the most irrelevant digit. If the price is listed as $300.00, we may have a totally different response to it.

This concept can be used with people as well, to usher them into a thinking state. For example, I'm sure most of us have seen emergency situations in real life or at least on television. Have you noticed how the paramedics and police talk in life-and-death situations? They often sound as though they are having dinner conversation. Even though they may be churning inside, they realize that if they demonstrate panic, they will greatly influence the level of anxiety in the victim. Their lowered tone of voice and calm demeanor can orient a victim to less panic. In essence, these professionals are anchoring the others and biasing not only overt behavior, but emotions as well.

As teachers, we can benefit from this understanding. Picture a teacher instructing as an irate student barges into the room, obviously furious about something that has recently happened, perhaps in the previous class:

STUDENT: *(In a loud, boisterous voice:)*
            I hate this school and all of you
            idiot teachers!

TEACHER: *(In a similarly loud voice:)* You can't come in here and talk like that. Either shut up or get out!

Further interaction between the two is predictable. If the kid doesn't stomp out of the room, the "conversation" will escalate verbally and, possibly, given the emotional factors, physically. At any rate, the situation will not be ripe for a solution.

The kid, who has a need to be angry, comes in at a given level; and the teacher, in a vain attempt to overpower, enters the foray at a slightly higher level. If the teacher's level isn't enough to subdue (and in this type of circumstance, the teacher hardly ever can be that forceful without crossing the line of verbal or physical abuse), his/her reaction only serves to propel the student to higher levels of emotional response.

Do you recall earlier in this book, when we mentioned a number of ideas that characterize the relationship between kids and adults, and one of these was that our "magic people" have more influence over us than we may readily perceive? And that what we see these magic people do has more power than what they say? In a sense, this is what happened in the scenario above. The teacher, one of this kid's magic people, was anchoring the student to higher and higher levels of emotion.

Let's suppose a different reaction on the part of the teacher:

STUDENT: *(In a loud, boisterous voice:)* I hate this school and all of you idiot teachers!

TEACHER: *(In a tone she wants the kid to model:)* Sounds like you're pretty mad. I'll be glad to visit with you when we are both calm. Would you rather cool off here in the room, or do you think someplace else would be better?

With the simple use of questions and anchoring, what would be a predictable response on the part of the kid? In most situations, the student would lower his/her voice, at least a little, and make some response to the question. Let's analyze why this strategy can be an excellent tool:

1. The student's self-concept remains intact. The teacher, regardless of the student's behavior, is offering dignity and respect (regardless of whether or not the behavior is condoned).

2. The teacher demonstrates model behavior for the student. In other words, the teacher is modeling how to act when caught up in a stressful situation. The teacher is demonstrating control over self, rather than control over others, knowing that self-control is a commodity valued by most everyone. The hope is that this student will say, "I want to be like that teacher."

3. The teacher has taken a potential struggle between the teacher and the student and put responsibility for solution in the student's head. This was accomplished with questions and choices, asked and given with calm interest.

The student becomes less agitated because he or she is forced, or induced, to think. Once thinking begins, calming is not far behind.

Developing the Attitude of Relearning

An important aspect of teaching kids to think is the concept of relearning. We had mentioned earlier that in today's world, and in the world we anticipate our kids will be living, simply learning a skill, or even several skills, is not enough to provide a basis for success. Those who will be successful will be able to *relearn*.

In the past, society and technology didn't change very quickly. Once a skill was learned, mastery was the ability to refine that particular skill. Even science was relatively stable. Once a particular concept was learned about the world, that's how it remained.

So much of what we learn now has to be significantly altered, whether it's a scientific theory, a social issue, or some minor day-to-day activity. People who do not have the capacity to relearn either become confused or rigid. They become unhappy at best; dysfunctional at worst.

I have a friend who is a wonderful woman, but she has learned only to learn. She learned to read, learned what it took to parent, how to manage a checkbook, and how to deal with those things that were necessary for life to go on. But times have changed for her.

Raising kids in today's society calls for different skills; therefore, some of her suggestions are ineffective. Electronic banking is the norm today, so simply being able to add and subtract is no longer all that is needed. She no longer has "a doctor"; instead, she has to see numerous "health specialists." As her world continues to change, just keeping her balance takes tremendous energy.

Coping with change is not the way to success. The act of "coping" can use up so much energy that little is left for enjoyment. However, if we have the skills to relearn, change is anticipated, frustration is reduced, and we are more likely to reach our potential.

This is so important for today's teacher. How many of us knew teachers who had one set of handouts and had used them for the last twenty years of their career? How many of us know teachers who are trying desperately to teach in a way that was successful for them even a decade ago but are facing burnout and frustration every time they enter the classroom today?

Relearning is an essential part of a mind-set for everyone—not only for children and the elderly.

How do we as teachers orient kids to this idea of relearning? I think it is not so much a skill as it is an attitude. It's what we as teachers and parents demonstrate to kids. Do you and I get frustrated when things don't work out the way we planned? Or do we adjust and, when given lemons, make lemonade?

This is not to say we should put kids in situations with feeble foundations and changing winds. Yet, if we are going to provide them with stability and values, this will have to be done within the context of the world in which they live. Of course, none of us wants to be shifting with every new theory, idea, or value that springs up.

For an attitude of relearning to be accepted, there needs to be, first, a sense of stability. Even relearning is done within a context of order. Just as teachers need to have a solid paradigm that allows for change, so do kids. The question is how to do this. Do we develop a curricu-

---

✎ LOVE AND LOGIC TIP #12:
Four Steps to Responsibility

Creating responsible students is a four-step process:

1. Give a student the chance to act responsibly. Let a student decide, for example, whether or not to bring his homework assignment in on time.

2. Hope and pray the student makes a mistake. This provides opportunities for the student to have a "real world" learning experience. If the student does not bring the homework assignment in on time, you can empathize, "I'm sorry you didn't get it here on time." But you don't offer any other alternatives. Allow the student to suffer the consequences.

3. Stand back and allow consequences, accompanied by liberal doses of empathy, to do the teaching. Students need to learn that their mistakes hurt them. Empathy or sorrow reduces the chance that the student will spend time thinking about anything but his/her own life and decisions instead of focusing on anger or other emotional reactions of the adult.

4. Give the same task again. This sends the unstated message that you believe he or she is wise enough to learn from the mistake that was made.

---

lum and be sure we have a certain number of hours for formal instruction? Probably not. When we look at other behaviors we have tried to change, formal instruction has often been expensive and has provided limited results.

I recall one school district that was going to "wage war" on teenage pregnancy by budgeting about $4,000,000 to the cause. That year, the pregnancy rate rose. Why? There are many possible contributing factors, but my guess is that the "instruction" probably focused on contraception—something kids already know. What these kids really needed was something besides sex and babies to validate themselves.

I know of no better way for kids to develop an understanding of those who are different from themselves—to be able to absorb change without being enslaved to it, to not become destructively frustrated over the faults of others, and to form values that will be both to their benefit and that of those around them—than to have their "magic people" show them how.

Share with your students that you are learning to teach through questions. Encourage them to develop with you a plan to assist your learning. Everyone in the classroom, including you, will profit from this attitude of learning and relearning.

PEARL
▼

Students need to learn to think. By giving them practice at thinking, teachers not only gain more control over the classroom, but also model the joy of relearning.

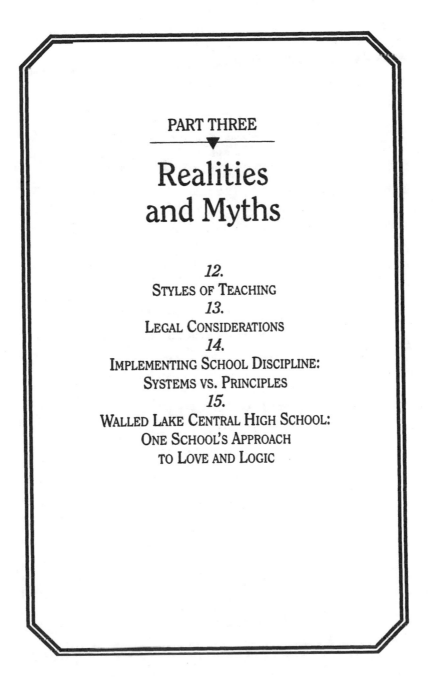

PART THREE

▼

Realities
and Myths

Love and Logic Experiment #15

STUDENT:

I don't need to wear my coat out to recess.

TEACHER:

You can either wear it or carry it.

STUDENT:

But I don't want to.

TEACHER:

I know. And what were the choices?

(Play broken record with this statement regardless of student's arguments.)

Love and Logic Experiment #16

STUDENT:

(Student is trying to argue.)

TEACHER:

I argue at 12:15 and 3:15 daily. What's best for you?

STUDENT:

But . . .

TEACHER:

Let me know what you decide.

(Turn and walk away.)

▼

CHAPTER TWELVE

Styles of
Teaching

*E*ducators have been inundated with styles of learning. It is anyone's guess when there will be a consistent understanding of them all and a strong consensus on which work for which kids. Educators are exposed to teaching styles to a far lesser degree, which places the responsibility on us.

How kids learn is certainly important, but how we teach may be more important in determining the effectiveness of a classroom and giving kids the opportunity to reach their own potential.

Helicopters, Drill Sergeants, and Consultants

Jim Fay identifies three styles of teaching: Helicopters, Drill Sergeants, and Consultants. We have had them all as teachers, and perhaps we have been them all. In any case, it is enlightening to examine how each one operates.

Helicopters. Helicopter teachers are fascinating to watch. Their primary goal is to hover and rescue. They take on many of the kids' responsibilities and make decisions for them that the kids could well make for themselves. Although Helicopters protect kids from having negative feelings and making mistakes, when kids mess up (as they are wont to do), these teachers tend to whine and infuse guilt in the hope that children will learn from being told what is right.

As a result, the kids of Helicopter teachers often feel they are incapable, or a burden. The teacher conveys overt and covert messages that say to the kids, "When will you ever learn?" "How could you do that, after all I've done for you?" Most of their messages tell kids: "You can't make it without me."

This brings us to the negative side of Helicopters. They have a tendency to create artificial situations in which they are needed and others are dependent upon them. It almost seems that deep down, they create these situations as a subconscious way of being needed.

David Funk offers his perspective on Jim Fay's styles of teaching, which he relates to personal experience.

Drill Sergeants. These teachers are also intriguing. They thrive on having power over others. Drill sergeant teachers make lots of demands and are prone to telling kids how they should behave and feel. Harsh words and sometimes harsher actions are the techniques of choice. Drill sergeant teachers give kids the unstated message, "You have low personal worth." "You are a burden, if not an out-and-out irritant."

As with Helicopter teachers, there is a negative side to Drill Sergeants. Their tendency to dominate lowers the self-worth of others. It almost seems that they need to bolster their own self-image by putting others "below" them, substituting domination over others for self-control.

Consultants. From the Love and Logic perspective, the most satisfying teaching style is that of the "Consultant." Consultant teachers are in education on purpose. They love kids and love learning. They recognize their own value and the influence they can have on kids. They focus on preparing their students for the real world by utilizing the Four Key Principles of Love and Logic (whether formally trained or not). Here is what consultant teachers do:

1. Set enforceable limits through enforceable statements.

2. Provide messages of personal worth, dignity, and strength through choices.

3. Provide consequences with empathy rather than punishment.

4. Demonstrate how to take good care of themselves and be responsible.

5. Share feelings about their personal performance and responsibilities.

6. Help people solve problems by exploring alternatives while allowing them to make their own decisions.

7. Provide latitude, within reasonable limits, for students to complete responsibilities.

✎ **LOVE AND LOGIC TIP #13:**
Styles of Teaching

HELICOPTERS

What they do:	• Rotate their lives around their students.
	• Do students' thinking and work for them.
	• Whirl, whine, and complain.
What they say:	• "Why can't you remember your homework?"
	• "I'll think through that problem for you."
Their hidden message:	• You are helpless.
	• You are unable to handle the hurdles in your life, so I have to rescue you.

DRILL SERGEANTS

What they do:	• Bark out orders and call out their list.
	• Turn up the volume and threaten.
	• Command their troops to follow their instructions.
What they say:	• "Don't talk that way in my classroom!"
	• "Don't leave without your pass!"
	• "When will you learn to hand in work on time?"
Their hidden message:	• I know better than you what's good for you.
	• You can't think for yourself.
	• Follow my orders and you'll be fine.

CONSULTANTS

What they do:	• Sympathize with the situation.
	• Listen and provide choices.
	• Leave the decision to the person with the problem.
What they say:	• "I'm sorry you forgot your homework."
	• "Are you planning to stay in class today?"
	• "I argue at 12:15 and 3:15 daily— which works best for you?"
Their hidden message:	• "I know you are strong and wise enough to handle the rough sections of your life."
	• "I care about you and I'm here to encourage you while you travel this path."

8. Induce thinking through questions and enforceable statements.

9. Use more actions than words to convey values.

10. Allow students to experience life's natural consequences, allow time to think through a problem, encourage shared thinking and shared control, and let them be teachers as well as students.

Raising the Odds for Student Learning

I saw one of my favorite examples of a consultant teacher some years ago. I was traveling from Milwaukee to Madison for a meeting and stopped at a fast-food restaurant to tank up on coffee. It was early in the afternoon, so I thought few people would be there, and I could get my coffee quickly and resume my travel.

When I walked in, I was surprised. The lobby was filled with kids. I realized at some point that these kids were cognitively disabled and, because of my special education background, decided to see how the teachers handled the group.

My eye caught one teacher standing with a kid, evidently just finishing his order. He was quite small and could barely see over the counter. There was food and a drink on his tray, and I heard the teacher ask, "And what do you do next?" in a voice that left no doubt that her highest priority was for this kid to learn some skills that would prepare him for the real world.

The kid handed the clerk his money and, after the change was received, the teacher asked, "And what do you do next?" At that point, the kid pulled the tray from the counter and turned to the teacher. As the tray tilted, the contents spilled all over her skirt, legs, and shoes. Her next statement, in the same tone of voice as before was, "And what do you do next?" As I watched her, I thought, "If all teachers could be that way in situations when kids mess up, education would be a wonderful place."

I had first become involved with Love and Logic because of the discipline emphasis. It did not take long, however, for me to realize that there were potential applications to other aspects of student performance, including achievement.

Ben "Gets It"

When I was first exposed to Love and Logic, I thought of a student, Ben, in my class at that time. My idea was that if I could make this work with Ben, it could probably work with anyone.

Ben was identified as "severely learning-disabled" and had not had a very successful school experience. Although he had been retained twice by seventh grade (he would be the only kid who could drive himself to school while in middle school), he was reading and doing math at about second-grade level.

The day I felt ready to try this new teaching style, Ben was right on cue. He walked into class with his usual slow saunter, held up his science worksheet (by this time a bit crumpled), and in a slow drawl said, "I don't get it." This was fairly predictible because Ben often said that, and I knew the scene was set for what I had rehearsed.

In the past, I would have told Ben I would help him with his work. This, of course, he interpreted as my eventually ending up doing it for him, just as so many teachers had done in the past. However, now armed with my new concept of "consultant teaching," I began my new approach. I asked Ben if he had read the worksheet. His response was, "No, but I know I won't get it."

At this point I asked Ben to take a seat at the study carrel and give some thought to how he could get the answer. After a couple of minutes, I went over to see how he was progressing. When I asked if he had any idea of how he could get the worksheet done, he didn't hesitate a second with his answer: "I could get the answers from someone else."

This answer was no surprise. Ben had used that often, not only with me, but with other teachers. Normally, this kind of response would start teachers moralizing about how Ben needed to do his own work and prophesying that if he always worked this way he would never be successful. I suppose these "birdwalks" were entertaining to Ben, and much more fun than doing the work.

I bit my lip, because my "natural" inclination was to go into a lecture about honesty, responsibility, and how it was not right to take advantage of others. Instead, I looked at Ben with "calm interest" and said, "Well, that would be one way. I wonder if you could fool somebody into giving you the answers." I emphasized "fool" just a bit, for the benefit of others in the class.

Ben took me up on this and went to every kid in my room who had science. However, no one was willing to be fooled into giving him the answer. Within a few minutes, Ben was back in his seat looking somewhat unhappy. I went over to him to ask about his success. In his despondent drawl, he said, "Nobody will give me the answer."

At this point I was curious to see what Ben would do next, so I asked him to give this problem more thought and call me over when he had an idea. Within a short time, I heard words coming from Ben that, frankly, made me a bit weak in the knees. From his carrel came, "Maybe I could find it (the answers) in the book."

I couldn't help myself. I went right over to him and told him I bet he *could* find "it" in the book and wished him well in this effort. At this point, Ben's learned helplessness kicked in again. He had mentioned "the book" but made no effort to obtain it. The book was on the shelf of his carrel; he wouldn't even have to stand to get it. But he was waiting for me to get it for him—something I would have done in the past.

Eventually, he did get the book, but not without a hint of manipulation. He started leafing through the book, page by page, beginning with page one. This was April, and the class was more than halfway through the text. I'm sure Ben was thinking that the teacher wouldn't be able to stand this page-by-page ploy and would surely show him the answer now.

Not wanting to revert to my previous behavior with Ben (which would have been to become frustrated with him and essentially do the work for him, just to get it done), I casually walked over to him and made the observation that there were several ways to find an answer in a book, one of which was to start at the beginning and read each page until the answer was discovered. I mentioned this might take a lot of time, but that it certainly was one way.

I then went to work with another kid, always keeping an ear open for Ben, just in case he came up with something legitimate. Soon, he spoke again, in his slow drawl, and said something that made my heart accelerate: "Maybe I could use the index."

Throwing caution to the wind I went right over to Ben and said that was a good idea. What I discovered was that although Ben had "index" within his vocabulary, he didn't really know how to use one. At that point I could do some real teaching. I showed him how to identify key words on the worksheet questions and how to locate these words in the index. He wanted to know what the numbers after the words meant, so that skill was taught. He realized that the chapter they were studying was within a certain page range and concluded that page numbers outside that range would probably not be relevant for answering the questions on his worksheet.

That day, as Ben left class, I did some reflection on my teaching with him. In the past, my "helping" him would have probably ended up with me doing the work for him. I was realizing that in the past, I had been "teaching" Ben many things he already knew. He knew he should get the answers himself, rather than getting them from someone else. He knew the answer was in the book. He needed some skill building in the use of an index. In the past, I probably would have never gotten to that point during class time.

My experience with Ben was a keen turning point in my career. I was in special education and achievement was a primary factor for me. I was beginning to realize that, although I was doing my job with all sincerity, I might have been hampering my students from learning some of the most valuable lessons—lessons that would prepare them for success after they left my class.

I realized that every time I did something for kids that they could do for themselves, I was limiting them in the long run.

This was a beginning. Eventually I began to understand that the Four Key Principles of Love and Logic were derived from observing what people both want and need and that they could be the pattern (or paradigm) for other aspects of the classroom. I understood that kids misbehave, to a large degree, because they want to hurt back or hide their weaknesses. I was beginning to understand that these factors were primary issues in their academic performance as well.

Consider the goal of giving all students the opportunity to reach their own potential without harboring resentment for those at other levels of development. If this were the norm, our classrooms would be filled with students who had retained the love of learning that they had when they were just starting school. However, if we were to see this happen on a global basis, we would have to seriously question some of the fundamental practices that often appear in the traditional system of education.

From experiences with my students and information from venerable educators, I realized that if my primary focus was on helping kids achieve, so much of what I wanted for them would be accomplished. What did I want for them?

- To feel legitimately good about themselves
- To have a respect for learning
- To be successful in their life's endeavors
- To spend their energies on learning, not on misbehavior

I began to realize that this could be accomplished if kids had a real sense that they were learning.

Achievement, then, became my goal. The Four Key Principles of Love and Logic were my roads to get there. The paradigm of these principles gave me a new understanding of many of the learning theories and teaching strategies I had been exposed to throughout my teaching career. A new formula for conducting my classroom was taking shape.

Although this book is not a treatise on school reform or curricular restructuring—that is the domain of others—we can consider how to utilize the Key Principles of Love and Logic in creating situations that increase the chances for student learning. Used effectively by teachers in the area of discipline and classroom management, these principles are also applicable to achievement and other aspects of academic performance.

The remainder of this chapter will consist of concepts and steps to take on the road to finding and using our best teaching style.

The Road to Achievement

The Four Key Principles of Love and Logic provide a pattern for enhancing the opportunity for students to achieve without violating established curricula, grading systems, or other expectations and obligations we have as teachers. To offer ideas that would necessitate radical change would, at best, be difficult and, at worst, be impossible.

Our intent is to offer information about application of Love and Logic principles that can be used in classrooms, regardless of the many variables present.

There is, however, one point of agreement to establish and that is the definition of achievement. Love and Logic advocates a definition that is "real world" oriented:

What Is Achievement?

1. Achievement is attaining a singular goal or standard rather than a relative position among peers. In other words, "How close did I get to the goal?" rather than "How much better am I than anyone else?"

2. Within the Love and Logic framework we emphasize "sustained, continuous achievement"—that is, learning that is incremental, built on previous learning, and sustained over the long term.

3. There are four elements of achievement:

- Ability
- Task difficulty
- Luck
- Effort

The most controllable by the student is effort. Successful completion of a learning task relies heavily on individual effort.

4. Students recognize that within the classroom, different ability levels occur in each learning area. The attribution of success is substantially under the control of the learner.

5. Students' aspirations for future achievement are based on their own previous performance. Students set their own learning goals, within parameters set by the teacher, without comparison with the aspirations, achievements, or goals set by others in the classroom.

6. Success is based on attainment of a standard rather than on a position relative to peers. Sufficient learning opportunities are available for all students to attain the levels of their choice.

7. Reduction of externalized loci of control factors are emphasized. Success is attributed to causes within a student's volitional control such as "working hard," "studying a long time," and "practicing" rather than luck, preferential treatment from a teacher, or "divine intervention."

8. The reason for lack of success is the result of elements within the students' command, such as lack of effort, watching television instead of studying, or not being serious about study, rather than attributing failure to luck, "teacher doesn't like me," or other excuses for not performing.

One way of accomplishing this is to utilize a cumulative point total, a system commonly used. A cumulative point total basically assigns a point value to grades. For example, 500 points might equal an A; 400 points, a B.

In classrooms where this system is utilized, kids do not "fail" a test. Instead, they may get a point for each correct answer. There may be no set number of homework problems; rather, students might get a point for each correct answer. Likewise, end-of-chapter questions are given a value and the points accomplished by the student are then added to the cumulative total for the grading period.

Utilizing this system, students are given a number of ways to demonstrate skill mastery and teachers are allowed to maintain academic integrity.

The Joy of Accomplishment

Regardless of the particulars developed, the contention of Love and Logic is that any program can be enhanced when conducted within the framework of the Four Key Principles of Love and Logic.

Enhancement of Self-Concept. We all have a need to have a sense of self-worth, and our worth is validated in our accomplishments. We feel capable when we have completed a project or learned a task, unless our accomplishment is compared with that of someone else. Competition is valuable, but not when it is the cause of lowered performance.

In everyday situations, we don't often relate a feeling of success with specific actual performance. But from what I can observe, the primary element that pushes us on to further achievement is a feeling of success.

I have had the opportunity to watch our grandson develop and, as it is with all young children, learning seems innately rewarding. They rejoice in their accomplishments and are spurred on with their successes. Watch a young child who has just accomplished putting three blocks on top of each other. His feeling good is obvious and he strives for increasing his skill. He feels good, not because he is better than someone else, but because he has mastered a task and has demonstrated increased skill over previous performances.

Adults are no different. I recall my first attempts in dealing with a computer. Each success gave me encouragement and an excitement to continue on. When I was basing my success on my own previous performance rather than comparing myself to the computer expert, I could hardly wait to learn more.

When I can be good only if I am better than someone

else, or when learning becomes a test of my worth, my attitude changes. If I have some innate ability that can ensure success over my peers, I can still feel relatively good, although this can become distorted into conceit. However, if I buy in to my worth being measured by my achievement, and I predict my achievement will be less than that of someone else, I am more than likely to make excuses for my failure, try to bring the other person down to my level, or quit altogether.

Why we think kids are different, I'm not sure. My observation is that they need the same support adults do when they are learning. Perhaps reading, writing, and arithmetic have become associative skills for adults. Have we forgotten what it was like when we were learning?

I didn't want to infuse negatives into my classroom. I wanted kids to feel good about learning. Taking my cue from Jim Fay's three-legged table of self-concept, I set out to provide an academic atmosphere that would enhance self-concept.

First, regardless of their performance, my students would have my unconditional respect and would be treated with dignity. Part of accomplishing this would be to make sure my expectations were enforceable. No longer could I be satisfied only if the kids met my standards or got good grades. I had to establish an expectation that I would *give them the opportunity* to do their best, rather than *make them* do their best.

Second, I would give kids lots of opportunities to use their individual abilities, interests, and learning styles in their academic learning. This would require planning a number of ways for them to demonstrate their skill mastery, devising as many ways for them to learn as I could think of, and letting the kids themselves decide what ways

Guidelines for Student/Teacher Interactions

1. Give messages of unconditional respect by interacting with kids as we would well-respected adults. Personally, I can think of very few instances within the school situation where kids should not be afforded dignity, even in situations of misbehavior.

2. Be mindful of the role of nonverbal language. As discussed earlier, nonverbal aspects of language carry the most meaning. An impatient facial expression is often remembered for a lifetime.

3. Model self-acceptance. One of the best ways for kids to accept their limitations and recognize that they have strengths is to see their teachers doing the same.

4. Concentrate on the development of trust. Components of trust when dealing with kids include having no ulterior motives, being consistent, and acknowledging mutual experiences—the same thing that applies to our relationships with adults.

5. Place emphasis on individual uniqueness rather than on some hierarchy within the class. Most people respond positively to those who treat them as respected individuals.

6. Give credibility to kids' feelings. Don't discount their emotions by such phrases as "You don't really feel that way, do you?" Of course, they do! This is not to say that we must condone all feelings, but to discount them as invalid is to attack the kid's very inner being.

7. Keep in mind that our self-worth is wrapped in our field of awareness. Teachers with the most "power" can change kids' fields of awareness and still allow the kids' perceptions to change on a volitional basis.

8. Remember that almost all misbehavior has a positive purpose. Most kids misbehave to hurt back or hide weakness. If we can address these issues rather than only the overt behavior, we are further ahead in the long run.

9. Attempt to understand a student's mind-set and world view. Be cautious about seeing kids' behavior through only your own colored glasses. The key to relationship building is to understand another's point of view. Again, this is not to condone a misperception or misbehavior, only to understand it so that effective action is possible.

10. Make kids' learning tasks manageable and put components of success within their grasp. This may be because of the students' ability or effort, but, nevertheless, make success available to them, regardless of the abilities or efforts of others in the classroom.

would be best for them. There is no question of academic integrity. The goal would be to demonstrate that they could learn a particular concept. How they demonstrated this would be their decision. Kids fly on their strengths.

Third, I would let kids experience the consequences of their own behavior. Teachers are part of a "helping profession" and, as such, mistakenly become uncomfortable when kids struggle. Sometimes I think we feel uncomfortable because we think the kids feel uncomfortable—and then they do. So often kids take the cue for how they should feel from the adult.

There would be some things a student would not be good at; I would show them that failures and struggles can be overcome, and when we overcome them, we feel capable—one of the world's best feelings. On the other hand, I wanted kids to be able to experience their successes and not rob them of that feeling by taking the credit.

Kids need to feel loved, capable, and unique. These were to become guidelines to my interactions with the students in my classroom. It seemed appropriate to address self-concept issues in a number of ways.

Shared Control. We have spoken at length about autonomy in terms of behavior management. Freedom can be an important factor in learning as well. There is a phenomenon that can be observed when people have control over their learning goals: When we are given the opportunity to choose, we will invariably choose a goal that is between two extremes—too easy to be satisfying and too difficult to be accomplished.

Our sense of success (or, for that matter, failure) is greatly determined by individually set goals and self-standards. When we self-regulate success in the classroom, we significantly increase the chances for involving kids in sustained achievement, because they have ownership and a vested interest in their learning.

Give kids as much control over their learning goals as possible, without violating the integrity of the classroom and what we are expected to teach.

The control we can give to kids is extensive. Consider how much control the kids would have over their own learning from the following teacher statements:

• "Do as many of the math homework problems as you need to convince yourself you understand the concept."

• "Decide what grade you will be working for. Also, if you earn more points than this grade requires, make a list of what you might do with the extra credit."

• "I have seven ways you could show you understand the causes of the Civil War. Choose one of these ways, unless you can think of another option that would be better for you."

When we allow kids to have some control over their own learning, they often amaze even the most experienced teacher. I recall one science teacher who decided to give her eighth-grade students this control. The assignment was to develop a science project concerning the solar system. She gave her students several ideas, one of which was to decide for themselves if they had a better idea than the ones the teacher had presented.

When it came time to present their projects, she was

amazed when one kid's dad wheeled in a washtub filled with clear gelatin. The kid had made a three dimensional "universe" using Jello as space! The teacher later told me that she never would have considered that way to demonstrate the universe—and she had a master's degree in education.

Certainly kids need to have parameters, whether for behavior or academics, but when we constrain them too much and take away control that could be given without detrimental effects, we can knock the creativity out of them or lock them in to bucking the system.

I recall a story Jim Fay shared with me some years ago about a college student in a physics class. The student was to answer a test question about how to use a barometer to determine the height of a building. The correct answer was to use the barometer to measure the difference in air pressure at the top and bottom of the building and then, using a formula, determine the height of the building.

The student had come up with a number of answers "using a barometer to determine the height of the building." One method was to drop the barometer from the roof and time its fall. Another was to use the barometer as a ruler and mark off "barometer units" up the side of the building. Still another was to ask the building superintendent how tall the building was, and then give him the barometer as a payment for the information. The student even knew a "physics" way of using the barometer, but having his professors constrain his learning is what caused him to rebel.

He was not the only student who has engaged in the Cycle of Defiance (see chart on page 153); we have probably all had one. This cycle is so subtle, we don't even realize we are involved. However, it is destructive not only to the classroom atmosphere, but kids' learning as well. When teachers and students dissipate their energies with

Guidelines for Avoiding Control Battles

1. Keep in mind that your students' feelings of success are a primary component of achievement. Also, these feelings of success do not have much relationship with actual performance unless kids are engaged in competitive achievement. When achievement is defined in terms of approximation of a goal rather than in a hierarchy compared to peers, positive connotations are present.

2. Make conscious attempts to avoid the Cycle of Defiance by giving kids alternatives, using questions, and speaking to them in the language of respect. If you find yourself in this cycle with a kid, you may need to initiate a unilateral "cease fire."

3. Follow the pattern for sustained, continuous achievement, which states that the student is responsible for his/her own progress, with aspirations in advance of current achievement, yet attainable through effort and practice.

4. Allow as much self-regulated learning as possible. Give students control of the learning elements within appropriate parameters that are, ideally, set by mutual agreement between students and teacher. There *is* an accountability element, and students at some point are responsible for demonstrating skill mastery.

5. Value judgments about a student's behavior or work can be made; however, generate these from the student, not from the teacher. Normally, this can be accomplished with such questions as "What did you think of your work on that project?"

6. The ideas of "fairness" and "equity" are identified as meeting individual needs, not treating everyone the same.

power struggles, everyone loses. How can we avoid this? The preceding chart has some suggestions.

Consequences. All people I have ever met (1) need some order and (2) learn better when a logical relationship exists between what they do and what happens to them as a result. When we have the opportunity to experience that our behavior affects our outcomes, learning internalizes. However, when this relationship is diffused with extrinsic rewards and/or punishments, risk-taking and the intrinsic value of learning tends to decrease.

In the classroom of a consultant teacher, consequences, with an equal balance of empathy, are common and visible. Consequences with empathy are equally applicable to success and failure. Kids soon learn that when they make good decisions, they feel good; when they make bad decisions, they feel bad. The teacher is there to guide and model appropriate behavior, but never to rob the kids of the experiences that will make them better adults.

An application of consequences often overlooked is in relationship to grades. How many times have we "hoped" for a certain grade or been pleasantly surprised or sorely disappointed when we opened a report card or got a test back? When this happens, grades become a reward or punishment.

When grades become a punishment, a student's natural response is to avoid that source of pain. This usually results in some kind of misbehavior or performance problem. If the grades are interpreted as a reward, a kid may tend to work for the reward and, at the extreme, become a reinforcement junky. How many kids have we known who refuse to perform because they are "going to get an F anyway" or who become devastated if they don't get straight A's.

When grades are a consequence, they are simply an efficient feedback mechanism to verify performance. Grades should never be a surprise. When they are, and they become a punishment or reward as a result, they are, in the long run, ineffective.

Love and Logic teachers often talk about grades with children like this: "Kids, I was at the football game last night. I discovered that the players, coaches, and fans for both teams were frequently angry with the field judge, but never with the scorekeeper.

"I decided that I'd rather be your scorekeeper than your judge when it comes to grades. I will help you keep score and help you translate the score into letter grades. You can come to me any time to talk about your score and progress. That way you will never be surprised about your grade."

Regardless of the system used to evaluate progress, within the Love and Logic framework grades represent attainment of a standard or goal, regardless of the goals or attainments of others. When kids have a sense of personal causation in terms of their learning, they become invested in their learning. They feel a logical connection between what they did and what happened as a result.

When teachers make rules,
assign criteria for grades with no student input,
and control what constitutes learning—
kids often lose interest.

Natural consequences, then, become an important part of orienting students to sustained achievement. Here are some general guidelines for maintaining them as a component of classroom atmosphere.

Guidelines for Utilizing Consequences in the Classroom

1. Combine consequences with empathy rather than with pity, blame, judgment, or anger.

2. Allow students to own their own problems. The teacher can guide a student in solving a problem but should never let the kid's problem become hers/his. When we see others highly involved in solving our problem, our tendency is to let them.

3. Hurting and struggling are part of gaining wisdom. However, there is a difference between making kids hurt and allowing them to hurt. When kids are allowed to experience the consequences of their own behavior, their "inside pain" forces them to make a decision about that behavior.

4. Reduce any opportunity for a student to transfer any of his/her hurt to the teacher after making a mistake. Too often adults, with high emotional overlay (e.g., anger, sarcasm, frustration), allow kids to focus on the adult's emotions rather than on their behavior.

5. Focus on effort as an attribute of success rather than luck, preferential treatment by a teacher, or other external loci of control issues.

6. Reduce "toxic" rewards. Be cautious about orienting kids toward working for grades or making grades a measure of the student's worth.

7. Measure success on the basis of approximation to an individual goal or objective standard rather than to relative rank with other students in the class.

8. Maintain consistency. Utilization of the Key Principles of Love and Logic significantly reduces the stress that interferes with consistency.

Shared Thinking. We all have a need to feel capable. Thinking through a problem, creating solutions, and developing ideas allows us to demonstrate (whether to ourselves or others) that we have ability. Thinking also allows us to feel unique. When kids cannot feel distinctive in their thinking, they are more than willing to substitute clothes, hairstyles, and behaviors adults consider typical of the "rebellious teenage years."

I'm convinced that thinking is rewarding,
something we innately want to do.
We quit thinking only when it has brought
negative consequences.

In the ideal world, the need to feel capable is fulfilled by exploring our environment and making conclusions. This is common with toddlers, as well as with adults working with hobbies, or engaging in political or sports talk. So sad is it that this curiosity and love for learning is reduced to near zero for some kids as they progress chronologically through school.

This phenomenon results from the fact that as kids move through school, there is a narrowing of acceptable responses, and the potential for high rewards becomes more and more restricted. Exploration, natural curiosity, and innate rewards for learning often drop out of the picture.

A kid in kindergarten who draws a blue tree
might cause a teacher to wonder at
the kid's fertile imagination.
Drawing a blue tree in sixth grade could get a kid
a referral for special education.

Strict conformity can result in student apathy for a number of reasons—boredom, fear of failure, or resistant behavior. Teachers who put inordinate emphasis on a particular method of demonstrating skill mastery (e.g., tests, projects, homework, class participation) will lose those kids who are not good at that particular method. Likewise, teachers who limit the opportunity for kids to think at a high cognitive level will also lose students.

To break out of this cycle is difficult, because most teachers are required to conform to given techniques and materials. However, even if certain parameters are in effect, effective interaction dynamics between student and teacher can increase the chances that kids will be heavily involved in their own learning.

There are innumerable ways to encourage kids to think. Asking questions, setting goals, and applying consequences with empathy have been discussed previously. Here are more specific suggestions.

✎ **LOVE AND LOGIC TIP #14:**
Affordable Price Tags

It's important for children to learn to make wise choices while they are young, when their mistakes have smaller price tags. If an adult loans a grade-school child money for rollerblades, the adult can create a real loan situation like "First National Bank," drawing up a promissory note with a payment due date and a repossession clause.

If the child misses the payment due date, the adult becomes the owner of a pair of rollerblades, and the child learns a lesson in financial responsibility—while the price is still affordable. Learning that lesson with a $100 set of wheels at age ten may save that child from having to learn that lesson over a $15,000 set of wheels later on.

Encouraging Students to Think

1. Ask high-level questions. Bloom's Taxonomy is but one guideline for obtaining ideas.

2. Allow students to solve problems that affect them. Certainly the teacher can be there to guide students and suggest alternatives, but does not have to unilaterally determine the solution.

3. Reduce judgmental respones. Within the Love and Logic philosophy, we believe the effect is much more long-term when judgments and perceptions are made by a kid, rather than by the adult doing it for them.

4. Allow time for kids to think. Too often we go for an immediate response. If we give kids sufficient time to process a situation, we give them the opportunity to arrive at the best solution.

To conclude this chapter, it seems appropriate to review the academic applications of the Four Key Principles of Love and Logic. The more we think about them and allow them to filter through our thought processes, the more we are able to digest them and, finally, use them to our teaching advantage.

Jim Fay worked with a middle school for a short time to help the staff implement Love and Logic. The staff was initially delighted with the results of using Love and Logic for their discipline program. Within a matter of months, the principal reported to Jim that office referrals for discipline had dropped by almost 90 percent. The staff was sold on their new approach to discipline.

Several months later, the principal contacted Jim. The staff was no longer sold on using Love and Logic. The teachers were saying that it was not working. Jim asked if kids were misbehaving and if the office referrals had gone back up. The principal said that office referrals had, in fact, continued to drop. He said that behavior was not the problem, but that Love and Logic was not working and that teachers were discouraged.

This did not make sense to Jim. How could discipline be better than ever, and yet the teachers were saying that the program was not working? As he worked with the principal, it became evident. The teachers had been so successful using Love and Logic as a disciplinary tool that they then thought it should work just as well to make kids do their assignments.

These staff members had the mistaken idea that discipline techniques will also solve problems related to underachievement and reluctance to perform written assignments.

Jim met with the staff once more and demonstrated to them that the techniques used to solve problems around learning and performance are distinctly different techniques than the ones used to solve discipline problems. Once the teachers realized this, they were happy to use Love and Logic to manage discipline and set out to learn the skills needed to solve the learning problems.

Don't fall into this trap of believing that techniques used to solve discipline problems are readily used for learning and performance problems.

It is easy to become so successful with discipline through the use of the techniques in this book that you make the assumption that these discipline techniques will also get kids to do their assignments. Nothing could be farther from the truth. Punishment, rewards, and consequences have never proven to be effective in making long-term changes with underachievers.

Love and Logic was designed to address behavior problems, not to make kids do their assignments.

As you read the following information about academic applications of Love and Logic, keep in mind that I am referring to the process of developing optimal learning environments. I am not referring to solving learning problems or dealing with reluctant or apathetic learners.

The following information and strategies will raise the odds for success with your students and give them the best possible opportunity to achieve.

Academic Applications of the Four Key Principles of Love and Logic

1. We all have a need to achieve. Achievement validates us, shows that we are capable, and allows us to demonstrate our unique characteristics.

2. Optimal achievement is an individual accomplishment. Within the Love and Logic approach, optimal achievement is attained from accomplishments that give a sense of satisfaction and closure. This feeling is determined on an individual basis, without negative reactions toward others who may have differing abilities or levels of mastery.

3. Any system that denies a feeling of success creates a negative reaction. Sometimes this reaction appears as student apathy or attempts to create a zero-sum classroom where successful students are "put in their place" by students who experience less success.

Although there are certainly factors outside the control of the teacher that affect student performance, there are thousands of classrooms throughout our nation in which disadvantaged kids are achieving and have a love of learning.

There seem to be some basic characteristics of classrooms with a positive atmosphere, and the variables do not seem to be curricula, equipment, or teaching strategies. Rather, the most essential characteristic seems to be the attitude of the teacher. I have had the opportunity to visit many classrooms. Those that are consistently productive have two primary characteristics:

1. Positive teacher/student relationship is a key factor. Productive classrooms have teachers who demonstrate self-control, consistency and respect for their students. These teachers model how a well-put-together adult behaves, even in the face of stress.

2. Achievement is defined as attainment of a goal. Students are involved in their own learning goals and are accountable for the attainment of those goals, without regard for how they compare with their fellow students. Opportunities are given to students to utilize their strengths, rather than to be reminded of their weaknesses.

Consultant teachers recognize faults in the system, but do not use these as an excuse to not teach. They also recognize that, although they may not be able to rectify all the problems that need to be addressed, they can work with a few and, in doing so, have a lasting influence on their students.

Among the faults in the system educators are recognizing more every day is the way legal issues are cropping up in the area of education. In the chapter that follows, we hope to familiarize you with what you may, but hopefully will not, need to know for future reference.

PEARL

▼

Those who believe it cannot be done need to get out of the way of those who are doing it.

Love and Logic Experiment #17

STUDENT:

(Other kids have been complaining that he causes problems on the playground. Teacher does not know what to believe, but tends to believe the complainers.)

TEACHER:

Jason, we are going to conduct a diagnostic experiment. That's where we diagnose the problem. I'm going to keep you off the playground for five days. If the problem stops, what do you think I'll think? If the problem continues even without you being on the playground, what do you think I'll think?

STUDENT:

But it's not fair.

TEACHER:

It's not punishment. It's an experiment.

STUDENT:

But it's just not fair.

TEACHER:

I'm sure that's true. And remember those other times when you didn't get caught? This will make up for some of them. Good luck with the experiment.

▼

CHAPTER THIRTEEN

Legal
Considerations

*I*t is an understatement to say we live in a litigious society. The United States has most of the world's lawyers, and millions of lawsuits are filed in this country each year. The rules surrounding legal issues are complicated. Many of us have been in court-related situations in which we felt very vulnerable because we had no idea what was going on, how the game was played, or what the rules were. We may not have even known the meaning of words that were being used.

The intent of this chapter is to offer information that may not be common knowledge to many educators. However, this is not to be construed as legal advice. We want to make clear from the outset that there is no substitute for competent, professional legal counsel when the situation demands.

The Bottom Line

Educators have, at least in the recent past, been barraged with new teaching concepts, social changes, and other pressures that impact on our classroom performance. We spend so much time on new curricula, technologies, and teaching strategies designed to improve our skills and help us be better teachers that we have little time to spend on reading the fine print of education law. As a result, the "bottom line" is ignored. Education's bottom line—the legal aspects of education—continues to have an increasingly significant effect on teachers. Yet, few teachers have had formal instruction on how education law can affect them; too many are woefully unknowledgeable about their professional liabilities.

Many teachers may also have the erroneous idea that if they are taken to trial and are found "not guilty," their troubles are over. This is hardly the case. Regardless of the findings of a court, teachers are subject to administrative hearings, and the rules for these are substantially different. Whereas rules of evidence prevail in a court, hearsay may be used in decisions made at an administrative hearing.

Awareness of legal liabilities is a subject David Funk feels strongly about. In this chapter he presents top-notch information that educators will find valuable and instructive.

It takes little research to find case after case of teachers who are negatively affected by legal proceedings. Educators have lost their careers from actions stemming from student accusations (some of which have been false), failure to maintain classroom control, and violating students' rights to due process.

When I teach a course called "Discipline With Love and Logic," we deal extensively with the legal aspects of discipline. Typically, after an hour or two of instruction, I ask for a raise of hands of those who know more about their legal liabilities now, after that brief amount of instruction, than they ever knew before. Virtually everyone responds. I have two emotions at that time: anxiety and annoyance. My anxiety comes from the fact that those in the class knew next to nothing about their liabilities, which makes them extremely vulnerable. My annoyance stems from the fact that I personally believe our teacher-training institutions, and districts employing these teachers, have a moral obligation to provide information about such issues that can have life-changing effects on the personal and professional lives of educators.

The Scope of Employment

In conversations I've had with teachers about their liabilities, often the comment is made that if educators are doing what is best for kids or the "morally" right thing, they feel they will be able to avoid legal penalties. It would be a wonderful world if this were true, but, frankly, it is a bit naive. The reality is that we can only guarantee protection for activities performed within the scope of employment.

Written Authorization. "Scope of employment" is a term that basically means we have job-related legal protection for activities we have been contracted or directed to do and that have been approved by some authority.

Teachers who do "good things"
that are outside of officially sanctioned activities
may be placing themselves in a position of
great vulnerability.

For instance, teachers who take it upon themselves (again, without obtaining approval from or sanction by school authorities) to take a special field trip, have a group meeting during non-school hours, or discipline a student outside the approved procedures, are setting themselves up for potential trouble. In such situations, master agreements generally allow disciplinary measures to be at the "discretion of the Board," a very loose term that can leave a teacher woefully unprotected.

Liability Insurance. Even such activities as transporting students for a school-related activity may put teachers in an unanticipated position. It would be wise for teachers engaging in such practices to look at their district's liability insurance policy. In those policies I have been made aware of, the indication is that those using private vehicles for school-related activities are covered by the district policies "in excess" of their own personal liability.

What this means is that the driver's insurance pays first, with the district's policy picking up any excess. Let's suppose that the driver's policy has a $300,000 liability limit and any suit is settled for $500,000. The two policies would probably keep the driver from any personal cost. However, we all know what happens when our insurance companies have to shell out that much money. A "we regret we cannot keep you" letter is sure to follow. Further, when application is made to a new insurance company, the typical question that company asks, which does us in every time, is: "Have you ever been denied insurance in the past?"

Protection for teachers, then, comes from ensuring that all activities are approved with a contract, or at least written authorization, from an administrator and making sure that other variables (e.g., insurance coverage) are well considered. Since courts usually consider those with higher authority as responsible, teachers can best protect themselves by obtaining a "contract" for incidental activities, even if no financial consideration is involved.

Educational Malpractice

For most of us, the concept of professional malpractice is confined to doctors who leave sponges in us after surgery. However, we must keep the following definition in mind:

Malpractice involves lack of skill in performing professional duties, no matter what the profession.

Because teachers are certified, the presumption is that they have at least a minimal level of competency. Those who fail, and, in some cases, organizations that hire them, can face serious consequences.

Lack of Skill. For instance, certified teachers are presumed to have acquired sufficient skills to maintain an environment conducive to learning and to convey knowledge and/or skills to their students. This is often summarized by the phrase "duty to supervise and instruct." When this is not accomplished, the accusation of "lack of skill" can be made.

Let's look at an analogy, using a doctor/patient relationship. Suppose you have a particular ailment and go to your doctor for treatment. A prescription is given and you faithfully do as instructed. Two weeks pass and you are feeling as bad, or worse, than before. You again see your doctor and are given the same prescription, but told to take twice as much as before. Given the idea that sometimes "more is better," you, again, faithfully do as instructed.

Two more weeks pass and you are still feeling as bad, or worse, than before and make a third appointment. At that appointment the doctor gives you the same prescription again. At this point you ask a pointed question:

YOU: "Why are you giving me this pill when it hasn't alleviated the problem?"

DOCTOR: "Well, it's really the only medication I know anything about, the pills are pretty cheap, and it has worked for some of my other patients in the past."

Most of us would be rather alarmed and would certainly consider the physician less than professional and probably guilty of at least some level of incompetence. If this were a pattern, the physician would be ripe for an accusation of malpractice.

Repeating Ineffective Procedures. Similar situations occur in schools every day. I am personally aware of a student who received 256 detentions in a single year. When I was made aware of this, my first question was, "How can a kid get that many detentions when there aren't even that many days in the school year?" The answer I got was, "When a kid misses a detention, the number is doubled." My second question was, "How many detentions do you have to give a kid before you realize they aren't working?" The answer, not nearly as pat as the first, basically was, "What else can we do? Besides, don't detentions work for some of the kids?"

Certainly, detentions work for some kids. The pill the doctor prescribed in the previous scenario probably worked for some people. But where is the justification for continuing with obviously ineffective procedures?

There are a number of activities, used in education from time immemorial, that, given the tenor of today's society, could be cause for concern. As parents become more legally savvy and focus on calling schools to task, teachers may want to give considerable thought before continuing some practices simply because they worked in the past.

Learning as Punishment. I know I am not the only kid who had to do extra math problems or copy page after page of the teacher's favorite *Webster's Dictionary*, for misbehaving in class. Such practices serve only to antagonize kids and have little remedial justification.

Using Grades to Control Behavior. Teachers would be well advised to reconsider using grades for anything except reflecting actual skill mastery, rather than effort, improvement, or other behavior. To be judicious, all grades should be equally accessible to every student.

Grading on a Curve. This may be another practice for reconsideration. It does not allow for equal accessibility to every student, and only indicates mastery relative to others in the grading pool. Also it does not always give an accurate indication of what skills the student does or does not have.

Ignoring Students' Individual Capacities. With the advent of special education and "504" legislation ("504" refers to the section of civil rights legislation that went into effect in 1973, which basically states that individuals cannot be discriminated against because of being handicapped), the courts are now increasingly involved in determining a definition for "appropriate instruction." This individualization may include modifying materials, giving additional time to complete tasks, and developing teaching strategies to address different ways of learning.

Student Access to the Results of Other Students' Work or Other Personally Identifiable Information. A teacher may unwittingly get into trouble, for example, trying to encourage one student by offering that student information about another student that is, in actuality, confidential. Since both tangible and intangible property (grades are considered intangible property) can be "taken away" only by due process, giving this information indiscreetly may be considered violation of a student's rights.

Punishing Special Education Students for Behavior Related to or Resulting from the Handicapping Condition. Here is another situation about which we want to caution teachers. We all know the level of annoyance a disturbed student can create, but, to a large degree, special education laws indicate that for a student to be punished because of his/her handicapping condition results in a discrimination against that student. This situation will be discussed further in a later section. Suffice it to say that we need to proceed with caution when it comes to disciplining special education students.

Discipline and Constitutional Rights

As mentioned in an earlier section of this book, discipline was not a very big concern for my teachers. Because kids didn't have the concept that they had "rights," teachers could generally use any method they determined to be effective. That often included restricting access to the classroom, confiscation of property, and even corporal punishment. That all changed in the late 1960s with a court decision commonly referred to as *Tinker vs. Des Moines Public Schools.*

Several students decided to protest the U.S. involvement in Vietnam by wearing black armbands. School officials addressed this threat of student protest by calling this action disruptive to the educational process and any students participating in this action were threatened with removal from school.

Several students, disregarding the direction of the school, did protest and were subsequently dismissed from school. Eventually the courts were involved and ultimately made a decision that affected schools' authority to regulate student conduct. The decision stated that students are people and people have rights, and these rights are not relinquished at school.

Prior to that decision, schools had virtually the same authority as parents—to make rules, regulate student behavior, and determine the criteria for students to remain in school. After that decision, regulations had to be weighed against the rights and freedoms protecting individuals as per the Constitution. For instance, prior to this decision, there had been no question that a school could regulate students' clothing, boys' hair length, and conduct.

How different that one aspect is in today's schools. How students dress, wear their hair, and what they put on their notebooks relies more on First Amendment rights than on what is "appropriate," and these rights can be reduced or removed, in the final assessment, only through due process.

Due Process: Two Kinds

Due process also regulates what is protected by the Fourteenth Amendment. That is, "life, liberty, and property" cannot be taken except by due process. Although "life" is usually not a question for schools, "liberty" and "property" certainly are and involve student speech, locker searches, dress codes, personal items, and evidence of learning.

Students in a vast majority of states have a constitutional right to an access to education. To reduce or deny this right involves due process.

"Due process" may be a familiar term to many, but usually few can verbalize what it means within the context of a classroom. There are two kinds of "due process"—substantive and procedural.

Substantive Due Process. Substantive due process simply refers to the substance or content of rules and regulations. Provided these regulations are not arbitrary or capricious, there is usually no need for concern.

Procedural Due Process. Procedural due process refers to the process itself. It is more complicated and, in my experience, more cause for concern.

For teachers who wish to ensure, to a high degree, that they are not violating due process, the following steps are recommended:

1. Have clear goals and expectations. Rules and regulations should be based on justifiable standards and must avoid any appearance of being arbitrary or capricious. These rules need to be conveyed to all involved, including parents and administrators. Suggestions for verifying dissemination include putting "rules" on the bulletin board, sending letters home (registered mail, if necessary), and notating in your lesson plan book when the rules were covered, such as in class or as a topic for an open house. You never want the accusation to hold that a "violator" did not know what the rules were.

2. Have evidence of student involvement. Involving students in a disciplinary process substantiates that they have had an opportunity to understand the effects of their conduct and have had input into what strategies would be most effective to address the situation. There are any number of ways to substantiate this involvement, including documenting conferences with the student, student involvement in determining the consequences of his/her behavior, or testimony of others serving as observers. One teacher I know utilizes a time-out procedure that requires the student to write answers to the following three questions: (1) What is the problem? (2) What are some solutions to the problem? and (3) What is the best solution? The student's responses are the basis for discussion and are filed as documentation.

3. Give opportunity to improve. Although schools are not obligated to indefinitely keep trying things that are not working, there is a need to give a student a chance to indicate his or her good-faith effort to improve. There has to be the opportunity to determine if a particular remedial or disciplinary technique is working. However, that is not to imply that the same ineffective procedure is to be used over and over, although a particular procedure could be modified to "up the ante."

For instance, a time-out procedure could be developed on a hierarchical scale: The first time, a student returns to class when she or he feels able to handle the rules. Should this not work, the contingency could increase to returning to class after the student had developed a written plan. Should this not work, the student could then be required to have a conference with the teacher before the return to class would be permitted.

This cycling of the same basic technique is effective with most kids. However, in my view, if this is done more than three times, this is a sign that the basic technique is not effective for this student. Giving kids an opportunity to improve is not synonymous with playing games.

4. Have written evidence to support the circumstance. Written evidence is of vital importance to (1) justify higher levels of intervention and (2) protect teachers. Such evidence may include documentation of the incidents involved, summaries of interactions from both teacher and student, and/or copies of letters to parents and administrators. All written evidence should be dated. If conversations are to be used as documentation, these should be summarized and reviewed with all parties to ascertain accuracy.

Compelling State Interests

We have spent a substantial portion of this chapter discussing rights of students. This is appropriate because they have more rights than teachers, who are considered agents of the state. However, educators are not helpless. We have a resource that has been secret to most, but will be no more: compelling state interests.

I recall a story told by a teacher some years ago about a student who was quite knowledgeable about his rights. He informed this teacher of his knowledge frequently. After we had discussed the concept of compelling state interests in class, she said she thought this would be a great tool to use to reach this particular student.

By the next Monday, she had her plan ready. Her student, whose name is Will, misbehaved and, before he could remind her that she better not violate any of his rights, she simply put a check on a paper she was carrying on her clipboard. She said nothing. She did note that Will, as predicted, was apparently quite interested in what the paper and check represented.

He was, however, too "important" to ask for himself, so he sent his "bodyguard." When asked what this procedure was all about, the teacher, very calmly, responded, "I know Will is very knowledgeable about his rights, so I am sure he is aware of 'compelling state interests.' I've decided to keep track of those violations instead of just the little irritations he causes in class, because those violations are much more likely to hold up in a hearing."

You can imagine the interest Will now took in his behavior. Obviously, he had no understanding of "compelling state interests" and, in fact, because of this situation, Will decided it would be in his best interest to interact with the teacher. She was able to make some real and constructive contact with him.

Although individual rights are of high priority, the law recognizes that there will be times when individual rights must be subordinate to what is best for the common good.

If we use "compelling state interests" as the foundation for rules that will limit individual rights, we will be developing fewer rules and regulations that will be challenged.

What are compelling state interests? They are fairly common sense and, if used properly, powerful tools for educators in their quest to have order in the classroom. They are:

1. Prevention of property loss or damage. Schools have the right to establish rules that will protect property from being stolen or damaged. Although rules against vandalism reduce what some students want to do, the rules are valid. Likewise, classroom rules based on treating the property of others with respect are on a sound foundation.

2. Preservation of health and safety. Rules and regulations based on the intent to preserve health and safety of students and teachers are not only obvious, but justifiable on the basis of maintaining the common good. Rules based on this premise are also on a good foundation.

3. Serving legitimate educational purposes. Although this may be a bit more esoteric than the previous two, it is just as valid. Requiring class attendance, setting grading standards, and requiring homework can fall within the parameters of this concept. The primary defense of regulations based on this compelling state interest is in the school's justification of the requirements.

4. Prevention of disruption to the educational process. There is the assumption that certain givens are necessary for learning to take place, including appropriate interaction, a safe environment, and freedom from disruption. Rules based on this premise, provided they are legitimate and not arbitrary or capricious, would most likely be upheld under judicious scrutiny.

Special Education

When I started teaching, special education was limited in scope. I was one of three special education teachers in a district of over 8,000 students. Twenty years later, with a school population of less than 5,000, there were nearly 100 staff and support personnel associated with special education.

This phenomenal growth is characteristic of school districts throughout the country. Society is changing, and we now have more students with disabilities than we have ever had. Babies born to drug-addicted mothers are on the rise. Children from the growing number of dysfunctional families are coming to school with problems that require more attention. Environmental insults that affect kids' learning are also a significant factor. However, although all these situations are becoming more and more prevalent, the primary reason for the increase in special education activity has been due to legislation.

In the early 1970s, laws were passed that identified specific handicapping conditions and mandated that schools be responsible for developing specially designed instruction to meet the educational needs of these students. Terms like "M-Team" (Multi-Disciplinary Team), "IEPs" (Individual Education Plans), and "learning disabilities" have become familiar educational vocabulary.

Although these laws are complicated and seem somewhat convoluted, there are basic concepts that all teachers should be familiar with in the consideration of special education issues.

The law states that students cannot be discriminated against because of a handicapping condition. Students identified as disabled and/or in need of special education have the right to specially designed instruction. This includes modification of curricula, materials, and teaching strategies. In addition, discipline of students must take their disability into consideration because of the restrictions on disciplining EEN (Exceptional Education Need) students for behaviors related to or resulting from their handicapping condition.

Section 504 of the Civil Rights Code

When discussing legal aspects of education with groups of teachers, I often ask how many have been trained to teach people with disabilities. There are usually a few special education teachers in attendance, and they are the only ones who respond.

When I ask the next question, "How many are expected to be teachers of people with disabilities?" there are usually some blank stares indicating that they have no idea what I mean. At that point, I tell them:

As of a 1991 decision by the Department of Education, all teachers have the responsibility to teach children with disabilities who wind up in their classrooms.

As we've already mentioned, the law commonly referred to as "504," which refers to the section of civil rights legislation that went into effect in 1973, states that individuals cannot be discriminated against because of a number of conditions, one of which is having a disability. Therefore, schools must provide an equal opportunity of access to education for all individuals.

Some have compared "504" with special education. There are certainly similarities, such as developing accommodations (that look very much like special education Individual Education Plans), need for an assessment basis, and requirements for periodic reevaluations. There are, however, some fundamental differences.

The first is that "504" defines "handicap" in a way that might be unfamiliar even to special education teachers. In special education, "handicap" is defined by specific criteria, usually established by some objective measure (e.g., test scores), which often results in the need for specially designed instruction.

In the case of "504," however, "handicap" is defined as any condition that causes a disruption of a major life activity, including walking, working, breathing, and learning. Several categories are identified but, in essence, it is an open list. When this fact is known, teachers are quick to comprehend that, without some parameters, the list of conditions could become overwhelming and include a significant number of students found in any classroom.

Lawyers for parents are not nearly as concerned about substance or content of individual education and accommodation plans as they are about the procedural.

*When dealing with either special education or
"504" issues, it is of primary importance
to be procedurally correct.
It is of vital importance that timelines, notifications,
and appropriate personnel be considered.*

Because of the requirements that special education and "504" students be educated with their peers to the extent appropriate, all educational areas—including academics, discipline, and extra-curricular activities—are affected.

The balance for most teachers will be to play it safe without compromising values and educational standards. We have addressed this issue in the section on consultant teaching (Chapter Twelve, Styles of Teaching) and would encourage readers to review it.

Protection from Liability

On a more global perspective, the following recommendations are given for your consideration.

Guidelines for Being Legally Prepared

1. Individualize whenever possible. In most cases, this is just good educational practice; with special education and "504" students, it is imperative. Within individualization, however, questions often arise about educational standards and grading. This is a legitimate concern because grades on a report card, or GPA upon graduation, ostensibly serve to identify skill mastery.

2. Document all occurrences, no matter how small. Documentation is a powerful tool for defending your actions, clarifying situations, and establishing your credibility.

3. Maintain and upgrade professional skills. Formal training places you at an advantage in terms of becoming an "expert" and giving your recommendations additional credibility.

4. Be aware of your vulnerability. We are victims of what we are not aware of. The legal realm is no exception. Many teachers have gone merrily on their way down a path that has been disastrous simply because they did not realize the jeopardy they were in. Teachers should regularly review professional materials that deal with legal issues.

5. Discuss potential legal situations only with supervisors, legal representation, and insurance agents. Teachers often openly discuss very sensitive issues in very public places. There are times I have cringed after hearing what teachers have talked about in the lounge or at social gatherings. I have also cringed after hearing what some teachers have told parents. Realize that whoever is privy to certain information can be subpoenaed in the event a case goes to hearing or court.

6. Be cautious about forcing a child to do something without due process and documentation. This is especially true for students who are enrolled in EEN programs, but can be just as true for all students. Disciplinary measures can be a trap for teachers if due process is violated or if the circumstances of the situation are the slightest bit hazy.

7. Legal and moral are not always synonymous. It is naive to believe that doing the "right" thing will exonerate teachers who violate policies or laws. Ignorance of the law is no excuse.

8. Make rules and safety precautions obvious and available to all. These can be posted in the room, sent to parents in an introductory letter, used as agenda items at open houses, and written into lesson plan books. The point is, make these as public as possible.

9. Modify "no exceptions" language. If teachers are required to "supervise halls outside their rooms" they may be liable for any incident that occurs in that area, even if they are engaged in some other valid activity. Eliminate this "locking in" by using language (rewrite teachers' guides, if necessary) that gives latitude. Wording on the hall question might be, "Teachers are *normally* expected to monitor halls outside their rooms."

10. Ensure that all staff are in-serviced in developing procedurally correct IEPs and "504" Accommodation Plans. Because teachers are usually responsible for implementation of these plans, they would be well advised to be intimately aware of what is expected.

11. Read your master agreement. What many master agreements say is at the discretion of the Board can be very revealing. Administrative hearings require far less evidence or compelling arguments than court hearings. Even "hearsay" has been used in administrative hearings to the detriment of a teacher.

12. Make strong requests to your district for training. Training, and requests for it, can reduce the liability of both teacher and district by demonstrating good-faith efforts to address specific problems.

We certainly have not addressed all the legal issues that affect teachers. Our intent is to bring this aspect of teaching to an awareness level in the hope that teachers will exercise their penchant for life-long learning to explore this area further.

We realize that few teachers are trained to interact comfortably within the legal system. However, those teachers who conduct their classroom interaction on the basis of the Four Key Principles of Love and Logic are, in all probability, acting in ways that reduce their liabilities. Efforts to maintain a student's self-concept, sharing control, instituting a program of consequences rather than punishment, and creating an environment in which students are encouraged to think about situations all establish an atmosphere that eliminates many antecedents that can provoke legal involvement.

PEARL
▼

Great teachers are terminally curious and have a penchant for life-long learning.

CHAPTER FOURTEEN

▼

Implementing
School Discipline

SYSTEMS VS. PRINCIPLES

*T*here are two basic approaches to implementing
school discipline in the United States today. I
(Betsy Geddes) would like to illustrate them by giving you
what I call "A Tale of Two Schools." The first, called the
Systems Approach school, exists in every state of this
nation, and yet it is proving to be more and more ineffective every day. The second, called the Principles Approach
school, is on the rise and, although less familiar, it is
proving to be highly effective.

---

*Dr. Betsy Geddes used the principles of Love and Logic
to turn around an inner-city school in Portland, Oregon.
She was so successful that she later became a highly
effective and popular educational consultant and public
speaker. Among her strengths is her ability to provide
practical techniques injected with humor. In this chapter
she addresses the challenge of implementing a school-
wide discipline plan based upon Love and Logic.*

Armed with the knowledge that discipline has never been more of a problem than it is today, and we need all the help we can get—let me begin by talking about the approach used in most schools right now and explain why I believe it is not working.

The Systems Approach

The Systems Approach school follows a pattern. The staff comes together and the principal stands up in front and says, "Okay, staff, what rules do we need in order to govern the school this year?" Across the United States, the answers tend to be fairly similar: "No hats." "No gum." "No running in the halls." "Keep your hands, feet, and other objects to yourself." "Be on time." "Respect your teachers." "Bring your materials." "Do your homework."

Once we decide on the rules, we ask ourselves as a group, "Okay, what are we going to do to these kids when they break the rules?" I call this "laying out the punishments." I am the adult; therefore, I am going to be the judge, jury, and executioner. When a student comes to school and breaks a rule, I am going to move in, judge the behavior, select a punishment from a list of many, and make sure that it is carried out.

Let me give you an example. In the lower grades, we do lots of take-aways: "Stay in from recess." "No lunch break for you." "Go to time-out." "Write fifty sentences." "Run twenty laps." In the upper grades we tend to use: "Go to detention." "You get an in-school suspension." "You get an out-of-school suspension." "Fill out a referral." "Go to the principal." "See the vice principal." "Get fixed before you come back here."

Who Is Doing All the Work?

In one particular school, the kids came to school and were given the rules right off the bat. When they broke the rules, they were given a warning. Actually, they were given two warnings. This was the procedure: Warning, warning, pink slip.

If the kid had received two warnings and gotten a pink slip, that kid had to stay after school. This was called "Go to Detention." Every night after school, different teachers had to take turns tending the detentions. The teacher of the week had to stand by the detention room. As the students came in with pink slips, the teacher would write down their names and check them off a master form. Then the students would sit down, look at the teacher, and the teacher would look at the students, and after thirty minutes of relative silence, the students would all get up and go home.

Now the real work begins. The teacher looks down the list and sees that three or four kids, who were supposed to come, didn't show up. What does the teacher have to do? Go down to the office, look up their regulation forms, find phone numbers, call the parents—half of who do not have regulation forms, the other half of who do not have phone numbers—and, most often, nobody is home.

If a kid missed one night, that kid then had to stay two other nights. If a kid missed two; he had to stay four. Someone once told me about a student who owed 1,935 detentions at the time of his graduation. Guess what? He graduated anyway.

My first question to you is: In this system of punishment, who is doing all the work? The answer, of course, is the teacher. Any kid who is any kind of kid at all, will drop in, play that teacher for thirty minutes—throwing spit wads, making noises, wiggling, acting up. Afterward, the kid goes off and says, "Hey! Not a bad use of time for thirty minutes!"

My second question to you is: What are the kids thinking while they're sitting there? Do you suppose any of them is thinking, "Boy, I'm never, ever going to mess up again at school so I don't have to come to detention"? Most kids are saying, "Well, I may get my homework in, I may straighten up, but, by golly, if I don't drive that teacher crazy the way I did yesterday, I've got to think of something new."

My third question is: Does it seem to you that the same kids come, day in, day out, year in, year out, to these detentions? The answer in general is, yes. Every once in a while, a kid drops in who has never been to detention before, looks around, maybe spends a night or two, and says, "Whoops! This isn't for me." And he never shows up again. In general, however, you see the same kids. There is a pattern here. In fact, there is a great likelihood that kids who are kept in after school in the first grade will be in detention halls when they get to high school.

Most of us focus on that one kid, the one who dropped in, straightened up after one or two tries, and then went on to be president of the high school class. We say, "Well, remember Josh way back in the third grade? If detention worked for that kid, why hasn't it worked for the hundreds of others who have passed through the detention halls?"

The System of Punishment

Another interesting aspect of trying to set up a system in school is that you always, always, always have teachers in your building who do not follow the plan. In the building that has a rule such as, "No gum," there will always be a teacher who, when a kid comes to class, will say,

"Hey, guys, in this class, it is okay to chew gum." The kids sit there the entire period and chomp away. They usually are given two conditions: "Just remember, if the principal comes in, close your mouths. And when you leave, be sure to spit the gum out."

After they have chomped the period away and the bell rings, and they have three minutes to dash to their lockers, spritz their hair, and flirt with members of the opposite sex—quite frankly they are not thinking about spitting out their gum. As they dash down the hall and into their next class, where do you suppose the eyes of that teacher are? You've got it! On their mouths. The scenario is started and finished in three words: "Gum!" "Gotcha!" "Detention!" Then the real fighting starts—not between kids and adults, but between the adults.

The teacher who allowed gum chewing usually gathers his or her friends someplace in the school and says, "Well, if all the other teachers in this building would just lighten up and not be so uptight, we would have no problem here." The other teacher, the one who was following the rules, gathers with his or her friends and says, "We formed a committee, we wrote these rules, we laminated them and hung them on the wall. We typed up copies and had the kids sign them and their parents sign them. How in the world can you expect me to discipline my class if all the other teachers in this building aren't going to follow the rules that we set up?"

At the end of the year, when we come together as a staff, the principal gets up one more time and says, "Well, guys, you know, discipline did not go well this year. What do you think we need next year?" In unison, we all chorus: "We need more rules and more punishments." And the cycle goes on and on and on.

This is the System Approach. What you get in this system is inconsistency, complaints, and disharmony.

The System of Reward

After a few years of this, most schools come to the conclusion that they need more positive aspects in interacting with kids. They set up another system. This system is based on positive reinforcement. We come together as a staff, we make a bunch of rules and then instead of deciding how we will punish them if they misbehave, we say, "Okay, when the kids do follow the rules, let's reward them. What are we going to give them?"

Across the United States, the responses tend to be fairly similar. We are going to give them free time, passes, popcorn and pizza parties, kickball games, stickers for their lockers. Some schools even opt for giving them pricey material objects, or money, if they follow the rules.

I know of a school that set up a self-management program as their reward system. The staff had elaborate charts that they hung on the wall, and teachers were expected to keep track of students' activities every single day. If a student did not get a referral that day from any teacher in the building, that student got a nice check after his or her name. If a student did get a referral, that kid got a big, black mark.

If a kid got fifteen checks in a row, then she or he got to wear a plastic badge that said "Self-Manager." And "Self-Manager" meant that the student could do extra things, such as extra duties for the teacher, and did not have to have a pass when going to the bathroom or the library. At the end of the month, that kid was rewarded with a big popcorn party in the gym, supervised by the principal and the vice principal.

If students did get a black mark, they would have their Self-Manager tag taken away and would have to work for at least fifteen more days before becoming eligible to have it returned.

What would be your guess as to how teachers followed these rules? Once again, some teachers never, ever, gave out Self-Manager tags. They found reasons to negate students' behavior every day. Other teachers gave Self-Manager tags to everybody, especially when it was time for the popcorn party! They said to themselves "Hmm, 45 minutes, no kids! You are all Self-Managers. Head for the gym and have a good time!"

As expected, the teachers turned on each other and said, "Well, how in the world can you expect any program to work if everybody in this school does not follow the same rules?"

Systems Are Difficult to Maintain

Beliefs Are Stronger Than Systems. When a school tries to set up a "system," it is very difficult to get everybody to follow it. When individual teachers go to their classrooms, close the doors, pull the shades, and no one is scheduled to come and observe, they interact with their kids in exactly the manner that fits their personality and their beliefs, no matter what system has been designed by their school.

Old Systems Die Hard. There are several other problems associated with trying to set up a system of reward and punishment. A system that has existed in a school for a long time is difficult to change. I know of one school that, after four years, had a punishment approach called "137 steps until you're out." In other words, each misbehavior brought a new punishment, each of which was added, and added, and added, because nobody knew how to stop the growth of this system.

It's the same with rewards; we reward and we reward; and if it took two stickers this year, the next year the kids say, "Well, I got two last year. How many do I need this year?" The reward grows and grows, until teachers find that not only is the school budget gone, but they themselves are spending a lot of money out of their own pockets.

Those Who Need to Change, Don't. Another problem in a system of reward and punishment is that it does not change the behavior of the kids whose behavior most needs changing. We see the same kids getting the punishments and the same kids, year in and year out, getting the rewards. The reason? These systems of reward and punishment are based on *external* control.

> *A kid will behave only as long as*
> *the threat of the punishment is severe enough,*
> *or the anticipation of the reward is great enough.*

If the threat of punishment means nothing to a kid, or the reward is not great enough, the kid reverts to the original behavior. There is no *internalized* behavior change.

I was talking to a girl in a high school in-school suspension room. I walked up to her and said, "Wow, this has got to be kind of boring sitting here for three days. How did you happen to come here?" "Well," she said, "I've been skipping school, and when I've skipped school for three days, they make me spend three days in the in-school suspension room." So I asked her, "What have you learned from this? Do you think you'll be doing it again?" And she said, "Oh, sure. You know, it's worth it. Sitting here for three days means nothing to me."

A kindergarten teacher I know was "controlling" her class using chocolate-covered peanuts. She would go around the room and say, "Now if you'll do this, I'll give you three peanuts; and if you do that, you'll get four." She had come to the end of the bag—in fact, she had two left and they were kind of chipped and mangy. But there was a little girl who needed to clean her desk, so she walked over with the mangled chocolate covered peanuts and said, "Hey, Susie, clean up your desk, and I'll give these to you." Susie took one look at the two peanuts, got a disgusted look on her face and said, "Never mind. I like my desk the way it is." And she walked away.

The truth about operating on a Systems Approach in this country today is that schools no longer have enough authority to punish kids severely enough to bring about compliance. Nor do we have enough money to provide the kind of rewards needed to bring about compliance.

Compliance achieved through reward or punishment has two interesting components:

- ✏ It is almost always temporary
- ✏ It is almost always malicious

In other words, a student will behave only as long as the fear of punishment is held over that student's head. I will do my work only as long as you hold out a reward that appeals to me and, even then, I won't do it well.

When a child has been misbehaving, you fill out a referral form and say, "Leave the room, please." The kid gets up, snatches the referral form and then, at a pace that would put a turtle to shame, begins to slowly, step by step, head for the door. When you say, "I told you to leave the room," the kid says, "I'm going. I'm going."

Then there's the child whose father gave him fifty cents for every smiley face he brought home in kindergarten and first grade. By the third grade, it was $3.00 for every A or B. By the time the kid hit sixteen, it became, "You either give me a car, or I'm going to flunk out of school."

These are examples of the Systems Approach, which, you most certainly have figured out by now, does not work.

The Principles Approach

The second approach to setting up school discipline for working with kids is called the Principles Approach. It is based on agreeing to a set of beliefs that are turned into principles. It is also called the Love and Logic way of working with kids in the classroom.

Let me set the scene. Once again, we come together as a staff and we make a bunch of rules. Everybody has rules—the Internal Revenue Service, the National Football League—everyone. So we make some rules, and the rules are pretty standard. But instead of asking, "What are we going to do to the kids when they misbehave?" or trying to figure out how we are going to reward the kids when they do what we want them to, we focus on a way of behaving—for us, the staff.

This way of behaving is based on a set of beliefs about our purpose in working with students. Once we agree on our core set of beliefs, we turn them into principles. "Principles," as defined by Stephen Covey in his book *Seven Habits of Highly Effective People*, are guidelines for human conduct that are proven to have enduring, permanent value.

✎ **LOVE AND LOGIC TIP #15:**
A Core of Beliefs

Empowering beliefs are beliefs based on developing an *internalized* sense of control in kids, rather than trying to control them with rewards and punishments.

Many school staffs want students to:

1. Be responsible for owning and solving their own problems, with some guidance.

2. Do more thinking than the adults.

3. Face logical consequences instead of punishment, whenever possible.

4. Learn to make a connection between their infraction and the action taken—a logical connection.

5. Learn to make decisions and then live with the consequences of those decisions.

6. Be able to take some control over their lives and yet have the school retain some control.

7. See adults as helpers, rather than judges who dole out punishment.

8. Learn in their school that problems are an opportunity for personal growth.

So, the staff comes together, and in front of each person is a set of discipline planning sheets that contain a series of beliefs or purposes that relate to teaching. Each person is asked to look over these beliefs and purposes and pick out four, five, or six that, in their heart of hearts, they feel are what they, as teachers, are about in their work with kids on a daily basis.

Let me give you an example. On the list was:

My purpose, when disciplining students, is for students to:

➠ **Be responsible in solving their own problems, with guidance."**

If I truly believe that is one of my purposes as a teacher, then I put a check after it. If I don't believe that, then I don't.

➠ **Learn that the adult is boss and in control.**

If I truly believe that, then I put a check after it.

Each teacher completes the worksheet him- or herself. Then we divide into small groups, either by grade level or by curriculum team, or however the school happens to be organized, and come to some rough consensus on four or five of the six beliefs. Then the small groups come together as a total staff and reach a similar consensus.

Once we have a general agreement on four, five, or six of these beliefs or purposes, they become the unchanging core around which all activity, all change, and all behavior in that school takes place.

Common Misbehaviors and How We Handle Them. Once a school has decided on a set of core beliefs—four, five, or six of them—they then come up with six to ten of the most common misbehaviors the staff deals with on a daily basis.

Frankly, most teachers do not deal with things like drugs, alcohol, sex, and violence on a daily basis. What they do deal with are talking back, making faces, no homework, disrespect, sitting, unmotivated, like a bump on a log, and making noises.

These behaviors are not life-threatening,
but, on a daily basis, they are very irritating.

Then, as a staff, we look at how we presently handle these misbehaviors. Let's say that a kid has come to school for five days in a row with no homework. What would be a way of handling this that sits well with our core of beliefs?

In a school that operates on a systems approach of punishment, teachers might react to no homework by requiring a student to stay after school for two days. The kid might be given a detention slip, and for two days be expected to show up and do the homework.

In a school operating on a systems approach of reward, the teacher might say, "Okay, no homework for five days? For every day you bring your homework, you get five points. When you have twenty points, I will give you a certificate to go get a pizza."

As you can quickly gather, the action taken, or the reaction to misbehavior, by using reward or punishment does not complement any of the core beliefs previously stated. Look at them again and ask yourself: Does a two-day detention slip mesh with helping a student learn to become responsible for his or her own problems? Does a 20-point pizza help a kid learn to make a decision and live with the consequences of that decision?

A major problem has been that we see the value in core beliefs, but we have not yet learned how to turn them into principles to live by on a daily basis.

It has been my experience that most schools in this country do select core beliefs based on empowering kids to develop an internalized sense of control. Yet, at the same time, our schools react to kids' behavior using external controls—rewards and punishments.

As the staff comes together, we go to the last part of the discipline planning sheet, which asks, "In the future, what kind of actions are we going to use with kids when they misbehave or break the rules that support our core beliefs?"

Core beliefs + Misbehavior = What Action?

Internalizing Responsibility

This is where discipline with Love and Logic comes in. Discipline with Love and Logic teaches prevention and intervention strategies that focus on developing an internalized sense of responsibility in the students with whom we work. It doesn't mean, however, that we drop all rewards and punishments. There is a time and a place for everything.

What it does mean is that we focus on developing, to the extent possible under our concurrent conditions, a sense of responsibility within each student that leaves that student with a feeling of shared control. What we wind up with is a set of principles, based on our core beliefs.

Guidelines for Human Conduct in the School

1. Every time I interact with a student, to the best of my ability I will give some control in order to retain some control.

2. Every time I interact with a student, to the best of my ability I'm going to share the thinking that's necessary. At the end of the day, I want the student going home exhausted from thinking instead of me.

3. Every time I interact with a student, to the best of my ability I'm going to let empathy and logical consequences do the teaching. Instead of anger, shame, blame, and guilt, I am going to express sadness when students do things that are not appropriate in school. Then I'm going to let logical consequences come out of the situation.

Now, all programs, all interactions, all new skills and techniques must answer to my core beliefs and basic principles. If I truly believe that my purpose when interacting or disciplining students is for them to be responsible for solving their own problems, with guidance, then when a student comes to me and says, "I haven't done any homework for five days," instead of sending him to detention or setting up a reward system, I'm going to look at him with great sadness and say, "How sad, hon. How do you plan to take care of that?" With nothing more than my sadness, questions, and guidance, that student is going to make a plan for dealing with *his* problem.

Those of us on staff must also internalize *our* responsibilities. Often our schools are visited by companies with programs to sell us. Let's say a representative from one of those companies comes into our building and offers us a great new program for motivating students. They say, "We have this program. We guarantee you it will really get kids excited, working, and behaving in your school. We are going to put big shields on every kid's locker and every time a student does something that is appropriate, the teachers will go around and put a little sticker on the shield and then pretty soon all the kids who are working and behaving will have lots of little stickies on their shields, which will motivate the other kids to get busy so that they can have their shield filled with stickies, too."

As a staff we sit down and ask, no matter how pretty those stickers look, "Does this program fit our core beliefs?"

The answer is no. One of the beliefs we did not select was getting kids to expect to be rewarded for good behavior. We want to help these kids and understand how they feel, but we don't want to reward good behavior by giving *external* rewards every time the kid does something we ask.

Implementing the Love and Logic philosophy in interacting with or disciplining students brings about consistency and harmony.

Consistency comes, not from trying to force everybody to do the same thing at the same time— but by living by a set of core beliefs.

Once we have our core beliefs, the principal can turn to the staff and say, "Next year you are welcome to interact with and discipline students in any way that works best for you, as long as you do not violate your core beliefs."

At first this sounds a little frightening, as if you are going to have fifty staff members all doing their own thing and running amok. One principal said, "I couldn't possibly say that. I'll lose all control." Jim Fay's famous response was, "You have no control anyway. What do you have to lose?"

We want to give teachers the same sense of control and autonomy that we hope teachers will give their students.

The school or administration will retain control by the choices or options they give. All behaviors, all programs implemented and used in our school, will be critiqued against our core beliefs. And when core beliefs are violated, we will discuss this. Not in terms of someone being a bad teacher or a bad student, but rather we will focus on what techniques we need to use to put behavior back in alignment with our beliefs. No one wants to hear,

"You are really bad." "That's not the way we behave in this school." Or, "That's not the right way to treat kids."

Empathy and Options

Let's go back to our tale of two schools and change it slightly to "Tale of Two Teachers." These teachers teach next door to each other. On one morning, two kids come to school—one goes to Classroom A, and one goes to Classroom B. Each kid has forgotten his materials. Student A walks into Classroom A and the teacher, standing at the door, smiles and says "Good morning, John." John says, "Hey, Teach, I forgot my materials today. I don't have anything to work with." The teacher says, "How sad, John. Feel free to see if you can borrow from a friend."

At the same moment, Student B goes into Classroom B. The teacher standing at the door, smiling, says, "Good morning, Mary." Mary says, "Good morning, Teacher. Guess what! I left my books in the car. My mother just drove off and I don't have them to work with today." The teacher smiles and says, "Oh, how upsetting that must be. You're welcome to borrow from the free pile at the back of the room." Or "You are welcome to sit and take a zero."

Each teacher reacts in a slightly different manner; yet, there are two common threads that run through both behaviors—both based on core beliefs. First, each teacher showed sadness or concern for what had happened to the student. Neither one went into "Well, how many times have I told you . . ." or "You'll never amount to anything . . ." or "When are you going to remember to . . .?" "See what happens if you don't get up and plan in the morning?" Second, each teacher gave the student options or choices.

Expecting a staff to work from a system—step one, step two, step three, step four—results in chaos, frustration, and confusion. Getting a staff to work from a common set of beliefs and principles results in consistency and harmony.

Becoming a Love and Logic school is not easy in the beginning. Let's face it. With any real, significant change there is pain. When students and adults are first handed their problems to own and solve, and when students and adults are asked to take responsibility for their behavior, most of them do not say, "Oh, thank you for this opportunity to become a responsible, problem-solving person." More likely, you will hear reactions like, "What workshop did *you* go to?" "What happened to the old person who used to yell and scream, who I knew and loved?" "What are you trying to do, use psychology on us?" "How long is this going to last?" It takes support, understanding, and fortitude to implement behavior change.

Implementing Change

Let's start with individual change. You are a teacher who has gone through the process we've been discussing. You have selected your beliefs, thought about your basic principles, and you say to yourself, "This is something I would really like to implement in my classroom."

There is something you should know. Bringing about individual change is like learning to do a high dive. First there is no awareness. You go off the board and you have no idea what went right and what went wrong. Only the pain of the belly flop makes you realize something was amiss. Your coach must give you feedback.

As you get better, you realize that you forgot to tuck in your head or keep your legs straight. Soon, about halfway through the dive, you become aware of some problems and make immediate adjustments. Finally, you reach the point where the moves are internalized and you can do the dive with ease. What originally was your desired dive has now become the norm—the dive you do well almost every time.

So it is with bringing about change in the classroom, whether the change is in your behavior or in that of your students. At first, there is no awareness.

Let's say you have been using rewards and punishments much the way you walk around humming a song. You've given as much thought to handing any control over to the kids and internalizing responsible behavior as you have to the tune you've been humming.

Now you have read this book. Some of it makes sense to you and you would like to get started. You look on your discipline planning sheet, down at the bottom where it says "Future Reactions to Student Misbehavior," and you pick one specific skill.

Let's say, for example, you are going to apply more choices. So, you write on a 3x5 card or a yellow sticky note, and place it somewhere you can see it, say on your lesson plan book, "This week I am going to give students choices." Let's get really specific and say that when a kid is disrupting other people in the group, you are going to walk up to the kid and say, "Please feel free to quiet down, or use the quiet table at the back of the room." You have mentally prepared.

Then, what actually happens the first time a student acts up is, you walk over and say, "Knock that off or I am going to send you to the back of the room."

That is an out-and-out threat. The minute you've said it, you say to yourself, "Hmmmm, I think I learned a better way." You take a quick look at your 3x5 card or your yellow sticky and you say, "Oh, yes. I gave a threat instead of giving choices."

Now pretty soon, if you do this enough, you'll walk over to a student and you'll start with, "Look, you either knock this off, or . . ." and halfway through the act, you realize you are back in the old threat cycle again. You simply say, "Excuse me," adjust your shoulders, and continue, "Feel free to straighten up at the table, or feel free to work quietly at the back table."

Eventually, over a period of time, you internalize this new behavior, so that as you walk around the classroom and students begin to act up, the first words that roll out of your mouth are choices. "Hey, Jennifer, feel free to knock that off or feel free to work by yourself at the back table today."

Guidelines for Changing Your Behavior

Get Feedback. It is important to structure a way to obtain feedback during the "no awareness" stage. You might want to use a tape recorder or videotape yourself. You might have a close friend whom you trust enough come in, watch you and look for specific behaviors.

Get your students to help. Many teachers have found success in involving their students in their professional growth. They say to the class, "Kids, I am learning a new skill. Let me tell you about it. From now on, I am going to try to give you more choices instead of being bossy.

"I'd like you to help me. If I forget to give you choices, you may say, 'Do I get any choices on this?' If possible, I'll try to think up some choices. However, you need to know that sometimes I will have to tell you there are no choices this time.

"Thanks for helping me learn new skills. Do you think it will work best for all of us if you are nasty or kind when you say, 'Do I get any choices on this?' Won't it be fun to find out?"

Find a Partner. It is also important to find someone you really feel comfortable with to be your partner. Then, on a daily basis, when you've tried some new skills, whether they work or whether they don't work, as soon as you can, you go and describe what happened to your friend and then you laugh, and laugh, and laugh.

Leave Room for Mistakes. A woman who was an administrative assistant in a school was trying to learn some new supervision skills. During the lunch hour, when she was supervising the cafeteria, she began to walk more often among the kids and say, "Move, move, move. Smile, smile, smile. Laugh, laugh, laugh. Chat, chat, chat"—trying to stay away from yelling and screaming into that microphone, telling kids what to do.

Every once in awhile, for some reason—maybe it was the phase of the moon, who knows?—the cafeteria would get out of control. It was just one of those days when everything went wrong at one time. This woman would forget herself and run to that microphone, grab it, and start yelling, "Look, you kids! Sit down and put your heads down! I want exactly ten minutes of quiet. Do you hear me? Not one person is leaving this cafeteria until I have ten minutes of quiet!"

After she'd finally gotten ten minutes of quiet, she would let the kids outside and she'd come dragging up the stairs, and her partner would say, "Wow, you really went off on them today!" And she'd say, "Yeah."

And her partner would say, "We could hear you all over the building." And then they would look at each other, and the lady would laugh and say, "Well, probably didn't do them any good, but I feel a lot better." Then the two of them would laugh and say, "Well, blew it today; tomorrow is another day."

The next day, when lunchtime came, she went back to the cafeteria: "Move, move, move. Smile, smile, smile. Chat, chat, chat."

Allow yourself to make some mistakes. Laugh at your mistakes, and talk about your mistakes. It's an amazing and wonderful way to learn.

Practice New Skills One at a Time. Take one skill at a time. It's like learning long division, one step at a time. Perhaps you will work a whole month just learning empathy. Or you'll work a whole month learning to ask a sincere question.

I take a skill and work on it for awhile. Then, when I begin to get comfortable with it, I move on to another skill. I remember the words of Foster W. Cline, M.D.:

> *"It takes a long time to bring about*
> *internalized behavior change.*
> *Be patient with yourself and be patient with the kids."*

On a school-wide level, it takes about three years to bring about internalized change in an organization. Let's say you have been working in a school that's been heavily involved in a systems approach based on punishing kids who misbehave. You have come together as a staff, picked four or five beliefs that are your unchanging core, and you have adopted the Love and Logic principles. As you begin to implement these principles, you find yourself in what I call "the dip of change." Another way of saying it is that things always get better before they get worse.

A prime example might be a school that has a tardy policy. In the staff's infinite wisdom, they set up a "Roundup" or "Lockout." This term varies around the country. In junior highs or high schools, at a certain period every day, when the tardy bell rings the administrator gets on the phone in the office and says, "Teachers, lock your doors."

At this time, administrators and counselors run through the halls and round up all the kids who are tardy, take them down to the library, have them fill out detention forms, and keep them after school.

At first, when this procedure starts, things tend to get better. Kids say, "Hey, it isn't worth the hassle, I think I'll just show up on time." After a few days, or maybe a week, everyone says, "Wow, we have the tardy problem licked. We don't need round-up anymore."

The minute the round-up procedure is dropped, what do you suppose happens to tardies? You've got it! Kids start being tardy again, because they say, "Ooo, those adults aren't bothering to punish us anymore. We might as well go back to being tardy."

Now in their even more infinite wisdom, staff members come together and say, "That doesn't work. Why don't we switch to a system of rewards. In every homeroom, each teacher will keep track, and if his class has twenty days in a row where there is no one tardy, we'll give that class an ice cream or pizza party."

Once again, everything tends to get better. Kids come on time. A pizza party sounds really good. But after awhile, the kids say, "Oh geeze, now it's only a pizza. I mean, that isn't very much!" Or the school runs out of money or, quite frankly, we just get tired of the program.

The minute the reward is taken away, what do you suppose happens to the tardy rate? Yes! It increases. And what do we do then? We go back to punishment. And when that stops working, we switch to reward. And what we find ourselves doing is hopping back and forth between short-term reward and punishment programs, over and over and over again—looking for a quick fix.

The Principles Approach to Tardiness

In the Love and Logic way of working with students, I ask myself, "How can we get students to want to come to school, to internalize wanting to come to class because they *want* to come to class?"

"Well," I ask myself, "what behaviors, on my part as an adult, are going to make a kid feel welcome?" Eye contact. Touch. Smile. Standing at your doorway welcoming kids into your world every morning. Reaching out and touching, or shaking hands. Starting the class period right on time with something interesting and vital. Moving around the classroom and building relationships with kids.

My tardy policy is based on my belief that kids want to come to school and learn, and that they are capable of solving their own problems, with a little bit of guidance.

When I first started this approach, what I found was that things got worse. The kids would say, "Those adults aren't doing a darn thing. We can be tardy all we want and nothing happens."

So tardies got worse as we fell deeply into the "dip of change." But it is the wise school that rides out that dip and waits until—all of a sudden—it may take a few months; it may even take a year—before kids say to themselves, "Oh boy, if those adults aren't going to do anything about my being tardy, maybe I might want to do something about it myself."

After a period of time, you find more and more kids coming on time; and over a one- to three-year period, you can change the norm from kids being habitually late to kids being mostly on time.

It is the ability to act in accordance with your beliefs, focus on making your classroom a vital place to be, ride out the dip of change, and be patient with this process that eventually brings about success.

Keeping the Process Alive

Anything not attended to tends to be ignored. Schools successful in becoming Love and Logic schools focus heavily, the first three years, on staff development. How they do it is that at least once every other week (but preferably once a week) part of every faculty meeting is devoted to learning Love and Logic skills.

Follow-Up Conversations. Let's say next week, in this building, we are going to focus on asking questions. Therefore, at the next faculty meeting we spend maybe fifteen minutes talking about:

- What went wrong?
- What did you try that didn't go well?
- What do you think we need to work on next week?

If the environment in the faculty meeting is not supportive of taking a risk or falling flat on your face, then there will not be a lot of learning of new skills. One school staff lived by the belief, "You either are doing it the Love and Logic way or the reward and punishment way."

When the principal goes to observe a teacher at work, the principal might see the teacher handing out scratch and sniff stickers to kids who completed their work.

In the follow-up conversation, the principal would say, "That was a great reward system handing out those stickers. Now, if we're operating on the principles of Love and Logic, what behavior might you use next time before you offer the students a sticker? What could you offer those kids instead of a sticker?"

In another situation, a principal walks into the classroom precisely when a teacher has absolutely lost control and says to a kid who is bothering another kid, "Knock that off now or you are going to the office!"

In that follow-up conversation, we might concur as a group, "That was a great punishment! Good threat-giving!" Then someone might say, "Next time, however, before you issue the threat, is there a skill available that supports one of our basic beliefs about kids owning and solving their own problems that you might use instead?"

Group Teachings. In-servicing these new skills and behaviors can be done one of two ways. It's nice to have big-time speakers come in and pep up the troops, refocusing the group. However, in between times there are several other effective ways of keeping the in-servicing going. Some schools assign the Love and Logic tapes to small groups of teachers, either by grade level or curriculum group. Once a month, that small group is responsible for teaching the content of that particular tape to the whole staff. It's based on the philosophy that "I've never truly learned something until I have taught it to someone else."

Jim Fay has produced a very effective training program for schools. Videos provide Jim's teaching and a course study guide provides opportunities for group discussion, experimentation with skills, and specific solutions and interventions.

Implementation of Love and Logic training is most successful when done in the following manner:

1. Don't require all staff members to adopt Love and Logic. This can be the "kiss of death" for any program.

2. Don't train all staff members the first year.

3. Introduce the program to all staff by allowing them to view the first part. Use your own judgment as to when to stop the tape during the first presentation, and then announce that further study will be on a voluntary basis.

4. Create a study group made up of the most enthusiastic teachers. These are the staff members who will get a study guide and will continue to work together in the study of Love and Logic the first year. Some schools have required that teachers apply to the building discipline committee for admittance into this group. Make the study of Love and Logic an honor, not a mandate.

5. Create additional study groups as the rest of the staff members catch the enthusiasm generated by the ones using the program.

This is the training model that has had the greatest degree of success in schools over my last fifteen years of consulting. I didn't design the model. It was created by many of the great school principals who were dedicated to long-term change in their schools.

Many schools are finding great success in training parents in Love and Logic. Parents who take the "Becoming A Love and Logic Parent" training course also become much more positive supporters of the teachers in that school.

One very successful approach has been to target parents new to the school and kindergarten parents. The school schedules two Love and Logic classes each year, one in the fall and one in the spring. This gives parents choices.

When the parents enroll their children, the school secretary says, "We like parents at this school to take a parenting course. Would you rather sign up for the spring class or the fall class?" Registration for the course is accomplished easily.

Principals consistently report that parents who take the course are not only thankful but they relate to the school personnel in more positive ways than do parents who do not take the course.

You may learn more about Love and Logic training programs by calling the Love and Logic Institute at the toll-free number 1-800-338-4065.

Love and Logic Newsletters. Other schools send Love and Logic letters home in newsletters to parents, and each week the focus is on a different Love and Logic skill. That skill becomes the focus of conversation in the faculty meeting.

Pearls of Wisdom Posters. Some schools take Love and Logic pearls of wisdom, make them into posters, hang them around the room, put them in the weekly faculty bulletins, and in weekly bulletins going home to parents.

✎ **LOVE AND LOGIC TIP #16:**
When Consequences Don't Work

Ask Yourself:

1. Did I implement the consequence with compassion? If not, the student focused on my emotions rather than on his/her problem.

2. Was I in the emotional state when I implemented the consequence? If so, the student focused on my emotions instead of the problem.

3. Did I deliver the consequence in a questioning manner? "Where are you going to eat now that you can't use the cafeteria?"

4. Did I try to reason with the student while he/she was still in the emotional state? This usually results in a power struggle.

5. Did I tie the time and location of the violation to the consequence? The consequence has to be reasonable in the mind of the student; otherwise, he/she will see it as retaliation.

6. Did I use the consequence to get even with the student? We cannot hide our intentions. Trying to get even will cause resentment. As a result, the consequence will lose its value.

7. Did I use a consequence when a disciplinary intervention would have solved the problem instead? Save consequences for the big lessons children need. Use quick and easy classroom interventions to break the emotional spell whenever you can.

8. Did my attitude or behavior indicate that I was trying to teach the student a lesson? We can't hide our attitudes from students. If they think we're implementing consequences to teach them lessons, they spend their time trying to show us that it won't work.

9. Did I implement the consequence immediately? Delayed consequences are usually much more effective than immediate ones. Take your time, talk it over with friends. Deliver consequences when both you and the student are in the thinking state.

10. Did I tell the student in advance what the consequence would be? Students either decide the consequence is worth it or act out to see if the teacher means what he/she says.

Unless there is constant attention to training and retraining, unless there is a feeling in the school building of support for people who are trying new skills, there probably will not be implementation of those new skills.

The tendency to slide toward rewards or punishments is always alive, waiting to kick in.

Becoming a Love and Logic school involves:

- Making a plan
- Following the plan
- Paying constant attention to the process
- Understanding that change happens only over time

Those individuals and those schools who do ride out the dip find joys in working with students that they never knew were possible.

Remember: There are a limited number of students who have not yet developed cause-and-effect thinking. They often do not have an internalized conscience. However, they still need to experience consequences on a consistent basis, mostly for the protection of the other students and the teacher.

PEARL

▼

You are either doing it the Love and Logic way, or you are doing it the reward and punishment way.

▼
———

CHAPTER FIFTEEN

Walled Lake Central High School

ONE SCHOOL'S APPROACH TO LOVE AND LOGIC

O ne of the three target goals of the North Central Association (NCA) accreditation process is to enhance student self-esteem in the school environment. Walled Lake Central High School, located thirty-five miles northwest of Detroit, Michigan, has been involved in this program since 1991.

Self-Esteem Planning Phase

An NCA committee of twenty-five teachers volunteered to research and identify strategies to enhance student self-esteem and implement them within their classrooms. Our approach was to offer what we felt would be

———

Jim McKee, who wrote this chapter, is a counselor at Walled Lake Central High School in Walled Lake, Michigan. His contribution to this book was chosen because it is an outstanding example of systems change. He and his committee implemented the principles of Love and Logic to move an entire staff to develop a Love and Logic school.

most effective for students, teachers, and the remaining staff. However, we felt strongly that although we could make choices for ourselves, we could not force others to make any they did not want to make. We believed that if we had only one teacher utilizing these strategies, it would be enough to have some positive effect on a student's self-esteem.

Every department was represented on the committee, which conveniently made available to others a consultant within their academic discipline. We developed a school within a school, operating from a set of core beliefs, which I will describe in this chapter.

Over this past year, our school has utilized a program called V.I.P., Vision In Progress, which structures our Wednesdays so that our regular school responsibilities do not begin until 9:30 a.m. Between 7:30 a.m. and 9:30 a.m., time is available for in-service and staff development. This block of time has allowed the Self-Esteem Committee to meet and process the principles we've been introducing.

Classroom Ecology

We function as a support group for one another, and the goal of our group involves three intervention strategies:

1. Integrate the five elements essential to enhance self-esteem in the classroom.

2. Manage the classroom through Love and Logic principles.

3. Deliver content with an understanding of whole-brain learning.

The implementation of these strategies has been labeled "classroom ecology," based upon maintaining a balance of shared control in the environment and providing a nurturing atmosphere to support building positive relationships. For an ecosystem to thrive, all living and nonliving factors of the environment must be present and in balance. For student self-esteem to survive and thrive within a classroom environment, all three strategies must be present and implemented in a balanced approach.

The Five Elements

The five elements essential for enhancing the academic self-esteem of a student and thereby developing healthy relationships, are adapted from the self-esteem work of Robert Reasoner (1991). In his research, the five elements he identifies are:

- Security
- Identity
- Belonging
- Purpose
- Competence

His primary belief, "Education is based on a relationship, not a procedure," relies on addressing each of these elements within the classroom. By so doing, the teacher establishes a foundation for healthy relationships to develop not only between teacher and student and student and student but also between student and self.

Love and Logic Principles

When the committee first began to search for a way to implement Reasoner's five elements essential for enhancing student self-esteem, we wondered: How could we best manage the environment and promote responsible, healthy behaviors and relationships? The committee decided the most effective way to work with adolescents is the Love and Logic approach.

Early in September 1993, we brought Jim Fay into our building to present his overview to our staff. He spent four hours with the entire staff, and the response to what he was presenting was so overwhelmingly positive, the staff was willing to stay after school for more. Later that evening, he spent two hours presenting Love and Logic to our parents. The staff and parents were intrigued by the way this approach would allow students to build a sense of competence and responsibility. They saw that:

The Love and Logic approach provides a critical component to the self-esteem process by creating real-world situations within the classroom in which opportunities for decision-making are experienced.

Following the presentation, the Self-Esteem Committee provided a bibliography of materials regarding Love and Logic to the entire staff. We reminded the staff of who the committee members were, so that interested staff members could contact them as consultants in this process. We continued to meet on V.I.P. mornings, and among ourselves discussed and practiced these new principles.

One of the primary reasons we adopted Love and Logic principles for use in the classroom was that we were looking for ways to avoid power struggles and saw new possibilities in managing the environment by sharing control. We began by learning the following three steps for teachers to master while managing their classrooms:

Always Take Good Care of Yourself in Front of the Students. The way to accomplish this is to:

- Tell students what *we* will do, rather than tell students what *they* should do, and make them familiar with what they can expect consistently from us in the classroom.
- Utilize actions consistent with enforceable statements—those statements that are possible to enforce.
- Use thinking words instead of fighting words.

Each teacher decides the boundaries and limits he or she wants to establish in the classroom. As teachers, we believe that establishing limits and boundaries and taking consistent action when necessary helps students feel a sense of safety. When teachers model behavior in which they take good care of themselves, they convey an essential component required in healthy relationships, both with self and with others.

Provide Choices for Students Whenever Possible. Giving students choices allows them to feel some control over time spent and decisions made within the classroom. It inherently sends the messages:

- I respect you.
- You are able to make choices that are in your best interest.
- You can think for yourself.

As always, the choices students are offered must be choices the teacher can live with, and must be consis-

---

✎ LOVE AND LOGIC TIP #17:
Setting Limits

Most people set limits on themselves. When they are unable to, but need to, limits must be set by others. To avoid limit-setting turning into a control battle, we can always give choices and allow consequences.

To ensure that the limits you are setting are effective, make certain:

- The limit is definitely needed. Otherwise, why set it?
- Consequences are possible.
- Enforcement of the consequences will change the behavior.

The most common mistakes teachers make are setting limits that:

- They cannot enforce.
- Do not consider consequences in advance.
- Are stated as demands.
- Have not been approved by the building administrator.

Remember to calmly state the limit in the form of an enforceable statement: "I'll accept all papers that are prepared in the correct form."

---

tent with the limits and boundaries established for the classroom.

These Love and Logic messages and choices enhance the odds of improving a student's self-esteem, because a classroom is then created in which many positive factors exist:

- Students are forced to think.
- The chance of a power struggle developing is reduced.

- The relationship between student and teacher is reinforced.
- Teachers trust students' ability to think for themselves.
- Students are taught to deal with the consequences of their choices.

It is natural for concerns to arise when new methods are about to be tested. When our teachers were first advised to offer choices wherever possible in the classroom, some felt faced with the following dilemmas, which we addressed:

1. How can learning take place in an environment that is not totally teacher-controlled?

Accepting that a student may be learning by watching or just thinking was difficult for some teachers because it required that they give up some of their control. We decided to accept as reality that if a student was not creating a problem for either the teacher or another student, learning was probably taking place.

2. What can teachers offer, when a student is disruptive, as a choice that would respect the rest of the students' right to learn and still allow the teacher to address this student's inability to function within the classroom limits?

A choice involved asking the student to take a seat in the hall for a short time-out, in order to refocus. Another choice was to report to a special room for the remainder of the hour.

The Time-Out Room

Since there were many differences in teachers' approaches and classroom content, we realized that there would be changing expectations and responsibilities should we create a "time-out" room. It was agreed that a few rules would be necessary to distinguish it from the attendance office.

Guidelines for a Time-Out Room

1. Only those teachers involved in the Love and Logic program who were willing to staff the time-out room either now or in the future could send students to the room.

2. Students who were angry and disruptive would be sent to the attendance office on a discipline referral. Those students who were unable to maintain self-control, emotional control, focused behavior, respect for others, or were otherwise unable to abide by expectations set for classroom, would use the time-out room.

3. Once sent to the time-out room, the student would stay for the remaining hour. If a teacher felt the student needed a short removal from class, then the hall was considered a better solution.

4. Teachers staffing the time-out room would note arrival time on 3x5 cards. They would also record student behavior and number of visits to the time-out room on student passes. They would place these passes in the sending teacher's mailbox. It was then the sending teacher's responsibility to address the student.

5. The time-out room was to be used only for student/teacher interaction issues, *not* tardies or illnesses.

6. It was up to teacher discretion whether or not students could make up work when they chose to go to the time-out room. The student would be made aware of this decision before he or she left to go to the time-out room.

7. When visits to time-out room exceeded three, the following rules would apply:

• *Fourth visit:* Within a 10-week marking period and from the same class, a mandatory call home was required by the sending teacher. The supervising teacher would note the dates of visit and remind the sending teacher that a call was expected.
• *Fifth visit:* A call home was required and a behavioral referral slip would be sent to the administrator by the sending teacher.
• *Sixth visit:* Student would go straight to the attendance office.

8. The rules for student behavior in the time-out room were as follows:

- If a stop was necessary for books, or the rest room, the sending teacher had to allow for that before the student arrived at the time-out room.
- Once a student arrived, he or she was expected to stay for the remainder of the period.
- Behavior had to comply with student code of conduct; no cards or headsets were allowed.

- Almost any behavior was okay in the time-out room, as long as it didn't create a problem for the teacher or other students.
- Out-of-bounds behavior resulted in a student being referred to the attendance office.

3. "Don't get mad. Get sad." Provide equal amounts of empathy with consequences.

One of the realities that we knew, as a group, we would have to accept was the fact that not all students would want to learn, regardless of what we did in the classroom. We needed to remain focused, in an adult state of mind, and not personalize their actions or comments.

As teachers, we recognized that the problem was not ours, but theirs, and we would shift the problem back to a student whenever possible. The life skill featured in this step was for students to learn that there are consequences for their choices and that they can learn from them.

An important lesson we were about to learn is that kids are willing to live with consequences when adults aren't rubbing salt into the wound by getting angry and lecturing.

Students accept consequences when we:

- Give them no opportunity to get angry, owing to our reaction to their choices.
- Accept that real learning will occur when, with our nonjudgmental support and guidance, they are left to answer the question: "What are you going to do about this?"

Developing and Practicing the Plan

In January 1994, our committee reported back to the entire staff in a two-hour in-service meeting to focus on the Love and Logic method of managing the classroom by building opportunity for trusting relationships to evolve and learning to occur based on responsible decision-making.

In a forty-five-minute presentation, the three rules of Love and Logic were discussed: (1) taking good care of yourself in front of your students; (2) providing choices whenever possible; and (3) providing empathy with consequences when necessary.

The following ninety minutes were spent in small groups (eight to ten teachers and two facilitators from the committee) focusing on a variety of potential power struggles within the classroom and possible ways of handling them using Love and Logic. A scenario would be described, then, beginning with the worst possible reaction, one that ensured a power struggle, the group practiced using enforceable statements, thinking words vs. fighting words, generating choices consistent with limits, and offering empathy instead of anger when consequences were appropriate.

By the end of the ninety minutes, these support groups were able to process five to eight scenarios. This in-service was timed so that it occurred just prior to the second semester. This provided the staff with the opportunity to begin using this new technique for classroom management, or at least some part of it.

As a committee we gave our staff the choice of trying just one of the three principles, if that was all they felt comfortable with. In order to assist them, we encouraged them to provide the committee with possible scenarios they had experienced or could foresee as a problem in their classroom. We offered to spend part of our V.I.P meetings processing these referrals and having the department liaison share our responses and feedback with the referring person.

Through this process, we were able to build positive relations between our committee members and other nontrusting staff. In many situations, we were able to recruit new staff to our committee's beliefs, principles, and practices.

A typical two-hour V.I.P. meeting would begin by calling for concerns from committee members regarding their own experiences in the classroom. After discussing these, we would process referrals that had been submitted by other staff members. Often we would role-play to practice different ways of responding and to experience for ourselves a comfort level utilizing Love and Logic techniques.

Following these concerns, new concepts relative to Love and Logic theories were discussed. It was reported that much of the practice of utilizing Love and Logic principles was done at home with children and family. The comfort level seemed safer there than in the classroom. After developing a comfort level, members would then begin introducing these principles in the classroom.

Having dealt with the issues of security, identity, a sense of belonging, and a feeling for the purpose of this program, its final portion of content and learning was spent on competence. The committee chose to work with the concept of whole-brain learning. Each committee member completed an inventory that produced an individual profile of learning style. It provided a visual tool by which members could see and understand their strength areas relative to the four quadrants of the brain.

Training was provided to help the staff work outside their strength areas and possibly raise the odds of reaching more students who might not come from this preferred learning/teaching style, which helps students feel a sense of belonging and safety, and allows purpose to be visualized.

The universal thrust of the three Love and Logic rules within the classroom—care of yourself (enforceable limits), choices within limits for students, and consequences with empathy—was to develop relationships between teacher and student, student and student, and, most important, student and self. Before we could change behavior, we would have to change self-concept.

Putting the Plan into Action

During the year, the Self-Esteem Committee moved into the action phase of its program. We began by surveying ninth-grade males and females using a Student Self-Esteem Inventory. Three areas of focus have received significant attention from the committee, and presentations have been made to staff and parents. These three areas include:

- The classroom environment
- Managing the environment
- Teaching approaches within the classroom environment

Each area has been researched, and all philosophy and practical approaches have been shared with staff and parents. Following is a description of the content of each area.

The Classroom Environment

As already mentioned, we adopted Robert Reasoner's *Five Components to Building Self-Esteem*. The components he considers essential are: security, identity, belonging, purpose, and competence. Explanations and strategies for each area were provided to the staff in reviewing their own classroom environment's effectiveness.

Managing the Environment

We adopted Jim Fay's approach to working with students. A "time-out" room was created to help facilitate this approach. Since the time Jim Fay spoke to our staff at an afternoon in-service gathering and then to parents the same evening about his Love and Logic approach, he has continued to act as a consultant to Walled Lake Central High School.

Teaching Approaches Within the Classroom Environment

Currently about thirty staff members participate in eight hours of in-service relative to different learning styles.

✎ **LOVE AND LOGIC TIP #18:**
Better Ways to Say "No"

The word "no" triggers resistance more easily than any other word in the English language. It's a student's call to arms. Kids hear it far too often—so often that it's the first word many kids learn to say.

When they hear "no," they often ignore it. Having heard it so much, they come to think it means "maybe." Other times they think it really means "yes." A good rule for "no" is to use it as seldom as possible. When you do use it, make sure you mean business. At other times, you can make a statement positively and still deny a request. You are saying "yes" instead of "no," but you are still in control. The behavior you want can be established without triggering resistance. Here is an example:

"No" Statement: "No, you may not watch television until the dishes are done."

"Yes" Statement: "Yes, you may watch television as soon as the dishes are done."

*What a difference a turn of the phrase can make
in how a child learns and responds!*

Each staff member has his or her own learning style identified in order to provide an awareness of specific preference.

Examining the whole-brain approach to teaching creates an awareness of learning styles that are different from our own. Strategies and techniques that address these different learning styles are offered to staff.

The committee believes that:

**When all three critical areas
are addressed in the classroom experience,
students are afforded optimal opportunity
to enhance their self-esteem and, thus, academic
achievement.**

Student reaction is:

**"All I want is to be recognized and valued as a person
and given the right to choose what I believe is best
for me, given my unique life circumstances."**

With these expectations recognized there is calming among students, much like the calm of the ocean at sunset. As always there is the student who, for whatever reason, cannot respect the rights of others. The general principle for extreme intervention, such as suspension or expulsion, would be applied in these circumstances. Such action is based on the principle that if another student endangers the safety of others, or impedes the learning of other students, his choices must be narrowed and we must be more corrective.

Small Group Work

The following is a representation of work that was done by one of the small groups of teachers.

January 1994, Staff In-Service Small-Group Work Utilizing Love and Logic Principles

Small Group: Following are six situations that typically require a response or reaction on the part of the teacher. If, during the time allotted, you exhaust this list, ask your group members to offer other situations.

- ✐ Included in each situation is an open-ended statement to be responded to in three different ways.
- ✐ Offer the situation to the group and then process the different approaches to the problem.
- ✐ Notice that answers have been provided for you if your group cannot generate a response.
- ✐ Have staff members use handouts as cheat sheets to formulate responses.
- ✐ Present guidelines for generating discussion.
- ✐ Always start off with responses that will not work or will result in a challenge, battle, or struggle for control; then work into effective responses.
- ✐ Always ask:
  1. Who owns the problem?
  2. How can we make it the student's problem?
  3. How can we force decision-making on the student?
  4. How do we get people to think in terms of options?

SITUATION #1:

During an assignment, where students are working together or individually, the noise level increases to intolerable levels. How can you respond?

Battle or Conflict Response: "Shut up, you're driving me nuts!"

Enforceable Statement: "I'll be glad to allow groups to continue working together when the noise level is lower."

Choices: "Would you rather continue to work at a reasonable noise level or would you like to work silently?"

Sadness: "What a bummer. Do you need to find another place to work?"

SITUATION #2:

During class, a student verbally abuses another student.

Battle or Conflict Response: "That was a mean thing to say. You're not very considerate!"

Enforceable Statement: "I will continue to teach when students can respect each other."

Choices: "Would you rather show respect for other students or find another place to work?"

Sadness: "That's sad, John. We have a rule in this class; we don't use put-downs." "I would like to talk to you after class." "I worry about you when I see you putting other kids down."

SITUATION #3:
A student wants to turn in homework late and feels that he has a legitimate reason for doing so.

Battle or Conflict Response: "You know the rules, and I don't want to talk about it anymore."

Enforceable Statement: "I give full credit to papers that are turned in on time."

Choice: "Would you rather turn your paper in on time and get full credit or turn it in late and get partial credit?"

Sadness: "It must be frustrating to do the work and not get full credit." "What a bummer. Do you suppose this will happen often?"

SITUATION #4:
A defiant student says, angrily, "You can't make me!"

Battle or Conflict Response: "You do it right now and I mean it!"

Enforceable Statement: "I'll listen as soon as your voice is calm." OR "You're welcome to stay as long as you don't create a problem for me or others."

Choice: "Would you rather work on the assignment with the rest of the class or would you rather move to the time-out room?"

Sadness: "You must really be angry about something." "Let's talk about this when we're both calm." "Do you think you can be with us now, or do you need to go to the time-out room to calm down?"

SITUATION #5:

During a cooperative learning group activity, such as a laboratory exercise, a student "goofs off" with another student and students touch each other.

Conflict or Battle Response: "You guys are always messing around. Why can't you grow up?"

Enforceable Statement: "I allow students to use equipment in this lab when they behave appropriately."

Choice: "Would you prefer to sit alone and not participate or stop fooling around and stay focused with your group?"

Sadness: "How sad not to be able to use the equipment. Would you rather go to the time-out room or sit alone?"

SITUATION #6:

The teacher directs students to take out a book and open it to page 69. One student just sits there.

Conflict or Battle Response: "You take out your book right now, or else!"

Enforceable Statement: "Students are welcome to remain in class when they come prepared and when they follow instructions."

Choice: "Joe, what would be best for you, to take out your book and open to page 69, or not understand what we're about to discuss?"

Sadness: "I'm sad that you're choosing not to participate in class today. Do you think you'll get it together in time for the test?"

In the following sections are generally recommended actions for your particular workshops. Each school, situation, staff, and set of students is different, but the following can assist you by providing a place to begin:

Create an Atmosphere for Learning

Any workshop has both an emotional and a physical climate that can enhance the learning environment.

To help achieve a positive emotional climate:

- Maintain a positive attitude.
- Accept participant ideas/behaviors as gifts to the program.
- Encourage participants to help each other.
- Make the experience pleasant by being friendly and using humor where appropriate.
- Establish trust, respect, and clear lines of communication and honesty.

For a comfortable physical climate:

- Select a workshop size (number of participants) that is comfortable for you.
- Select a room appropriate to group size that facilitates discussion and viewing of video cassettes.
- Align participant seating so that you can clearly see all participants.

Things to Avoid While Facilitating Learning

When we are put in positions in which we are passing on new information to others, we sometimes develop overwhelming expectations of ourselves that reach far beyond what we may be capable of doing. While facilitating learning, avoid:

- **Being made the "expert."** Don't expect yourself to know everything and to be able to answer all questions immediately. Your primary role is to introduce new knowledge and facilitate learning.

- **Expecting yourself to be the "perfect facilitator."** You will improve with experience. The more prepared you are ahead of time, the more successful you will be.

- **Being made the "parent."** Avoid situations in which participants seek approval and information from you alone. Encourage participants to help each other.

- **Giving participant resistance too much "air time."** It is important to recognize and acknowledge resistance, but too much attention will increase it.

- **Attempting too early in the workshop to impress participants with what this program provides.** When participants have some experience with the principles, they will be more open to them.

Common Questions and Answers

Question #1: *"I don't understand . . . my parents bossed me around and it worked fine. I didn't rebel like my kids. Why doesn't it work for me?"*

Times have changed. When my father yelled at me and bossed me around, I thought that parents were supposed to do that. Now when kids complain that their parents are ordering them around, they are told modern-society messages, such as, "You have rights. If your parents loved you, they wouldn't do that."

Question #2: *"When kids solve their own problems, what if they choose a bad solution?*

When this happens, they have the opportunity for a double learning lesson. When their bad choices fail, they are forced to look for new solutions.

Question #3: *"When I think about the Love and Logic philosophy and the new techniques and strategies I've learned from this program, I get overwhelmed . . . and frustrated. There's so much to remember!"*

The road to change is always under construction. It is slow and full of imperfection. Change takes time. Practice infers mistakes. Be patient with yourself. Begin the process by focusing on a single behavior you'd like to change, or by practicing a single new technique.

Sometimes discussing concerns and questions can appease our anxieties and fears that relate to trying something new. For additional discussion of common concerns, it may be helpful to review the Love and Logic Parenting Pearls contained in the book *Parenting With Love and Logic* by Jim Fay and Foster W. Cline, M.D. These Pearls represent common questions raised by parents.

Conclusions

As the end of the school year neared, much had been accomplished through the Self-Esteem Committee's efforts. Teachers reported that their practice of Love and Logic principles at home with spouses and children had been helpful. Most felt they had redefined the dynamics by which they interacted with family members, and results were overwhelmingly positive.

The teachers experienced less conflict with regard to power struggles, and less stress because controlling others gave way to guidance, support, and respect for others' right to choose and live with the consequences of their actions. Everyone became aware that although learning is sometimes painful, it provides a real picture for children of what to expect in the world in which they live. All of these experiences enhanced the quality of trust in a nurturing, but firm, relationship.

I believe it was the personal work as well as the practice and support within our committee's weekly meetings that provided the impetus for the staff to restructure their classrooms.

Some did more than others, but in the end we all had integrated the core beliefs of Love and Logic into our daily approach to all relationships.

At parent/teacher conferences, we explained our core belief that a class ought to be run as much like the real world as possible. We asked parents if they would like to know more about Love and Logic and provided handouts for them to better understand its principles. We made sure they understood that learning how to become a Love and Logic parent was always an option for them to consider.

In a number of different classes (psychology, sociology, health, business) teachers practiced turning fighting words into thinking words; turning unenforceable statements into enforceable statements; providing choices instead of giving orders; and providing empathy responses before focusing on self. Role-reversal was used in which students were asked to act out the part of a parent and address scenarios from the home utilizing Love and Logic principles. Students often provided the best responses because they were often receivers of such responses and knew best what would work with them.

Throughout the year many staff members from outside the committee approached us for help on how to deal with a particular problem or student; many came for literature to research Love and Logic more thoroughly; and others came to practice the principles at home or with friends.

Currently, within the Walled Lake School District, a strategic plan exists, which includes a Parenting Education Committee. The primary purpose is to provide education in support of parents who are frustrated with their children. The Love and Logic principles found in the program entitled, "Becoming a Love and Logic Parent," are being utilized. The Walled Lake educational cable channel has aired the Jim Fay parent presentation of September 1993 repeatedly during this school year for viewing by parents.

PEARL
▼

*Education is based on a relationship,
not a procedure.*

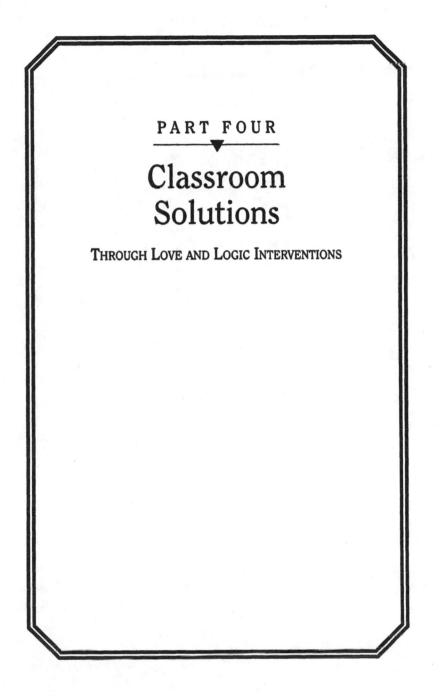

PART FOUR

Classroom
Solutions

THROUGH LOVE AND LOGIC INTERVENTIONS

Some Basic Love and Logic Disciplinary Actions

*E*ven though the goal of teaching is teaching and learning, most teachers today will state that a great deal of their time is spent on discipline. Throughout this book, we have emphasized efficiency in classroom management, the point of which is that the more effective you become, the less time you spend on discipline and the more time you spend on teaching.

> ***An important factor in efficient classroom management is your ability to put a stop to disruptive behavior before it becomes serious enough to necessitate applying consequences.***

Breaking the Emotional Spell

Love and Logic offers disciplinary interventions as positive techniques that will often bring a student back into appropriate behavior without having to make the situation into a major issue. These interventions usually allow the teacher to restore order without "breaking stride." Many of these interventions are so subtle that the casual observer is not aware that the teacher is actually involved in discipline.

Don't be fooled by the benign appearance of the first ten interventions. Experiment with them and you will be amazed at their power.

Before entering the presentation of these interventions, it is important to remember the following:

No technique can be effective if it is not delivered with genuine passion.

It is also important to remember:

1. These interventions are not designed to teach children the important lessons of life. They are intended to "break the emotional spell" of the moment, eliminate a disruption before it intensifies, and allow the teacher to continue teaching.

2. The teacher must be circulating in the room. These interventions don't work for teachers who sit at their desks and try to bark orders.

3. These interventions are designed to show students that the teacher is capable of handling kids without stopping the teaching process.

4. Even though the presentation begins with the least severe and moves to the most severe, these interventions are not intended to be used in a step-by-step process. Effective teachers pick the intervention that is the least severe, but still powerful enough to fit the situation.

5. These interventions are designed to enhance the teacher/student relationship. As kids see teachers using these techniques, they feel less threatened, are not embarrassed as frequently, and develop more positive feelings for their teachers.

For years, teachers have been listening to my (Jim Fay's) presentations and applying these strategies to the children in their own classrooms. The feedback I've received is that these interventions help teachers learn to move toward engaging children in working through problems as opposed to old techniques that encourage the teacher to move away from the student. Teachers have also discovered that these strategies improve the quality of their relationships with kids and reduce the number of times a kid acts up.

Getting Them to Fall in Love with You

There are some additional thoughts on teachers and kids I want to pass on before we delve into the interventions. I was reminded of these some time ago when I went to Las Vegas to give a keynote address. Between sessions, I had an opportunity to listen to other presenters, some of whom were excellent teachers who were not experienced speakers. I heard one teacher who was considered one of the outstanding teachers in the inner city schools of Los Angeles. She taught problem students in what was, in essence, an alternative program within a conventional high school. She had all the kids that nobody wanted— the ones who couldn't read or write and the tough kids of the school.

In her presentation, this teacher was using slides, overheads, audios, and visuals—equipment and techniques she had seen at her staff development academy—and was attempting to impart information she had gathered from a lot of research. The audience, however, was bored. In fact, one guy, who was rather straightforward and apparently insensitive, said, "Can it! If you're supposed to be so good, tell us one thing we can take away from this conference that we can use with our kids right away."

This comment, as you can imagine, threw her back. When she recovered, she started talking from the heart and said:

"I guess if there was only one thing I could depend on, it would be relationships. All the kids I work with are bigger and tougher than I am, so I can't threaten them with anything. They're not scared of anybody. So I have to rely on getting them to fall in love with me.

"I know there are many of you who believe that kids are supposed to respect you and that we get to do anything, because we are adults and they are kids," she went on. "But with tough kids, I've got to get them to fall in love with me so deeply that they will do things for me that they would not do for anybody else—including themselves.

"In fact," she said, "I have to get them to care so much for me that they're willing to take on the greatest risk that they will ever take on in their lives. That's not whipping out a knife and taking on some kid out in the alley, which is day-to-day operation with those kids. The biggest risk is to try to do something in front of their peers that they know they cannot do, like show that they can read something or write it down. I'm at a point with these kids where I can say, 'Hey, Jon, will you do it for me, please? I know you can do it.' And they will.

"There's only one way I know to get that done. On the very first day of school, you will see me out in front of my door, shaking hands with those kids, looking in their eyes, smiling, and saying,'I'm glad you're going to be in my room.' Right away, they suspect something crazy. Nobody's ever said that to them before.

"I get them doing something in the room that anybody could do, so they can keep busy while I meet every one of those kids before they come into the room. From that day on, I'm out there saying, "Gimme five," giving handshakes and smiles, looking at them, and showing them I care. I want to be human and show them I care about them as people far more than I care about them as students.

"Then I start noticing things about them and asking questions. 'Did your sister get back from the hospital yet?' 'How's your mom doing with the new baby?' 'Did you get to play ball this week?' 'Are you driving yet?' I ask about those kinds of personal things so that they start to know that I know them as a person.

"Largely because of this relationship I have with my kids, I have a special privilege at school. I am the only person on that staff who can leave the faculty meeting before the principal finishes talking. We have a staff meeting every Wednesday morning and we have a long-winded principal, so he often does not finish on schedule.

"The first time he didn't end on time, I got up and said, 'I have to leave; I have to meet my kids at the door.' He looked a bit indignant and said, 'This is important. Stay here.' To that I said, 'If I can't meet those kids ahead of time, then somebody else on this staff is going to have to teach them.' At that point, all of the teachers said in unison, 'Send her. It's okay. We'll share the information with her later.' I'm the only person who can get by with that. I'm also the only person on the staff who doesn't have to worry about my car in the parking lot. Those kids take care of that for me."

This teacher's "presentation," was a gentle reminder that teaching is building positive relationships with kids so that they want to do what we ask them to do. Doing this well is an art.

Who knows what has happened in students' lives in the morning, before they come to school. One may need desperately to have a power struggle with someone to regain a sense of self-concept. We may be working with variables we had not anticipated at breakfast that morning or on our way to work. A particular strategy may work on some kids and not on others. Or, a strategy may work on a specific kid at one time and not at another. If we have sufficient tools in our "bag of tricks," we can raise the odds that we will find something effective for nearly any situation.

The following interventions, from least to most intense, is not a list to be followed step by step. It's possible that a particular situation might call for an immediate jump to a relatively intense intervention. The only action I would caution against is sending a kid to the principal right away. I think it's a rather dangerous jump from "Give 'em the evil eye" (the first intervention) to "Send 'em to the principal" (the fourteenth).

> *As a teacher I have had more pride when*
> *I've been able to say to my principal,*
> *"I've tried these thirteen different things before*
> *I ever considered sending this kid to you."*

Another caution. It is easy to assume that if we have a "system," we no longer have to rely upon good relationships with kids. Nothing could be farther from the truth. There are few things that work, especially as kids get bigger, if we don't have a positive relationship with them. If you're going to remember only one factor, this should be the one.

Intervention 1
THE EVIL EYE

Let's suppose I have just started teaching a lesson from the front of the class and "Al" is fooling around. What is the most benign little thing I could do? Give him the "evil eye"! Probably nobody needs help with this because we have all had ample opportunity to learn this technique from our own parents and teachers. A higher level of sophistication is to give the student a smile and a wink (a hug from across the room).

Intervention 2
MOVING IN ON THE STUDENT

So far we have discussed techniques designed to allow me to continue teaching and utilize a minimum of confrontation. The integrity of the teaching environment is maintained. So, I move in on Al once more while I'm still teaching and this time I place a very gentle hand on his shoulder. I have not looked at him yet. I'm simply teaching with a gentle hand on the shoulder—no pinched nerves and no intent to embarrass or overpower. This is done in an absentminded manner, almost as if I don't recognize Al's misbehavior.

When using this technique, I have been known to teach leaning on the kid while I'm instructing—if I have a really good relationship going. More than likely the kid looks up at me. I look upon that as an opportunity for us to smile and grin at each other. The reciprocal smile is my clue that things are starting to fit together. I want to say in a nonverbal manner, "These actions on my part are designed to enhance our relationship, not create a confrontation."

Professional judgment is the key. There are some kids I could go up to, rest my hand on their shoulder, and everything would be fine. There are also certain kids who, if I make even benign physical contact, will turn and say, "What'd I do?" or "I didn't do anything!" "What're you doing?!" Whatever the words used, the message is, "Don't touch me." If this were to happen, I would move away without a word, almost as if I had not heard at all.

To be most effective, before I walk up to a kid, I will need to have a good idea ahead of time of whether or not I'm going to make things better or worse by touching him. That takes insight that is developed from experience and professional training.

Intervention 3
PROXIMITY

The third strategy has to do with proximity. Suppose I have given Al "the look" and it didn't work. What I will probably do next is walk toward him. I will not immediately try to make eye contact. Instead, I'm going to teach more intensely than before. I'll start asking questions of kids on one side of the room and check on what some kids are doing on the other side.

Where are my eyes? Not on Al, yet. He's not going to get any eye contact as I move gently and casually toward him. And what's on my face? A frown or a smile? A smile, of course! So now I am teaching closer to Al, but I still have not looked at him.

I have known kids who ended up in the principal's office when all that might have been necessary was for the teacher to move away from the desk and walk into the student's area to teach. If this doesn't work, I may decide to stand closer. Will it work then? Depends on the kid and what's going on that day. I have been known to stand right next to Al's chair, making it difficult for him to feel comfortable with his misbehavior.

Intervention 4
EYE CONTACT AND "NO" HEAD-SHAKE

If I see that standing close is not working or that it's escalating the behavior, I move away. But I will do something different with my eyes. I'm going to catch Al's eye out of the corner of mine and when I do, there's going to be a quick little shake of the head.

With this strategy we send the strong, unstated message: "I don't want to embarrass you, but that's enough of that." Will a kid appreciate the fact that the teacher does not want to embarrass him? In some cases, the answer is yes. Will it work? Although we don't know for sure, it takes so little time and effort that it's certainly worth a try.

Intervention 5
LET'S TALK ABOUT THIS LATER

What if, by chance, I misread the situation on a particular day? Is that possible? Absolutely! Because on some days, Al can be touched, and other days he cannot. What if I touch him and he whirls on me and says, "Get your hands off me," or worse, "What did I do?" Ever have a kid say, "What did I do?" That's a hook kids use to say, "Let's have a big power struggle right now, in front of all my peers." Then, if you do, exluding all the details, he tells his mother how mean you are.

If he does yell, "Don't touch me!" or "What did I do?" I'm going to quickly move away, to ease up this private space he needs. Then I'm going to whisper, so nobody else hears, "Let's talk about this later." He may not, however, give up that easily. He may say, "I want to talk about it right now!" My reaction is, with a calm, quiet voice, to repeat, "Let's talk about this later," or "I'll be glad to talk about this later."

If Al insists on having a power struggle, I may then confront him with, "That sounds like an argument. If it is, I schedule arguments at 12:15 and 3:15 daily. Which time would be best for you? Let me know later, thanks." I move away immediately to minimize the problem. It's harder to have a power struggle when we're having to make choices. Will this work? Once again, there's no guarantee.

Intervention 6
CAN YOU SAVE THAT? THANKS.

In the event no intervention has worked, I'm going to have to finally say something to Al. Although he's pushing the issue, I still want to say something that will enhance our relationship. I'd like to say something that tells him, "You're okay, Al, but the behavior is not." I love the one-liner that says, "Just because I like you, should I let you get away with that? Thank you." Once more, I walk away before Al can answer. This shows an assumption of compliance.

I need to be cautious because so often I can start the power struggle just by embarrassing a kid in front of his friends and then he has no choice left. In those situations, his only recourse would be to take me on. If Al decides to do this in the classroom, with thirty of his peers standing around smiling, "Yeah, yeah, go for it!" I wouldn't have a very good chance of avoiding a win/lose situation.

Depending on the relationship, I might say, "Al, is this necessary? Thank you." And what's happening to my face while I'm saying that? There's a smile that is natural and sincere and relays the message that since our relationship is cemented, this behavior we're currently addressing should no longer be a problem. The smile is important, because if I ask, "Is this necessary?" with a frown, he might say, "Yes, it is." At this point, we will both have a problem.

In situations of potential confrontation, any number of statements can be used, but the basic message that the teacher needs to convey is: "The two of us still have a relationship; we are okay. Your behavior isn't."

Experiment with this one-liner: "Al, could you save that for Mr. Larson's class? Thank you." I bet Al will have to grin and you can continue your teaching.

Intervention 7
CHANGING LOCATION

It's often easier and more effective to change a kid's location than it is to change the kid's behavior. Although I have not been able to determine the psychological reasons why, from my observations it seems there is some kind of magic involved when we change where the kid is placed. I've seen it work time and again. The only thing I have been able to figure out is that somehow, when the location is changed, the emotional spell is broken.

I first took note of this phenomenon at an airport. Waiting for an airplane, I saw a man standing next to an ice cream stand, holding a three-year-old. This kid was going crazy. "I want ice cream! Why can't I have some ice cream? You've got some money. I know you've got money!"

As I watched, I thought, "That guy is probably going through a lot of stress right now, but anyone dumb

enough to put a little kid in that situation deserves everything he gets."

My respect for this gentleman changed in an instant. I
saw him, without a single word, put the child down on
the floor, take her hand, and, in a very determined way,
just start walking away from there. The kid was trailing
along behind and with every step, the volume of that
whining little voice got softer and softer until, six or
seven steps away, the kid became completely quiet. The
man then picked up the child and deliberately walked
right back to the ice cream stand. I thought the kid would
start all over again, but that never happened.

I've seen this same phenomenon in classrooms where
I have done demonstration teaching. I show how to use
some of our Love and Logic techniques by teaching an
actual class. To balance the situation, I tell the school
that they can choose the class, and I get to choose the
subject matter.

I usually set up a game that's competitive between two
sides of the room. I might change all the chairs and desks
around so that we have all the makings for chaos. Then I
set up a lot of rules that are somewhat difficult to follow
and, if not followed, allow the other team bonus points.

Teachers like to challenge me by planting some rough
kids. Then the teachers wait to see what the "expert" will
do with these kids who have been driving them up the
wall all year.

What humors me is that it is fairly easy to find out
who these transplanted kids are, because the others are
looking at them and saying, "What are you doing here
today?" The funny part is that those kids hardly ever act
up, because the teachers have already done for me what I
might do if I were confronted by a disruptive kid: change

their location. For a short period of time, they're a bit off balance and they don't act up. Instead, they watch, listen and don't cause a problem at all.

Teachers' reactions also humor me. They will watch with great anticipation and afterward ask, with a bit of reverence, "What did you do with those kids? We want to know!" I almost feel like saying, "Well, it's classified information." But after basking for a moment in their awe of my skills, I have to tell them that they were really the ones responsible for changing the kids' behavior. The reason? Changed location!

From time to time, there will be a disruptive kid who starts to act up. The technique of changing a student's location has worked thirty-five times in a row. This is not to say it will work the thirty-sixth time, but thirty-five times in a row, I have gone, in a calm fashion, with a smile on my face, to one of these kids and asked, "Would you mind sitting over there? Thank you." Every time the kid has moved before he figured out what was going on and before he thought to ask himself what he was doing there. By the time he figured it out, his behavior had changed.

Let's remember that our goal with behavior management is to change the offending behavior. It's not to do therapy. This technique will not work for the long term; but for right now, the tone of what's going on has changed, which not only gives you additional time, but the opportunity to work on the relationship.

One eventuality is that some kids will say, "No. I'm not moving." In these cases, is it better to talk first and smile later or smile first and talk later? I would go for a smile, then say something like, "Would you humor me?" And the best way to say that is in a whisper, so that he knows our conversation is as private as I can make it.

When a kid says no is when we especially need to buy some time and get the kid to do the thinking.

I like to rely on questions. One of my favorites in a situation like this one is, "Did I ask in a nice way?" If I have been treating the kid with dignity and truly asked in a nice way, the kid is pretty obligated to say, "Yeah, you asked in a nice way." I follow that up with, "And you're still not going to do it? Wow. Really? That's hard for me to believe."

Is this kid eventually going to grin? I don't know. If he does, the behavior has changed. Then I have a new opportunity to build a relationship. In fact, right now, this kid may not be acting up anymore because he's so busy listening.

There is always the chance that, with a really tough kid, I may not be able to avoid a power struggle pursuing this line of interaction. At that point, I may say, "That's okay. I've changed my mind." I'm still okay, because I didn't just snap, "Hey! Do it now! I mean it!" That would sound like an indictment of the kid. If I say, "Hey, move!" to a kid who is not going to move—no way, no how—I'm the one who will pay the biggest price.

What is the secret? Why will kids so often accept when you say, "Would you mind . . . ?" or "Would you consider . . . ?" It is a simple matter of choices, respect, and control. A question is not a command. I will not guarantee that choices always work, but I firmly believe that using them significantly raises the odds that you will engage in a win/win situation.

When I ask a question, I don't wait for an immediate answer. When I do go back to the student, and he or she says, "No way, I'm not going to do it," my response will probably be, "Did I ask in a nice way?" There is rhythm and movement to this process that takes no more than a few seconds. It takes far longer to describe than it takes in actual class time. I'm in tune with the rest of the group and my teaching has not stopped. I would not like for a kid to think that I'm going to make such a big deal over behavior that I would take time out from teaching the class.

> *The message I like to send in a disciplinary situation is, "This is a piece of cake! I won't have to take a lot of time out from my teaching for this."*

If the other kids want to know what I've said to this student, I would probably say, "You know I would never share with the rest of the class the things I say to a kid in private. But thanks for asking."

My partner, Foster Cline, teaches a concept called "the assumption of compliance" that is incorporated into the techniques we've been discussing.

> *When we talk to a kid in a way that appears that we assume there will be compliance, the odds are raised immensely that the kid will do what we ask.*

When I smile and say, "Thank you" at the end of a request and then move right on to what I was doing, I have given the unstated message of expectation that the kid will cooperate.

The assumption of compliance is just as powerful in the negative sense. If I say, "We'll talk about that later" and then stare at the kid, I am basically saying, "I don't believe you're going to do what I'm asking. Let's have our power struggle right now." The messages have been nonverbal, but they are definitely there. Our nonverbal messages are much more powerful than words could ever be.

As a final thought on changing a kid's location, it is essential for us to give a message that says, "There are actions I want you to take, but this is not a threat." To do this, we need to use words that will convey respect and dignity.

Dave Funk says, "The language of respect is how you speak to your kids when the superintendent is observing your teaching." Isn't it amazing that when we speak this way to kids and have good results, we attribute them to the fact that the principal was in the room, when, in all probability, the kid's behavior was related to the use of respectful language?

Intervention 8
IS THIS THE RIGHT PLACE FOR THAT?

Virginia Satir has done extraordinary work with people all over the nation. In her counseling, she has placed emphasis on the questions: "Does the behavior fit?" "Is it working for you?" She does not dwell on whether or not the behavior is good or bad.

Most of the kids I work with know that the behaviors they get into trouble for in the classroom are not usually bad or evil—simply misplaced. The behaviors that sometimes get kids into trouble would never be a serious concern for an adult. Have you ever seen an adult in trouble for talking out in a class? Nevertheless, many of us believe that we can't have talking in a school classroom.

Do adults get into trouble for suddenly visiting with a friend because they notice something they just learned and want to share it? Do they get into trouble for chewing gum? Does it make sense, then, that kids are sharp enough to understand that some behaviors are simply misplaced and not innately bad? Does it also make sense that they would appreciate having a teacher who, just as smart, realizes this too and acts accordingly?

There is often a question about the best thing to do when a student acts up when an administrator is observing in the classroom. Do I stop instructing, knowing my principal is really into time on task, or do I continue to teach while the disruption continues in the back of the class?

My emphatic opinion is that you're still a good teacher, regardless of who may be visiting or observing, if you say to the students you are working with, "Pardon me. There's something going on that I need to deal with. I appreciate your patience. I'll be right back."

Then I would head back to the kid doing the disrupting, without angry body language, smiling as I go. I want all of the kids to believe that this is easy and that I'm not upset about having to deal with classroom disturbances.

Depending on the kid and the circumstances, I might whisper, "Hey could you save that for the playground?" Or, "Just because I like you, should I let you get away with that?" Or, "Does that fit in this class?" Then I would walk back to the group I was working with and apologize. "I'm sorry, guys. I know it's harder to get things done when I have to leave. Let's pick up where we left off."

I've seen many teachers who are experts at handling disruptions in a way that doesn't lose the class. Each has his or her individual way of doing this, but all show a level of sophistication based on a balance of respect for kids and for learning.

I observed one teacher in a situation similar to the one we have been discussing. When it was evident that the disruption needed intervention, she said to the kids she was working with, "Okay, group, please read the next paragraph and find the word that shows how the main character was feeling. As soon as you have it, put your fingers on your ears so I know you've got it."

While the other kids were engaged in this activity, she walked back to the offending student, talked with him, and got right back to the rest of the class without missing a beat. She said, "Looks like almost everybody's done . . . all but four . . . now all but two . . ." And, even though she had dealt with a behavior problem, she never quit teaching. As I was watching, I thought, "That's pretty cool teaching."

Intervention 9:
"I" MESSAGES

As with any technique, there are cautions to consider when using "I Messages." These are tough for even the best of us because we have to make ourselves vulnerable. Somebody might reject us. We might pour out our heart and soul to someone whose response is, "Who cares?"

Shortly after "I Messages" were introduced, several myths started to surface. One of them is that these messages are the only way to communicate your feelings. Actually, there are a lot of different ways to communicate with others. This is just one technique we put in our bag of teaching tricks.

Ray, the School Custodian

When I was a principal, Ray was the custodian in my school and was a good worker if he had the right motivation. If I had used "I Messages" with him, he would have thought I was a wimp. How do I know that? Simple. I tried an "I Message" with him once, and he thought I was a wimp.

One day, out of my bag of tricks I took a technique I seldom used. I went to him, and said, "Dammit, Ray, when I tell you to do something, that's what I expect you to do; and if you don't like it, find yourself another place to work!" The day I did that, he started going around the school saying that I was getting easier to respect. Ray had a certain level of disdain for those who didn't talk the way he did.

I would not dare speak that way to anybody else on the staff, but I needed that "technique" for Ray. I could never go over to him and say, "I feel discounted when you don't do what I ask."

Information in a Nonthreatening Way

We've heard some say that "I Messages" *make* people do things. I think this myth got started because simply giving information can be a very powerful psychological tool. In fact, the best that "I Messages" can do is provide an opportunity to share information without telling the other person what to do about it.

Tony the Tyrant

The best story I have on that subject comes out of a special education class. Tony the Tyrant could turn the best teacher into jelly. He could hook nearly anybody into a power struggle. There were diagnosed unattachment problems with this kid, and he was a master manipulator.

One day Tony invited his teacher into a power struggle, whereupon she said, "Tony, go into the time-out area." To this, Tony said, "I'm not going. You can't make me." And she said, "Yes, you are. I *can* make you." And he said. "I'm not going," and she said, "Yes you are." At that point, Tony gave himself a little control and said, "If you make me go, I'm taking off my clothes."

This teacher was sharp, but by now she realized she was heavily into this power struggle, and she backed off immediately. She said, "Whatever turns you on, Tony. See you in the time-out area."

He went, but pretty soon up over the top of the area came these little clothes. First, a shirt, then his socks; after that came the shoes. Finally, sailing over the top was a tiny pair of jockey shorts. At that point, the teacher said to the class, "I think this would be a good time for us to go down and play with the computers. Everybody line up."

On her way to the computer lab she stopped by the teacher next door and said, "Tony's in the time-out area. If you would just keep an eye on him and make sure he's okay until I get some help, I'd appreciate it." She did not, however, tell this teacher what Tony was up to.

She walked the class past my office and, as she passed, she poked her head in and said, "Jim, there's a naked kid in the time-out area. We're on our way to play with the computers." Then she walked off with the kids.

This provided me with a lot of information without telling me what to do with it. What did I do? I went right down to the time-out room and, on my way, I was thinking, "Somebody better do something about this—quickly!"

Let's consider what might have happened if that teacher had passed my office and said, "Jim, there's a naked kid in the time-out area. You're the principal and it's your job to take care of situations like this. You'd better do something about it now before that kid gets this school some bad press."

I can imagine all sorts of things I would want to say: "That's what we pay *you* to do. You go do it. That's your job. If you were a better teacher, this wouldn't have happened in the first place. I'm going to write this up for your personnel file!"

For some strange reason, when people tell us what to do about something, we pick up a message that attacks our self-concept. That message basically states, "You're so dumb, you can't figure out what to do on your own." It's an implied put-down and we react defensively to this kind of insult.

As I went to the room, I was hoping Tony was still in the time-out area. I was also thinking that I didn't want to get into a power struggle with him. I did have one advantage I could use in this situation. There were only twenty minutes of school left for that day, so as I entered the classroom I called out, "Tony! The bus will be leaving in about twenty minutes. It will be interesting to see what you look like when you leave." Then I left, waiting in an adjoining room.

We saw Tony going to the bus later on. He was a spectacle. There was a sock hanging out of each of his pockets. His shoes were on, but they were not tied, the laces flapping in the breeze. His shirt was on, but it was buttoned out of sequence, with one end sticking way down and the other way up.

By simply giving Tony information and stopping short of telling him what he should do, we allowed him to flow into a thinking state rather than stay locked in an emotional state. He had been in a power struggle for control. In the way we gave him information, he was allowed some control. There was no longer any point for him to continue. Because he was now in the thinking state, he was more able to make decisions that were good for him and that did not engage the adults in conflict.

That teacher was pretty sharp, wasn't she? She got me to act. How did she do it? Certainly not by telling me what to do. Rather, she just provided me with some valuable information. That's what "I Messages" are all about.

> *"I Messages" don't make people do things.*
> *Rather, they provide the opportunity to eliminate*
> *power struggles that are based on self-concept*
> *and autonomy issues.*

Another myth some people have come to believe is that if you do "I Messages" *right*, they will work. Not always. First, we have to hope that the other person cares. Although they often do work, "I Messages" don't work every time. They are not guaranteed any more than other things in life. They remain, however, the best way I know to give information in a nonthreatening way.

Allowing Space and Time—Critical Elements

Some people believe that good communicators can come up with an "I Message" right on the spot. Let's shatter that fantasy right now. If an "I Message" is needed, it's important enough to practice. We may need to give this technique some thought and rehearse it before we get into a potential conflict situation.

A teacher named Sally told me a story about "I

Messages" that provides additional insight into this technique.

The Pencil Tapper

A student who had a history of behavior problems had been assigned to her class. This guy used to test Sally's annoyance level by tapping his pencil. Sally was involved in studying the effectiveness of "I Messages" at that time and decided this would be a good time to experiment. The first time she responded to the pencil tapping she went up to the student, frowned and said, in a fairly harsh tone, "Quit that—now!"

His reaction to this was to tap louder and to grin at Sally. His unstated message was, "I don't have to quit!" Because she was simply doing research at this time, she just walked away. This kid was in her class full time, and she knew she would be able to continue her research.

What was the first thing he started to do the next time he came to class? Tap his pencil, of course. But Sally did something different this time. She smiled, casually wandered back to him, and whispered, "I don't know if you realize it or not, but I get distracted when there are pencils tapping." He looked up, and in order to save face he said, "This class is boring."

Sally, still in her quiet voice said, "If you think it's boring now at ten o'clock, you ought to see how bad I am at two." Then she walked off. He kept tapping his pencil, but what Sally noticed was the longer he tapped, the slower and softer it got. For whatever reason, this kid needed to be able to save face by saying, "I stop when I say stop, not when you say stop."

Sometimes we purposely give kids the last word so they can show others they are not intimidated by adults. Often there must be that space and that time.

What if Sally had delivered that wonderful "I message" and then stood there and stared at him? What would he have done? More than likely, he would have continued the tapping and escalated the power struggle. Sally gave us another valuable lesson: Sometimes when we deliver an "I Message" there may be some anger, also some face-saving activities right on the spot. Rather than interpreting this as antithetical to positive results, it may simply mean we are on the way to a solution.

Steve's Mom

Marge came to me one day and said she needed a good "I Message." She said her mother-in-law was coming for a visit and every time she visited, she would always find a way to remind Bob, Marge's husband, that he could have married "better." We came up with several "I Messages" to fit different potential situations.

Marge's in-laws came, and that evening they went out to a restaurant. Marge's mother-in-law looked around and said, "This is really an expensive restaurant. Look at these prices." Then she said, "We wouldn't need to go to an expensive restaurant like this if Bob had married somebody who could cook."

At that point, Marge said it was a good thing she had practiced. In a fairly calm voice she said, "Mom, I don't know if you realize it or not, but I'm pretty sensitive about my cooking ability. When it gets brought up, I get depressed." And then she said, "I know I shouldn't do it, but when I get depressed I find myself taking it out on Bob."

That was a penetrating "I Message" because it said, "I don't know if you know it or not, but you just shot yourself in the foot. You just sabotaged your basic intentions here." This kind of "I Message" has to be well delivered, with absolute sincerity and no sarcasm.

Marge called me up the next day to tell me how things had worked out. To my surprise she had no thanks for my advice. Instead she said, "Jim, you sold me down the river. It didn't work. My mother-in-law just got mad. She stomped out of the restaurant and made a big scene."

I didn't know what to say and was feeling really bad for Marge. All I could think to say was, "Could you give it a little time and see what happens?" Three weeks later Marge called. She said, "I got a strange card today, from my mother-in-law. And all it said was, 'Nice to have you for a daughter-in-law.'"

The letter didn't say anything about being sorry, but Marge got a whole series of those cards afterwards. So often the "I Message," if delivered well, does not work on the spot. It may sting and cause hurt because it enlists some legitimate guilt, which often needs space and time to seek a resolution.

The Three Parts of "I Messages"

Another myth is that you always have to use all three parts of an "I Message" for it to work well. We can shatter that one because we have seen teacher after teacher effectively using "I Messages" with only two parts. But for the time being, let's discuss the three-part "I Message."

Part 1: Describe what is happening.
Part 2: Describe how that makes you feel.
Part 3: Identify the tangible effect of the other person's behavior.

Sometimes Up, Sometimes Down

I've always had a weight problem. Sometimes I'm up; sometimes I'm down. When I was in the National Guard I had to have three different-sized uniforms. A friend, Bill, was always quick to remind me of any weight change and when I needed a different uniform. Not only would he make remarks, but he would poke me in the stomach a little bit with his finger. I used to say to him, "Don't rub it in. That hurts. That's painful." But he would still do it.

I delivered a three-part "I Message" to Bill one night. I said, "When my weight gets mentioned, I get depressed. And when I get depressed, I find myself going home and getting in the refrigerator. Before I know it, I've eaten everything I can find, and I'm fatter than I ever was."

Bill's response was, "Gee, Jim, I wouldn't hurt you for the world."

That was the night he quit mentioning my weight problem.

The Chronic Liar

When we talk about "I Messages," I'm often asked about the specific situation in which we have a chronic liar. This is the kid who says his dog died and gets a lot of sympathy. Later we find out the story was not true. How do we feel? As if we were played for a patsy.

When a lie catches us unaware, we often don't see the important things that are going on. To redeem this circumstance, we could use it as an opportunity to teach a kid a valuable lesson for life about the benefits of being trustworthy.

There are two kinds of liars—those who lie and never get caught, and those who lie and get caught. When kids lie, they present us with an ideal situation for an "I Message."

> *When I know a kid has lied, I might say,*
> *"When I hear stories from you that I later find out*
> *are not true, it takes away my fun of listening*
> *to what you have to say."*

Some teachers would say that sounds wimpy. There may be teachers who think that when a kid makes a trip to the principal's office for lying, or any other infraction for that matter, the experience hasn't been effective if there is no trail of blood as the kid leaves. Without an understanding of "I Messages," it's easy to say that they are not effective.

What is our goal is when working with kids? Do we want them to be burdened with heavy guilt or do we want them to consider the long-term consequences of their behavior and make a volitional decision to change? Do we want to lock kids in to the emotional state or do we want to usher them into the thinking state?

If a kid wants you to listen to his stories and now realizes that, because of his lying, you have much less interest in hearing them, my guess is that he will do some deep thinking about what he is doing. He already knows the lecture on trust. To repeat a moral harangue may simply lock him more deeply into his behavior.

Getting the Last Word

When Thomas Gordon, author of *Parent Effectiveness Training*, taught people how to use effective "I Messages," the problem arose of other people ending up having the last word. This left a situation in which the listener could neutralize the effect of the "I Message" by ending the interaction on a negative note.

So the question is: How can you have the last word without escalating a power struggle or otherwise compromising the value of the "I Message"? There are times when you do need to get the last word in. Not so much to save face, but to indicate to the kid that he doesn't have unilateral control of the situation. Or, perhaps, to bring closure to the situation quickly.

For instance, let's suppose I say to a kid, "I get distracted when there are pencils tapping." This is a respectable beginning to the "I Message" to which I could reasonably expect a cordial reply. However, instead of reciprocating my respect, the kid says, "I like distracting you; besides, I can think better when I'm tapping my pencil. So bug off."

To have the final word in these situations, I need to use a self-referencing statement, one that will be difficult to counter as invalid.

*I might say, "I just wanted you to know how I felt,
and I hope you will give it some thought. Thank you."
With this statement, I haven't ordered him to stop.
I have given him some information.*

It would be satisfying if, every time we made a statement like this, we had the last word and had clean, final closure on the interaction. But you and I know it isn't always going to happen that way. The reason it won't is that people will respond the way they do for any number of reasons: to save face in front of their pals, to strike out, to gain control, and sometimes as a simple knee-jerk reaction.

Whatever the reason, we need to be prepared with a continuation of the self-referencing statement.

*We can say, "That's probably true,
and I was hoping that telling you how I felt
would make a difference."*

The purpose here is to apply the Four Key Principles of Love and Logic in a way that makes everyone a winner.

Intervention 10:
ENFORCEABLE STATEMENTS

The next intervention involves the teacher setting limits by describing what she or he will allow or provide. We have used the term "enforceable statement" to describe this. Some examples are:

- "I listen to people who raise their hands."
- "I give credit for all papers on my desk at 3:15."
- "I dismiss people as soon as I see their desks are cleared."

When I use enforceable statements
I talk about what I will do, and I involve only what
I have absolute control over—me.

People have a hard time arguing with those limits. About the most they could say would be, "Well, you shouldn't do that," to which I can always reply, "Maybe you're right. And I do." That's another enforceable statement.

Intervention 11:
PROVIDING CHOICES

We have discussed choices at length elsewhere in this book, so suffice it to say that when we give choices, they must be legitimate and equally acceptable to ourselves. I would also encourage you to listen to the audiotapes *The Science of Control* and *Helicopters, Drill Sergeants and Consultants* for further information.

Intervention 12:
REMOVING STUDENT TO TIME-OUT

Time-out has been terribly abused in America. I would never tell parents I used time-out in my classroom, because they have probably heard some wild horror stories. Because the term has a negative connotation, I would call it the "office of productive thinking," the "think-it-over place," or, better yet, I'd have the kids name it.

The kids in my classroom named our time-out
"Australia." It was behind the filing cabinet and was
topped with a big sign the kids made themselves that
said "Australia" in huge letters. It had a picture
of a beach and palm trees.

Originally, time-out was a strategy advocated by a school of psychology that determined that kids need to have an opportunity to get away from their teacher for a while, and vice-versa. It was intended as a way to maintain the integrity of the teaching environment.

Time-out became abused when people did not pay attention to the options and choices associated with it.

The original intent was that the student could come back when he or she felt able to handle the limits placed upon the group. Therefore, a kid could stay there for thirty seconds, or thirty days. The kid was in control of that.

It wasn't long before people started to abuse time-out and give kids an opportunity to use it as a means to escalate the power struggle with their teachers. Teachers did this by saying, "You go there and stay until I tell you to come back." Or, "You go there for twenty minutes," or "You go there for an hour."

Then they started giving students additional opportunities to resist by saying, "Do your work while you're in there." This really gave kids more fuel for their fire. The sad part for those people who use time-out in this way is not knowing that often a kid can get himself together in three or four minutes. Put in time-out for an hour, a kid has plenty of time to figure out how to get even.

Fifty-Seven Minutes for Revenge

I had a little girl back in the days when I myself did not understand appropriate use of time-out. I had sent her to time-out with the instruction to stay until I was ready for her to return to class.

About an hour later I went back for her. I found that what she did with all that extra time was $370 damage to a solid oak door with a nail she had picked up somewhere. Nobody heard it; nobody saw it. She didn't have the money to replace it, and neither did her parents.

As I look back on the situation, I realize that she had probably gotten herself together in three minutes and had fifty-seven minutes left to figure out how to get revenge.

Common Questions

Many educators ask if work should be sent to time-out with the kid. I prefer not. Time-out is a think-it-over place. Others ask if we prescribe a certain amount of time. I prefer to have the kid in charge of when to come back. Shared control can avert a needless power struggle.

A tricky question is whether a kid should be counseled after returning from a time-out session. My answer to this is that counseling is not always necessary. For some kids, it's appropriate and they will respond positively; but for most, I would say probably no. However, I would emphasize that this is a judgment call, based on the circumstances and the kid.

Another commonly asked question is: What if I don't have room for a time-out area? If that is the case, I would suggest making one. I know of one teacher who brought a beach umbrella to school and just put it down on the floor in the back of her room. This was big enough to provide a visual barrier for a kid who went behind it. Some people move bookcases around so there's a little place where a kid can sit, be alone, and have no visual contact with buddies.

If you have a student who prefers to be in time-out for massive amounts of time, that kid is telling you something. She/he has a problem that may not be solvable within a classroom setting; perhaps this is a time for professional help. Basically, kids want to be around other kids.

Parental Involvement

Another issue that can arise involves a kid who is repeatedly sent to time-out, comes back on his own accord, and starts acting up again. If this happens, an alternative action is needed. A more intense level of time-out is a possibility. If this is the case, you will want to involve the parents.

When I mention parental involvement, I may strike a nerve with a number of teachers. To assuage teachers' anxiety, I have prepared a sample script to use in situations that involve the parent:

JIM: *(Addressing the parent)* I'd like to have a talk with Joyce (the student). I realize you know her better than I do, so when I'm done with this conference with her, I'd like to get your reactions to our discussion.

Notice how that comment gives the parents their role. It's well defined. Then I get close to Joyce with good eye contact, smile, with a positive attitude.

JIM: Joyce, do you think I've been sending you to time-out because you've been misbehaving or because I just can't teach when there are distractions? What's your guess?

JOYCE: Misbehaving?

JIM: No. I'm sending you because I get distracted. When I get distracted, do you think I teach well, or not teach well?

JOYCE: Not well?

JIM: Exactly. I don't teach well. Now we've established that I'm not sending you there because you're bad, but so that I can teach. So, then, who's in charge of deciding how long you stay there? Have I been deciding or have you?

JOYCE: Me.

JIM: Right. So, you come back when you decide. And lately I've noticed that you've been coming and going quite a bit. Would you say you're spending a lot of time, or not much time going out there?

JOYCE: Lots of time.

At this point, Joyce's mother needs to hear about the amount of time being spent in time-out from Joyce's mouth, not mine. She'll believe Joyce. So I would continue, this time involving the parent.

JIM: So I guess what we're here to decide is what would be a reasonable number of times to go to the time-out in one day. If you went x number of times, you might say, "Well, that's pretty normal for a kid." But if you went one additional time, it would be saying, "I guess I can't handle class today." So how many times do you think would be reasonable? Two? Three?

JOYCE: Three.

JIM: I guess I could put up with three easily enough. Would you say that's reasonable?

JOYCE: Yes.

JIM: Then, if I'm hearing you right, if you went on to a fourth time, it would be like waving a flag and saying, "Guess class is too hard for me to handle today." Does that sound reasonable?

JOYCE: Yes, it does.

JIM: Well, put it there. *(Jim and Joyce shake hands; then Jim turns to the parent).* Looks like Joyce is saying that three times would be reasonable; the fourth time would be saying that she can't handle class today. You tell me how

that affects you, because we don't want
to make a problem for you just because
Joyce is creating a problem in the
classroom. Does this seem fair to you?

MOTHER: I think it's fair.

JIM: *(To Mother)* What seems to work the
best is if we could have you say, "Joyce,
when this happens, go to the phone,
call home, I'll come over, take you
home, and let you sit in your room the
rest of the day and think this over so
you can get ready to go back the next
day." This would be said with no
questions, no lectures—nothing but
sadness—"Oh, that's sad that it didn't
work out." This seems to be what works
best. She could also do some chores to
make up for the inconvenience this
creates for you. How does this
affect you?

MOTHER: Since I don't have a job now, it should
work out all right.

JIM: It might work out all right while you're
not working. What I hear you say is
that if you go to work, we might have
to change, is that right?

MOTHER: That's correct.

JIM: Since that might happen, let's discuss the next best way, just in case we need to know it. We have a room in school that is unsupervised, but safe. We could, at your written request, allow Joyce to go there for the rest of the day, then try regular school the next day. We would give no lectures, no threats, no telling her how bad she is—none of that. Would that feel better to you or not better?

MOTHER: That would work out well, especially if I were out and you couldn't get me.

JIM: So, what I'm hearing is that it would work out well if we couldn't reach you. Okay. Thank you. *(Turning to Joyce)* Joyce, is there anything else we need to talk about? Can you think of anything else you'd like to say here?

JOYCE: No.

JIM: Are you feeling this is fair or not fair?

JOYCE: I guess it's fair.

JIM: Well, let's shake on that, too. Thank you.

Notice throughout this entire scenario, although I have not said that Joyce would have to stay in time-out for a given amount of time, I have given a strong implied message of how long that might be. For instance, I could have determined the amount of time by saying, "You can go there and think it over and then you're welcome to come back the next day."

The way you deliver the message can take a lot of threat out of the penalty.

Primary School Time-Out Area

What should the time-out area be like in a primary school? I think the ideal would be a little room with a bare light bulb and a chair. However, we don't have a lot of those rooms available. At any rate, I prefer not to put in a bean-bag chair where a kid can get too comfortable. I also don't want it to be a negative place. So any place where there is no human contact, but a place where the student can easily get out, would be appropriate.

One of the most effective time-out areas involves a reciprocal agreement with other teachers. In other words, teachers make an agreement to use each other's rooms for a time-out spot. There may be some agreements to be reached, such as stipulating that only one kid at a time can be sent or, if the kid is disruptive in the time-out area, he can be immediately returned to the original teacher.

This method is effective because it involves engaging another factor we talked about previously: changing location. Using another teacher's room is usually more acceptable to the principal because it's a place where the kids are supervised.

High School Time-Out Area

At the high school level, time-out takes a totally different form. There, the message is, "I don't want to force you to be in class; I don't want to make life tough for you. Please feel free to be somewhere else." We need to negotiate with administrators to discover where an acceptable place would be for a kid to be in this school when he's not in your classroom.

I once visited with some kids at a high school in the Portland (Oregon) area. That day I talked to the eight toughest kids in that high school.

One of my questions was, "What kind of teachers do you like?" Their answer surprised me. They said, "We like teachers who try to understand us and give us help when we ask for it." That's all they were asking for. Somebody who knew and responded to them as people, cared about them, and treated them with respect.

The bottom line for all of the interventions we have been discussing is: Treat kids with dignity and talk to them in the language of respect, the same way we would talk to a best friend.

That day I also asked them what kind of teacher they most disliked. They had a quick answer. "The ones who only know how to say three things: "Sit down." "Shut up." "Go to the principal's office."

They had some opinions about teachers that I thought were insightful. I found that they didn't have impossibly high standards. Overall, they just wanted a teacher who knew them personally, liked having them in the classroom, and was willing to answer their questions when they had problems. What they definitely didn't like were people whose sole purpose seemed to be to make them be or act in a certain way.

That was an enjoyable, informative day. Often, disruptive kids appear to know more about the real world than kids who behave all the time.

Negative Messages and Kids with Damaged Self-Concepts

Many kids today come to school already thinking that they're not so great. Their self-concept is damaged and they have a tendency to listen for messages teachers send that confirm this view of themselves. Even sadder, they tend to not hear the messages from teachers who tell them that they're okay. The teacher with a kid who is always looking for the negative message is going to have to be especially aware to keep this cycle from repeating.

I am painfully aware that this cycle often begins in the early elementary years. We have even seen some begin in kindergarten. Students who quit school when they were sixteen probably mentally dropped out in the second grade. It simply took several more years for their bodies to be removed.

As soon as kids say things like, "School is not for me," "The other kids are better students," "Teachers like the other kids better," "I have no place here," they have dropped out. When they can no longer stand the pain, they leave.

The positive way we handle time-out can go a long way toward reducing the negative feelings students have toward school and teachers.

Intervention 13:
EVALUATING TIME-OUT

To enhance the effectiveness of time-out, I will often focus the kids' thinking by asking the following five questions:

1. What happened?
2. How did you feel?
3. What did you do?
4. How did it work out?
5. What are you going to do next time?

I allow the student to go to time-out and either think through the answers to these questions or write them down. Notice that the questions are oriented toward getting students to think about a cause-and-effect relationship. These questions also focus students on how they have reacted in the past as well as on whether they think it's best for them to continue their current behavior.

Sometimes there will be a student who wants to act as if time-out is a joke and try to sabotage the technique by peeking around the corner or yelling out to friends. I simply say that this is a quiet, think-it-over place, and that we do have another place to go if that student needs to do so.

I may need to negotiate with the principal on a different time-out place for those kids—one that is secluded, but safe. Ordinarily this would require involvement with a parent. When all are in agreement, we can sit down and say, "Sometimes kids need safe places where they can swear, stomp their feet, jump up and down, kick, scream, and peek around corners. We have a perfect place right outside. You're welcome to go there when you need to; then, you're welcome to either be in class or in the quiet time-out once you get all of those behaviors out of your system."

Intervention 14:
USE OF THE BUILDING ADMINISTRATOR

I was a teacher for fourteen years and an administrator for seventeen. If I went back to teaching tomorrow, I would absolutely not allow a student to go to the principal's office for a cooling-off period unless I had a solemn promise that the kid would not be counseled at that time.

This is based on the fact that, in all those years, I never had a student show up at the office saying, "Mr. Fay, I don't know how that teacher put up with me for so long. She should have sent me here a long time ago." Usually the kid has a sophisticated excuse that places the blame on the teacher. Then, the principal has to make a value judgment about who is right. As a result, a lot of unnecessary energy is spent.

If I were a teacher, I would like to be able to send students to the office occasionally, for a short cool-down time, long enough for both the kid and me to get a different perspective.

> *The most I would want the principal to say is, "Looks like you got in trouble with that teacher. Good luck. Hope you get it worked out."*

The reason? My goal is to remain the ultimate authority figure in that child's life. I give that away when I send a student to the principal. It doesn't matter how skillfully I remove the kid from my classroom to the office; that action still imparts the implied message, "I can't handle you, pal."

In my last days of classroom teaching, I had a lot of fun. I had been an assistant principal for a period of time and chose to go back to the classroom for a while. When I got there, one of the first comments I made to the kids was that they never had to worry about being sent to the principal. Their only worry was that they might wind up *wishing* they could go to the principal. We were going to solve all problems here.

I wanted to constantly send the message that I considered teaching them and managing their behavior an important part of my responsibilities in educating that class. They would be dealing with me. I wanted to have a tough line with a soft touch. Although I would like the option of sending a kid to the office for a short cool-down time, I wanted the kid to plan on eventually coming back to my classroom to work out the problem.

Vision of Support

If I have a serious problem, I like the option of conferring for counsel and advice with an administrator, and I prefer that to be on the condition that I appear *with* the youngster. I want to be there to say, "Here's what I tried so far, here are the kid's reactions, and here are the kinds of things that are happening. What are your thoughts?"

While getting the additional thoughts of that administrator, I like the student to see that the administrator and the teacher are united.

The only way that happens ordinarily is if I can meet with the principal sometime in advance so we can discuss the specifics of the situation and work on a mutually agreeable direction. I don't want any surprises, and I want the student to leave thinking that I am still the authority figure to deal with.

This provides an additional benefit. By the time we meet as a team, all of us have clear heads. This is far better than making decisions while the student and I are in the emotional state.

From time to time, I talk to teachers who say, "I don't get the kind of support that I should have from my principal." When I hear that, I often say something that doesn't make me a big hero.

It's alright to complain about having no
support from the principal, provided you can describe
what support looks like to you.
This presents the opportunity to find out
if support looks the same to the principal.

During my years as a principal, there were times when
I did not support teachers, but it was never on purpose.
The problem was that my view of support was different
from that particular teacher's. I thought I was being supportive, only to discover later that the teacher thought I
was not.

Have you discussed your vision of support with your
principal? Have you done any negotiating on
definitions and specific cases?

If you have and the support does not come, you have a
perfect right to say, "You promised that you would support
me. It didn't happen. What are your thoughts about this?"

One of the questions that often comes about is: Does
this mean that every time a student gets into trouble in
the hall or on the playground, I have to appear in the
principal's office? My answer is no. I'm talking only about
the period of time when that kid is directly responsible to
you in the classroom. If you're having difficulty with that,
that's the time I want to appear with the child, and I want
to do it on an appointment basis. That means the student,
the principal, and I will get there when we are all in the
thinking state.

Intervention 15:
GIVING AN APPOINTMENT

Giving a student an appointment to talk about the problem is especially effective for kids who use hit-and-run techniques. Have you seen those in the classroom? They shout and when you say, "Stop that!" they say, "I'm not doing anything." In those situations, effective consequences are extremely difficult to think of and administer on the spot.

That's the time when I want to cruise by and, in a very quiet way, say, "We'll have an appointment to discuss that." Then I give the kid some control by saying, "School is out at 3:00 and I could meet you at 3:15 or 3:30. Which would be better for you?" If he says, "School is out at 3:00. Why can't we meet then?" I simply respond, "My early appointment is at 3:15 today. Yesterday it was after the faculty meeting, at 4:30. Today, it's at 3:15. What's your choice?"

When the child—let's call him Al—comes in for the appointment, the dialogue will probably go something like this:

JIM: Al, thanks for coming in for the appointment. I just wanted to let you know this afternoon when you were shouting in class that I got so distracted, you probably noticed I did a crummy job of teaching. So I just wanted to share that with you. Thanks for coming in. You have a nice evening.

AL: You kept me here all this time just to say that?

JIM:	Well, I wanted to say it when I was calm. You have a nice evening.

Is Al going to think about that a little? I hope so. Does that mean the problem's cured? Probably not. Al might need another appointment down the line. If the problem recurs, I would set up another appointment in the same way. This time the dialogue would be something like:

JIM:	Al, thanks for coming in. You remember the discussion we had last time about shouting in class?
AL:	No.
JIM:	No? Well, there's the problem right there. Thanks for being honest. Let me go over it again. When I hear shouting, I get distracted, and then what?
AL:	You can't teach.
JIM:	At least I can't teach well. So that's what this meeting is about. Did I not do a good job of explaining that to you last time, or did you decide to be disruptive anyway? I'm curious to know where you are on this. Have I done something that makes you so mad that you want to get even with me? If so, maybe you might want to share that with me. Maybe I can change. Any thoughts on this?

AL: Not now.

JIM: Not now? Maybe this is a bad time to talk about it. I have a lot of papers to grade. Why don't I just give you a quiet place to think and maybe later on you might have some thoughts on it. Take your time. There's no big hurry.

At that point I will probably start working on my papers. If, by the time I am ready to go home, Al still doesn't have any thoughts, I might continue the dialogue.

JIM: Still don't have any thoughts?

AL: No.

JIM: Tell me, are you planning to continue shouting in class, or not continuing to shout?

AL: No.

JIM: What does "no" mean?

AL: No shouting.

JIM: You're not going to shout anymore. Well, I appreciate that. Thank you for coming in.

People will sometimes ask, "But what if Al doesn't show up?" Well, that's a possibility for many of the more resistant kids. The nice thing about school is that the kid will probably show up sometime. I haven't lost my opportunity to work with this kid. I could get my blood pressure up and go home tonight and eat holes in the bottom of my stomach with all the black bile that I create over this whole issue, or I could call the parent and say, "Al didn't show up for our appointment today. With your permission, I would like to reschedule for tomorrow. Please don't mention that I called, but I just wanted to let you know that I plan to have this discussion after our last class."

I work out necessary details with the parent, such as transportation or being late to other activities. The next day I let Al get all the way through to the last class period. Prior to that time I have made arrangements with the last hour teacher to hold Al for me. Then, I meet the student at the class and say, "Hey, remember the appointment yesterday? We didn't get it done. Let's do it now."

Typically, kids will kick in their most creative powers at these times to think of a way this plan could get the teacher in trouble, by involving another teacher, activity, or even a parent. This is why pre-planning is so important. When the kid says, "But I've got football practice and the coach would be really mad and the team would be let down, so I can't come now," I say, "No problem. I talked with your mom and the coach. They both said being late for practice would be alright and that you could go after we have our discussion."

If the youngster is worth his salt, he won't give up. We can expect him to say, "Well, this is stupid!" If you remember, we've rehearsed for this kind of comment before. What do we say when he says this? "I know, and you are free to go to practice when we've had our talk." Maybe he will say, "But I ride the bus." My reply would be,

"No big deal. Your mom said she would come over and pick you up. By the way, she also said you should be prepared to pay for her gas and time."

When we have used this technique a few times, we learn to cover all the bases ahead of time. We can out-think kids if we don't do it in the heat of battle. If we try to make decisions when we are in an emotional state, all of our other responsibilities will come to mind and the kids will out-think us.

Intervention 16:
CREATING A NEW PLAN

Basically, what this strategy entails is my sitting down with a student and having a little conference. At that time I would say, "You're welcome to go back out on the playground, just as soon as you have a written plan that identifies what you will do instead of hitting the next time you feel like fighting. No hurry. Take your time."

Having kids submit a written plan sometimes works well, and sometimes it doesn't. A kid can come up with a wonderful idea and then find that it doesn't work for him. If so, then we move on to this intervention, where he is still restricted from the area, but on different terms. Once he comes up with his new plan of action and describes to you what he's going to do, instead of whatever the infraction was, he is given permission to go out on the playground one day at a time.

Each successful day earns him one more day, but he does not assume that he has this privilege on a permanent basis. He is on a schedule that reviews his performance daily. The following dialogue might be typical:

JIM:	Okay, Jon, we are going to have you go out on Thursday. If you have a good day on Thursday, what's your guess about Friday?
JON:	I get to play.
JIM:	Right! And if you have a good day on Friday, what about Monday?
JON:	I get to play again.
JIM:	Right! And if you blow it on Monday, what's your guess about Tuesday?
JON:	I don't go out.
JIM:	Good thinking. Hope it works out for you.

We may need some additional instruction at this point. Jon has come up with a new action plan to manage personal behavior and it's in line with what you want.

It may seem, at first glance, that Jon is now seeing playground time as a reward earned for good behavior or as something you restrict as punishment. I see the situation a little differently.

I'm not looking at going to the playground as something he has earned. First of all, he has a new behavior, but it's an action plan he developed. He says, "Here's what I'm going to do instead of the old behavior." The odds are that he's going to be able to behave a little better now. But, when he does go back onto the playground, what we're really looking for is proof from him that demonstrates his establishment of self-control and trustworthiness. We're not saying he's earning a privilege; he's merely showing that he can demonstrate self-control on a day-to-day basis.

As you read this, I assume you are thinking of adapting these interventions to various situations you have experienced. I want to interject an additional thought:

The trick is to have the child do the adapting.

All you do is say:

1. "That's not working out well in the classroom. You're welcome to come back when you can figure out a new behavior."

2. "That's not working well in the halls. Glad to let you use the halls when you can come up with a new behavior."

3. "That's not working well in the lunchroom. Feel free to come back when you've got a new plan of action."

These are all opportunities for the kids to do some thinking. It orients them to internalizing controls.

Intervention 17:
APPLYING CONSEQUENCES

In this intervention, the key word is "empathy."

Imagine that Al has been caught fighting in the parking lot and has been sent to the principal's office. Let's further suppose that the school rule for this behavior is a three-day suspension. If we were going to issue a negative content message ("You're out of school"), we could balance it with a positive ego message ("We'll miss you"). The following conversation would be typical:

JIM: Looks like you got caught fighting again. What a bummer. Those guys must have really made you mad to fight like that. I bet I would have felt the same way. A fight like that will earn you how many days' suspension?

AL: Three.

JIM: Three. That's right. So we'll get to see you when?

AL: Monday.

JIM: Monday. Well, I'll look forward to seeing you back here. I'd appreciate having you stop by when you get back, okay?

The consequence has fallen and Al will be out for three days. If he is like most kids, he will be hurting inside and will be asking himself, "Who caused all this pain for me?" In all likelihood he will run down the list of possibilities. When he gets to the principal, he will probably say, "It's not him. He was concerned for me and looking forward to my return."

With Love and Logic, the adult is the "good guy"; the misplaced behavior is the "bad guy."

Our hope is that his ultimate answer will be, "This pain was caused by my bad decision." This acknowledgement of responsibility is a key to internalizing control, and the conditions to encourage this acceptance can be determined largely by the interaction of the adult.

The key to this orientation is empathy in conjunction with the consequence. So often we dispense the consequence with anger, retaliation, or threats. And then what happens? Imagine the same scenario if the principal, in "attack mode," had said to Al, "You're not going to fight around here, understand? That's three days' suspension! You're out of here. Don't come back until Monday! We've had it with you! We're not putting up with that stuff! You're history!"

As the kid leaves the classroom, he will probably ask the same question as in the first example, "I'm hurting. Who caused this pain for me?" There will be no question in his mind that the principal is responsible. When that is established, the kid is more than likely to seek revenge, through vandalism or other acts of retaliation.

Intervention 18:
INFORMATIONAL LETTERS

Informational telephone calls and letters have about the same effect, so it doesn't matter which we use. However, it does take professional judgment for us to decide: Is it going to be better for this student to call his parents to notify them of his behavior and tell them about his plan of action so he can involve them in his thoughts, or better for him to write it all down? Some kids are better off writing everything down because the written word sinks in more deeply than the spoken word. Further, you then have more control over what they actually deliver to their parents.

If they are going to make an informational phone call, I would recommend contacting the parents ahead of time. Fill them in about the situation and what their child is going to be talking about. Be sure to tell them that you don't want them to take on the problem. Instead, ask if they could just listen to their child talk about the problem and his possible solution. Then, when he finishes telling them all about it, ask the parents to end the conversation by saying, "Thanks for sharing that with me. Is there any way I can help?" When that happens, we have a truly informational phone call.

If the parents agree to cooperate, I ask them to not let the kid know that I called ahead. It's interesting to see what happens if the child has a different story from the one that actually happened, because most people will believe the first person they hear on a given subject. I've heard kids scolded during a phone call, and I've been delighted that I wasn't the one who had to do it. Then I can be the good guy with empathy: "Wow. It sounds like your parent is really mad. Is there any way I can help?"

Sometimes those informational letters need to go to businesses or to neighbors, because a lot of older kids are adept at stopping by the mailbox to see if anything has a return address from school. We can out-think the kids on that if we take our time and act while we're in the thinking state.

One experienced teacher told me about some wonderful informational letters. One of them said, "Dear Mom, you're right, it happened again. I'm going to get an 'F' in French. Please don't blame my teacher. She's worked hard. I've just been messing around too much. I'm going to get my act together." It was signed, "Daniel, who loves you dearly." It's amazing the impact these letters and calls can have.

Intervention 19:
SYSTEMATIC SUSPENSION

Increasingly restrictive interventions involve appointments made with an administrator for consultation, parent conferences, and students suspended from school. A very specific technique, systematic suspension, has to be used with considerable forethought.

The elements of systematic suspension are the principal, the teacher, the parents, and the student. All need to get together to draw up the arrangement. If the student is enrolled in a special education program or a "504" accommodation plan, we already have a potential vehicle for this strategy. In other cases, a contract can be formulated. Whatever is used, the plan basically says this student is allowed in school for as many minutes or hours per day as he can be there without interrupting what's going on in the classroom. We will identify specific behaviors and when we see these, it is time for this child to go home for the rest of the day.

That is not something the teacher can do unilaterally. It's going to be tough, because parents may attack us and say, "But if my kid is out of school, that's just what he wants. He's not learning a thing."

If this happens, we need to say, "You are absolutely right. That's what we're worried about, too. When he's out of school, he's not learning anything. We've also discovered something else. When he's at school acting as he has been, he's not learning anything either. We're beginning to wonder if it matters where he *does not* learn. What matters is that we can still run school and other people can learn."

*When we get to that point where we fear
the parent who sends responsible kids to school
as much as we fear the parent who sends us
irresponsible kids, we will turn this nation around.*

We have too many kids in class today creating situations in which they do not learn and nobody else learns because we're afraid to enact a systematic suspension.

For every technique you can imagine, you can find a kid for whom it will not work. When teachers say it didn't work, what they often mean is that it didn't do therapy for the kid. He is not now cured of his problem.

Some kids bring problems to school that will only be cured with some pretty intensive therapy. Some kids come to school and their life has been so bad that there isn't a technique in the world that would work, other than putting them somewhere and letting them calm down for awhile.

✏ ✏ ✏

The interventions we have just covered will not do therapy. We need to always be aware that some kids may still need intensive and specialized professional help. These interventions will, however, help maintain the classroom. And they will build better relationships.

I have no doubt that you will soon realize, if you haven't already, that these interventions are based on nothing more than working to uphold the Four Key Principles of Love and Logic. You will soon discover additional interventions, as you come up with your own unique applications of the principles. I hope you'll let us know what you find.

▼

Supportive Theory
and Research

FOR TEACHING WITH LOVE AND LOGIC

*T*he following section is recommended to help you continue your study of discipline. This collection of research and readings was compiled by Charles Fay at the University of South Carolina. While Charles was working on his Ph.D. in psychology, he spent considerable time working with me in the analysis of Love and Logic and was instrumental in verifying the concepts taught in this book.

The outline below lists the concepts found in each chapter. Immediately following the outline is the list of research and readings, which further elaborate each concept.

CHAPTER ONE
The Purpose of Love and Logic

1. Consequences Need Not Be Immediate
2. Human Control Needs
3. The Importance of Student Involvement and Choice
4. Factors Affecting One's Ability to Obtain Cooperation
5. Adults Serve as Models for Children's Emotions
6. The Importance of Limit-Setting Combined with Love

7. The Importance of Struggle in the Development
of Self-Concept

CHAPTER TWO
Confronting the Myths About Discipline

1. The Importance of Student Involvement and Choice
2. Factors Affecting Students' School-Related Self-Concept
3. Relations of Self-Concept to Learning and Motivation
4. Using Control Needs to Reduce Unwanted Behaviors
5. The Importance of Positive Teacher-Student Relationships
6. The Importance of Limit-Setting Combined with Love
7. The Effects of Emotions on Reasoning
8. Consequences Need Not Be Immediate
9. The Importance of Struggle in the Development
of Self-Concept

CHAPTER THREE
Three Rules of Love and Logic

1. The Importance of Student Involvement and Choice
2. The Relations of Self-Concept to Learning and Motivation
3. The Causes and Effects of Learned Helplessness
4. The Effectiveness of Internal Versus External Consequences
5. The Importance of Limit-Setting Combined with Love
6. The Importance of Struggle in the Development
of Self-Concept

CHAPTERS FOUR AND FIVE
Finding Time for Love and Logic Discipline
and Discipline and Control

1. The Importance of Student Involvement and Choice
2. Factors Affecting Change in School-Based Systems
3. The Importance of Positive Teacher-Student Relationships
4. Human Control Needs
5. The Importance of Limit-Setting Combined with Love
6. Consequences Need Not Be Immediate

7. The Importance of Empathy and Acceptance
8. Factors Affecting Students' School-Related Self-Concept
9. Relations of Self-Concept to Learning and Motivation
10. Different Styles of Parenting, Teaching
11. The Development of Self-Regulatory Skills

CHAPTER SIX
Perception and Behavior

1. Human Control Needs
2. The Communicative Functions of Nonverbal Behavior
3. Students' Awareness of Teachers' Concealed Attitudes
4. Factors Affecting Students' Perceptions of Teachers and Peers
5. The Relationship Between Self-Concept Maintenance
   Attempts and Behavior
6. The Effects of Teacher Expectations
7. Adults Serve as Models for Children's Emotions

CHAPTER SEVEN
Principles vs. Systems

1. Factors Affecting Change in School-Based Systems
2. Learning Styles Research
3. Importance of Student Involvement and Choice
4. Human Control Needs
5. Factors Affecting Students' School-Related Self-Concept
6. The Importance of Empathy

CHAPTER EIGHT
Principle 1: The Enhancement of Self-Concept

1. The Importance of Empathy
2. Factors Affecting Students' School-Related Self-Concept
3. Relations of Self-Concept to Learning and Motivation
4. The Relationship Between Self-Concept Maintenance
   Attempts and Students' Behavior
5. The Effects of Teachers' Expectations

6. The Causes and Effects of Learned Helplessness
7. The Importance of Positive Teacher-Student Relationships
8. The Importance of Struggle in the Development
   of Self-Concept

CHAPTER NINE
Principle 2: Shared Control

1. Human Control Needs
2. The Importance of Student Involvement and Choice
3. The Importance of Empathy
4. The Importance of Trust
5. Using Control Needs to Reduce Unwanted Behaviors
6. The Effectiveness of Internal Versus External Consequences
7. The Importance of Limit-Setting Combined with Love

CHAPTER TEN
Principle 3: Consequences with Empathy

1. The Importance of Limit-Setting Combined with Love
2. The Importance of Empathy

CHAPTER ELEVEN
Principle 4: Shared Thinking

1. Human Control Needs
2. The Importance of Student Involvement and Choice
3. The Importance of Trust
4. Factors Affecting Change in School-Based Systems

CHAPTER TWELVE
Styles of Teaching

1. The Importance of Trust
2. Relations of Self-Concept to Learning and Motivation
3. The Causes and Effects of Learned Helplessness
4. Learning Styles Research
5. Different Styles of Parenting, Teaching
6. Characteristics of Effective Schools

7. The Importance of Positive Teacher-Student Relationships
8. Obtaining Cooperation from Others
9. The Importance of Empathy

CHAPTER THIRTEEN
Legal Considerations

1. School Law, Ethics, and Related Policies

CHAPTER FOURTEEN
Implementing School Discipline: Systems vs. Principles

1. Factors Affecting Change in School-Based Systems
2. The Importance of Student Involvement and Choice
3. The Importance of Empathy
4. The Importance of Trust
5. The Importance of Positive Teacher-Student Relationships
6. The Effectiveness of Internal Versus External Consequences
7. The Importance of Limit-Setting Combined with Love
8. The Development of Self-Regulatory Skills

CHAPTER FIFTEEN
Walled Lake Central High School:
One School's Approach to Love and Logic

1. The Importance of Student Involvement and Choice
2. Factors Affecting Students' School-Related Self-Concept
3. Relations of Self-Concept to Learning and Motivation
4. The Relationship Between Self-Concept Maintenance
   Attempts and Students' Behavior
5. Obtaining Cooperation from Others
6. The Importance of Limit-Setting Combined with Love
7. Factors Affecting Change in School-Based Systems
8. Learning Styles Research
9. Different Styles of Parenting, Teaching,
10. The Importance of Trust

PART FOUR
Classroom Solutions Through Love and Logic Interventions

1. Human Control Needs
2. The Importance of Student Involvement and Choice
3. The Importance of Empathy
4. Using Control Needs to Reduce Unwanted Behaviors
5. The Importance of Positive Teacher-Student Relationships
6. The Importance of Limit-Setting Combined with Love
7. Consequences Need Not Be Immediate

Research
and Readings

Human Control Needs

Brehm, S. S., and J. W. Brehm (1981). *Responses to loss of freedom: A theory of psychological reactance.* Morristown, NJ: General Learning Press.

Glass, D. C., J. D. McKnight, and H. Valdinardo (1993). Depression, burnout, and perceptions of control in hospital nurses. *Journal of Consulting and Clinical Psychology*, 61, 147–155.

Glass, D. C., J. E. Singer, H. S. Leonard, D. Krantz, S. Cohen, and H. Cummings (1973). Perceived control of aversive stimulation and the reduction of stress responses. *Journal of Personality*, 41, 577–595.

Glasser, W. (1969). *Schools without failure.* New York: Harper & Row.

Glasser, W. (1985). *Control theory: A new explanation of how we control our lives.* New York: Harper & Row.

Langer, E. J. and J. Rodin (1976). The effects of choice and enhanced personal responsibility for the aged: A field experiment in an institutional setting. *Journal of Personality and Social Psychology*, 34, 191–198.

Mercer, S., and R. A. Kane (1979). Helplessness and hopelessness among the institutionalized aged: An experiment. *Health and Social Work*, 4, 90–116.

Rodin, J. (1976). Crowding, perceived choice and response to controllable and uncontrollable outcomes. *Journal of Experimental Social Psychology*, 12, 564–578.

Rodin, J. (1978). Crowding and helplessness: Potential consequences of density and loss of control. In A. Baum and Y. Epstein (Eds.) *Human response to crowding*. Hillsdale, NJ: Erlbaum

Rodin, J., and E. Langer (1977). Long-term effects of control-relevant interventions with the institutionalized aged. *Journal of Personality and Social Psychology*, 35, 897–902.

Rodin, J., S. Solomon, and J. Metcalf (1978). Role of control in mediating perceptions of density. *Journal of Personality and Social Psychology*, 36, 989–999.

Schulz, R. (1976). The effects of control and preditability on the psychological and physical well-being of the institutionalized aged. *Journal of Personality and Social Psychology*, 33, 563–573.

Watson, J. S. (1967). Memory and "contingency analysis" in infant learning. *Merril-Palmer Quarterly*, 13, 55–76.

The Importance of Student Involvement and Choice

Aronson, E., N. Blaney, C. Stephan, J. Sikes, and M. Snapp, (1978). *The jig-saw classroom*. London: Sage.

Glasser, W. (1969). *Schools without failure*. New York: Harper & Row.

Sapona, R. H., A. M. Bauer, and L. J. Philips (1989). Facilitative stance: Responsive teaching of students with special needs. *Academic Therapy*, 25, 245–252.

Slavin, R. E. (1985). Cooperative learning: Applying contact theory in desegrated schools. *Journal of Social Issues*, 16, 169–180.

Snapp, M., Hickman, J. & Conoley, J. C. (1990). Systems interventions in the schools: Case studies. In. T. B. Gutkin and C. R. Reynolds (Eds.), *Handbook of school psychology*. (2nd ed., pp. 920–934.). New York: John Wiley & Sons

The Importance of Empathy and Acceptance in Helping Relationships

Carkhuff, R. R. and W. A. Anthony (1979). *The skills of helping*. Amherst, NJ: Human Resource Development Press.

Egan, G. (1990). *The skilled helper: Model, skills, and methods for effective helping.* (4th ed.). Pacific Grove CA: Brooks-Cole.

Glasser, W. (1969). *Schools without failure.* New York: Harper & Row.

Hammer, A. (1983). Matching perceptual predicates: Effect of perceived empathy in a counseling analogue. *Journal of Counseling Psychology*, 30, 172–179.

Maurer, R. E., and J. H. Tindall (1983). Effect of postural congruence on client's perception of counselor empathy. *Journal of Counseling Psychology*, 30, 158–163.

Rogers, C. R. (1958). The characteristics of a helping relationship. *Personnel and Guidance Journal*, 37, 6–16.

Rogers, C. R. (1961). *On becoming a person.* Boston, MA: Houghton-Mifflin Co.

The Importance of Trust in Helping Relationships

Fong, M. L., and B. G. Cox (1983). Trust as an underlying dynamic in the counseling process: How clients test trust. *Personnel and Guidance Journal*, 62, 163–166.

LaFranboise, J. D., and D. M. Dixon (1981). American Indian perception of trustworthiness in a counseling interview. *Journal of Counseling Psychology*, 28, 135–139.

The Communicative Functions of Nonverbal Behavior

Birdwhistell, R. L. (1970). *Kinesics and context.* Philadelphia, PA: University of Pennsylvania Press.

Ekman, P., and W. V. Friesen (1969a). Nonverbal leakage and clues to deception. *Psychiatry*, 32, 88–106.

Ekman, P., and W. V. Friesen (1974). Detecting deception from the body or face. *Journal of Personality and Social Psychology*, 29, 288–298.

Ekman, P., W. V. Friesen, and P. Ellsworth (1972). *Emotion and the human face: Guidlines for research and an integration of findings.* New York: Pregamon Press.

Knapp, M. L. (1978). *Nonverbal communication in human interaction.* New York: Holt, Rinehart, & Winston.

Mehrabian, A. (1972). *Nonverbal communication.* Chicago: Aldine-Atherton.

Students' Awareness of Teachers' Concealed Attitudes and Emotions

Babad, E. (1990). Measuring and changing teachers' differential behavior as perceived by students and teachers. *Journal of Educational Psychology*, 82, 683–690.

Babad. E., F. Bernieri, and R. Rosenthal (1989). Nonverbal communication and leakage in the behavior of biased and unbiased teachers. *Journal of Personality and Social Psychology*, 56, 89–94.

Babad, E., F. Bernieri, and R. Rosenthal (1991). Students as judges of teachers' verbal and nonverbal behavior. *American Educational Research Journal*, 28, 211–234.

Brophy, T., and T. Good (1970). Teachers' communication of differential expectations for children's classroom performance: Some behavioral data. *Journal of Educational Psychology*, 61, 365–374.

Zuckerman, M., R. DeFrank, J. Hall, and R. Rosenthal (1978). Accuracy of nonverbal communication as determinant of interpersonal expectancy effects. *Environmental Psychology and Nonverbal Behavior*, 2, 206–214.

Factors Affecting Student's Perceptions of Teachers and Peers: Perceptions Affect Interpersonal Behavior

Crick, N. R., and K. A. Dodge (1994). A review and reformulation of social information-processing mechanisms in children's social adjustment. *Psychological Bulletin*, 115, 74–101.

Dodge, K. A., J. M. Price, J. A. Bachorowski, and J. P. Newman (1990). Hostile attributional biases in serverly aggressive adolescents. *Journal of Abnormal Psychology*, 99, 385–392.

Dodge, K. A. and D. R. Somberg (1987). Hostile attributional biases among aggressive boys are exacerbated under conditions of threats to the self. *Child Development*, 58, 213–224.

Factors Affecting Students' School-Related Self-Concept: School Experiences Affect the Self-Concept

Cooley, C. H. (1902). *Human nature and the social order*. New York: Scribner.

Harter, S. (1984). Developmental perspectives on the self-system. In P. H. Mussen (Ed.), *Handbook of Child Psychology*. (vol. 4, pp. 276–384). New York: Wiley.

Harter, S. (1986). Processes underlying the construction, maintenance, and enhancement of the self-concept in children. In J. Suls and A. C. Greenwald (Eds.), *Psychological perspectives on the self*. (vol. 3, pp. 137–181). Hillsdale, NJ: Lawrence Erlbaum Associates Inc.

Harter, S. (1990a). Causes, correlates and the functional role of self-worth: A life-span perspective. In R. J. Sterberg and J. Kolligian (Eds.), *Competence considered*. (pp. 67–97). New Haven, CT: Yale University Press.

Harter, S. (1990b). Processes underlying adolescent self-concept formation. In R. Motemayor, G. R. Adams, and T. P. Gulliton (Eds.) *From childhood to adolescence: A transitional period?* (pp. 205–239). Newbury Park, CA: Sage Publications.

Hayes, N., J. Comer, M. Hamilton-Lee, J. Boger, and D. Rollock, (1987). An analysis of the relationship between children's self-concept and their teachers' assessments of their behavior: Implications for prediction and intervention. *Journal of School Psychology*, 25, 393–397.

Roberts, T. (1991). Gender and the influence of evaluations on self-assessments in achievement settings. *Psychological Bulletin*, 109, 297–308.

Wigfield, A., and M. Karpathian (1991). Who am I and what can I do? Children's self-concepts and motivation in achievement situations. *Educational Psychologist*, 26, 233–261.

Relations of Self-Concept to Learning and Motivation

Calsyn, R. and D. Kenny (1977). Self-concept of ability and perceived evaluations by others: Cause or effect of academic achievement? *Journal of Educational Psychology*, 69, 136–145.

Dean, R. (1977). Effects of self-concept on learning with gifted children. *Journal of Educational Research*, 70, 315–318.

Dweck, C., and E. Leggett (1988). A social-cognitive approach to motivation and personality. *Psychological Review*, 95, 256–273.

Eccles, J. S., and A. Wigfield (1985). Teacher expectancies and student motivation. In J. B. Dusek (Ed.), *Teacher expectancies* (pp. 185–226). Hillsdale, NJ: Lawrence Erlbaum Associates, Inc.

Harter, S. (1978). Effectance motivation reconsidered: Toward a developmental model. *Human Development*, 21, 34–64.

Harter, S. (1981). A model of intrinsic mastery motivation in children: Individual differences and developmental change. In W. A. Collins (Ed.), *Minnesota symposia on child psychology.* (vol. 14, 99. 215–255). Hillsdale, NJ: Lawrence Erlbaum Associates Inc.

White, R. (1959). Motivation reconsidered: The concept of competence. *Psychological Review*, 66, 297–323.

Wigfield, A., and J. S. Eccles (1989). Test anxiety in elementary and secondary school students. *Educational Psychologist*, 24, 159–183.

The Relationship Between Self-Concept Maintenance Attempts and Students' Behavior

Bandura, A. (1977). Self-efficacy: Toward a unifying theory of behavioral change. *Psychological Review*, 84, 191–215.

Bandura, A. (1986). *Social foundations of thought and action: A social cognitive theory*. Englewood Cliffs, NJ: Prentice-Hall.

Bandura, A. (1989). Human agency in social cognitive theory. *American Psychologist*, 44, 1175–1184.

Covington, M. V. (1984). The motive for self-worth. In R. Ames and C. Ames (Eds.), *Research on motivation in education.* (vol. 1, 77–113). New York: Academic.

Greenwald, A. G. (1980). The totalitarian ego: Fabrication and revision of personal history. *American Psychologist*, 35, 603–618.

Harter, S. (1985a). Competence as a dimension of self-evaluation: Toward a comprehensive model of self-worth. In R. Leahy (Ed.), *The development of self* (pp. 55–121). New York: Academic.

Harter, S. (1986). Processes underlying the construction, maintenance and enhancement of the self-concept in children. In J. Suls and A. C. Greenwald (Eds.), *Psychological perspectives on the self.* (vol. 3, 137–181). Hillsdale, NJ: Lawrence Erlbaum Associates, Inc.

Nicholls, J. G., and A. T. Miller (1984). Development and its discontents: The differentiation of the concept of ability. In J. G. Nicolls (Ed.), *The development of achievement motivation*. Greenwich, CT: JAI.

Using Control Needs to Reduce Unwanted Behaviors: Paradoxical Interventions

Dowd, E. T., and C. T. Milne (1986). Paradoxical interventions in counseling psychology. *The Counseling Psychologist*, 14, 237–282.

Jesse, E., and L. L'Abate (1980). The use of paradox with children in an inpatient treatment setting. *Family Process*, 19, 59–64.

Raskin, D., and Z. Klein (1976). Losing a symptom through keeping it. A review of paradoxical treatment techniques and rationale. *Archives of General Psychiatry*, 33, 548–555.

Obtaining Cooperation from Others: Variables Affecting One's Social Influence

Cartwright, D., and A. Zander (1968). *Group dynamics*. London: Tavistock.

Corrigan, J. D., D. M. Dell, K. N. Lewis, and L. D. Schmidt (1980). Counseling as a social influence process: A review. *Journal of Counseling Psychology*, 27, 395–441.

French, J. P., and B. H. Raven (1959). The bases of social power. In D. Cartwright (Ed.), *Studies in social power*. Ann Arbor, MI: Institute of Social Research.

Hollander, E. P. (1985). Leadership and power. In G. Linndzey and E. Aronson (Eds.), *The handbook of social psychology*, (vol. 2, 3rd ed.), New York: Random House.

Ng, S. H. (1980). *The social psychology of power*. London: Academic Press.

Strong, S. R. (1968). Counseling: An interpersonal influence process. *Journal of Counseling Psychology*, 15, 215–224.

Thibaut, J. W. and Kelley, H. H. (1959). *The social psychology of groups*. New York: John Wiley.

The Effects of Teachers' Expectations on Students: Teachers' Perceptions of Students and Self-Fulfilling Prophesy Effects

Algozinne, B. and T. Curran (1979). Teachers' predictions of childrens school success as a function of their behavioral tolerances. *Journal of Educational Research*, 72, 344–347.

Babad, E., J. Inbar, and R. Rosenthal (1982). Pygmalion, galatea, and golem: Investigations of biased and unbiased teachers. *Journal of Educational Psychology*, 74, 459–474.

Bennett, R., R. Gottesman, R. Rock, and F. Cerullo (1993). Influence of behavior perceptions on teachers' judgments of students' academic skill. *Journal of Educational Psychology*, 86, 347–356.

Blatchford, P., J. Burke, C. Farquhar, and I. Plewis (1989). Teacher expectations in infant school: Associations with attainment and progress. *British Journal of Educational Psychology*, 59, 19–30.

Brophy, J. (1983). Research on the self-fulfilling prophesy and teacher expectations. *Journal of Educational Psychology*, 75, 631–661.

Harris, M. J., and R. Rosenthal (1974). Mediation of interpersonal expectancy effects: Thirty-one meta-analyses. *Psychological Bulletin*, 97, 363–386.

Jussim, L. (1986). Self-fulfilling prophecies: A theoretical and integrative review. *Psychological Review*, 93, 429–445.

Quicke, J. and C. Winter (1994). Labelling and learning: An interactionist perspective. *Support for Learning*, 9, 16–21.

The Causes and Effects of Learned Helplessness/ External Locus of Control

Abramson, L. Y., M. E. P. Seligman, and J. D. Teasedale (1978). Learned helplessness: Critique and reformulation. *Journal of Abnormal Psychology*, 87, 49–74.

Dweck, C. S. (1975). The role of expectations and attributions in the alleviation of learned helplessness. *Journal of Personality and Social Psychology*, 31, 675–685.

Heyman, G., C. Dweck, and K. Cain (1992). Young children's vulnerability to self-blame and helplessness: Relationship to beliefs about goodness. *Child Development*, 63, 401–415.

Stipek, D. J., and J. R. Weisz (1981). Perceived personal control and academic achievement. *Review of Educational Research*, 51, 101–137.

Weiner, B. (1974). *Achievement motivation and attributional theory*. Morristown, NJ: General Learning Press.

Weiner, B. (1976). An attributional approach for educational psychology. In L. Shulman (Ed), *Review of research in education*. (vol. 4). Itasca, IL: F. E. Peacock.

The Importance of Struggle in the Development of Self-Concept/Self-Efficacy

Bandura, A. (1977). Self-efficacy: Toward a unifying theory of behavioral change. *Psychological Review*, 84, 191–215.

Bandura, A. (1981). Self-referent thought: A developmental analysis of self-efficacy in J. H. Flavell and L. Ross. (Eds.), *Social cognitive development: Frontiers and possible futures* (pp. 200–239). New York: Cambridge University Press.

Bandura, A. (1986). *Social foundations of thought and action: A social cognitive theory*. Englewood Cliffs, NJ: Prentice-Hall.

The Importance of Positive Teacher-Student Relationships

Anderman, E. M., and M. L. Maehr (1994). Motivation and schooling in the middle grades. *Review of Educational Research*, 64, 287–309.

Brophy, J., and T. Good (1974). *Teacher-student relationships: Causes and consequences*. New York: Holt, Rinehart, & Winston.

Eccles, J., C. Midgley, A. Wigfield, C. Miller-Buchanan, D. Reuman, C. Flanagan, and D. MacIver (1993). Development during adolescence: The impact of stage-environment fit on young adolescents' experiences in schools and families. *American Psychologist*, 48, 90–98.

Gipps, C., and H. Gross (1987). Children with special needs in the primary school: Where are we now? *Support for Learning*, 2, 43–48.

Glasser, W. (1969). *Schools without failure*. New York: Harper & Row.

Glasser, W. (1986). *Control theory in the classroom*. New York: Perennial Library.

Kramer-Schlosser, L. (1992). Teacher distance and student disengagement: School lives on the margin. *Journal of Teacher Education*, 43, 128–140.

Sapona, R. H., A. M. Bauer, and L. J. Philips (1989). Facilitative stance: Responsive teaching of students with special needs. *Academic Therapy*, 25, 245–252.

Schwartz, G., D. Merten, and R. J. Bursic (1987). Teaching styles and performance varlues in junior high school: The impersonal, nonpersonal, and personal. *American Journal of Education*, 95, 346–370.

The Effectiveness of Internal vs. External Consequences on Motivation and Learning: A Focus on Mastery vs Performance Goals and Intrinsic vs Extrinsic Reinforcement

Ames, C. (1984). Achievement attributions and self-instructions under competitive and individualistic goal structures. *Journal of Educational Psychology*, 76, 478–487.

Ames, C., R. Ames, and D. W. Felker (1977). Effects of competitive reward structure and valence of outcome on childen's achievement attributions. *Journal of Educational Psychology*, 69, 1–8.

Ames, C., and J. Archer (1988). Achievement goals in the classroom: Students' learning strategies and motivation processes. *Journal of Educational Psychology*, 80, 260–267.

Dickenson, M. M. (1989). The detrimental effects of extrinsic reinforcement on intrinsic motivation. *Behavior Analyst*, 12, 1–15.

Diener, C. I., and C. S. Dweck (1978). An analysis of learned helplessness: Continuous change in performance, strategy and achievement cognitions following failure. *Journal of Personality and Social Psychology*, 36, 451–462.

Dweck, C. S., and E. S. Elliot (1983). Achievement motivation. In P. H. Mussen (Gen. Ed.) and E. M. Hetherington (Vol. Ed.), *Handbook of child psychology: Vol. IV. Social and personality development* (pp. 643–691). New York: Wiley.

Dweck, C. S., and E. L. Leggett (1988). A social-cognitive approach to motivation and personality. *Psychological Review*, 256–273.

Dweck, C. S., and N. D. Reppucci (1973). Learned helplessness and reinforcement responsibility in children. *Journal of Personality and Social Psychology*, 25, 109–116.

Gambro, J. S. and H. M. Smitzky (1991). Motivational orientation and self-regulation in young children. *Early Child Development and Care*, 70, 45–51.

Lepper, M. R. (1981). Intrinsic and extrinsic motivation in children: Detrimental effects of superfluous social controls. In W. A. Collins (Ed.), *Minnesota symposia on child psychology*, (vol. 14), Hillsdale, NJ: Erlbaum.

Lepper, M. R., D. Greene, and R. E. Nisbett (1973). Undermining children's intrinsic interest with extrinsic rewards. *Journal of*

Personality and Social Psychology, 28, 129–137.

Rummel, A., and R. Feinberg (1988). Cognitive evaluation theory: A meta-analytic review of the literature. *Social Behavior and Personality*, 16, 147–164

Characteristics of Effective Schools

Austin, G. R. and H. Garber (Eds.) *Research on exemplary schools*. New York: Academic Press.

Bickel, W. E. (1990). The effective schools literature: Implications for research and practice. In T. B. Gutkin and C. R. Reynolds (Eds.), *The handbook of school psychology* (2nd ed., pp. 847–867). New York: John Wiley & Sons.

Glasser, W. (1969). *Schools without failure*. New York: Harper & Row.

Glasser, W. (1986). *Control theory in the classroom*. New York: Perennial Library.

Purkey, S., and M. Smith (1982). Synthesis of research on effective schools. *Educational Leadership*, 40, 64–69.

The Importance of Limit-Setting
Combined With Love

Allen, F. H. (1942). *Psychotherapy with children*. New York: Norton.

Axline, V. M. (1947). *Play therapy*. Boston: Houghton-Mifflin.

Bixler, R. H. (1981). Limits are therapy. In C. E. Schaefer (Ed.), *The therapeutic use of children's play*. (3rd ed., pp. 263–278). New York: Aronson.

Ginot, H. (1981). Therapeutic intervention in child treatment. In C. E. Schaefer (Ed.), *The therapeutic use of children's play*. (3rd. ed., pp. 279–290). New York: Aronson.

Glasser, W. (1969). *Schools without failure*. New York: Harper & Row.

Rogers, C. R. (1942). *Counseling and psychotherapy*. Boston: Houghton-Mifflin.

Adults Serve as Models for Children's Emotions

Bandura, A., D. Ross, and S. A. Ross (1961). Transmission of aggression through imitation of aggressive models. *Journal of Abnormal and Social Psychology*, 63, 575–582.

Hatfield, E., J. T. Cacioppo, and R. L. Rapson (1993). Emotional contagion. *Current Directions is Psychological Science*, 2, 96–99.

Hsee, C. K., E. Hatfield, and J. E. Carlson (1990). The effect of poser on susceptibility to emotional contagion. *Cognition and Emotion*, 4, 327–340.

Maccoby, E. (1992). The role of parents in the socialization of children: An historical overview. *Developmental Psychology*, 28, 1006–1017.

Consequences Need Not Be Immediate as Long as They are Linked Meaninfully to Children's Behavior

Bandura, A. (1986). *Social foundations of thought and action: A social cognitive theory.* Englewood Cliffs, NJ: Prentice-Hall.

Rescorla, R. A. (1988). Pavlovian conditioning: Its not what you think it is. *American Psychologist*, 43, 151–160.

Rescorla, R. A., and A. R. Wagner (1972). A theory of Pavlovian conditioning: Variations in the effectiveness of reinforcement and non-reinforcement. In A. H. Black and W. F. Prokasy (Eds.), *Classical Conditioning II*. New York: Appleton-Century-Crofts.

Seligman, M. E. P., and J. C. Johnston (1973). A cognitive theory of avoidance learning. In F. J. McGuigan & D. B. Lumsden (Eds.), *Contemporary approaches to conditioning and learning.* Washington, DC: Winston-Wiley.

School Law, Ethics, and Related Policies

American Psychological Association (1992). Ethical principles of psychologists and code of conduct. *American Psychologist*.

Bersoff, D. N., and P. T. Hofer (1990). The legal regulation of school psychology. In T. B. Gutkin and C. R. Reynolds (Eds.), *The handbook of school psychology* (2nd ed., pp. 937–961). New York: John Wiley & Sons.

Duke, D. L., and R. L. Canady (1991). *School Policy*. New York: Mcgraw-Hill Inc.

Koocher, G. P., and P. C. Keith-Speigel (1990). *Children, ethics, and the law*. Lincoln, NE: University of Nebraska Press.

National Association of School Psychologists (1992). *Professional conduct manual.* Colesville, MA: NASP Publications

Noll, J. W. (1989). *Taking sides: Clashing views on controversial educational issues.* (5th Ed.). Guilford, CT: Duskin Publishing Group Inc.

Overcast, T. D., B. Sales, and D. M. Sacken (1990). Students' rights in the public schools. In T. B. Gutkin and C. R. Reynolds (Eds.), *The handbook of school psychology* (2nd ed., pp. 962–990). New York: John Wiley & Sons.

Prasse, D. P. (1990). Best practices in legal and ethical considerations. In A. Thomas and J. Grimes (Eds.), *Best practices in school Psychology* (2nd ed., pp. 469–490). Washington, DC: National Association of School Psychologists.

Rothstein, L. F. (1990). *Special Education Law.* White Plains, NY: Longman.

Different Styles of Parenting, Teaching, and General Leadership

Baumrind, D. (1966). Effects of authoritative control on child behavior. *Child Development*, 37, 887–907.

Baumrind, D. (1967). Child care practices anteceding three patterns of preschool behavior. *Genetic Psychology Monographs*, 75, 43–88.

Baumrind, D. (1968). Authoritarian v. authoritative parental control. *Adolescence.* 3, 255–272.

Baumrind, D. (1978). Parental disciplinary patterns and social competence in children. *Youth and Society*, 9, 239–276.

Baumrind, D. (1989). Rearing competent children. In W. Damon (Ed.), *Child development today and tomorrow* (pp. 349–378). San Fransisco: Jossey-Bass.

Chang, C. (1988). Matching teaching styles and learning styles and verification of student's learning adaptation model. *Bulletin of Educational Psychology*, 113–172.

Dunn, K., and E. R. Frazier (1990). Teaching styles. *Journal of Reading, Writing, and Learning Disabilities International*, 6, 347–367.

Dunn, R. (1990). Understanding the Dunn and Dunn Learning Styles Model and the need for individual diagnosis and prescription. *Journal of Reading, Writing, and Learning Disabilities International*, 6, 223–241.

Fiedler, F. E. (1978). A contingency model of leadership effectiveness. In L. Berkowitz (Ed.), *Advances in experimental social psychology* (vol. 2), New York: Academic Press.

French, J. R. P., and B. H. Raven (1959). The bases of social power. In D. Cartwright (Ed.), *Studies in social power*. Ann Arbor MI: Institute of Social Research.

Glasser, W. (1993). *The quality school teacher*. New York: Harper-Perennial.

Hayes, J., and C. W. Allinson (1993). Matching learning style and instructional strategy: An application of the person-environment interaction paradigm. *Perceptual and Motor Skills*, 76, 63–79.

Kaplan, E. J. and D. A. Kies (1993). Together: Teaching styles and learning styles improving college instruction. *College Student Journal*, 27, 509–513.

Ng, S. H. (1980). *The social psychology of power*. London: Academic Press.

Pratt, M. W., P. Kerig, P. A. Cowan, and C. P. Cowan (1988). Mothers and fathers teaching 3-year-olds: Authoritative parenting and adult scaffolding of young children's learning. *Developmental Psychology*, 24, 832–839.

Quicke, J. and C. Winter (1994). Labelling and learning: An interactionist perspective. *Support for Learning*, 9, 16–21.

Schwartz, G., D. Merten, and R. J. Bursic (1987). Teaching styles and performance varlues in junior high school: The impersonal, non-personal, and personal. *American Journal of Education*, 95, 346–370.

Learning Styles Research and Individualized Instruction

Chang, C. (1988). Matching teaching styles and learning styles and verification of student's learing adaptation model. *Bulletin of Educational Psychology*, 113–172.

Dunn, K., and E. R. Frazier (1990). Teaching styles. *Journal of Reading, Writing, and Learning Disabilities International*, 6, 347–367.

Dunn, R. (1990). Understanding the Dunn and Dunn Learning Styles Model and the need for individual diagnosis and prescription. *Journal of Reading, Writing, and Learning Disabilities International*, 6, 223–241.

Gipps, C. and H. Gross (1987). Children with special needs in the primary school: Where are we now? *Support for Learning*, 2, 43–48.

Hayes, J., and C. W. Allinson (1993). Matching learning style and instructional strategy: An application of the person-environment interaction paradigm. *Perceptual and Motor Skills*, 76, 63–79.

Kaplan, E. J. and D. A. Kies (1993). Together: Teaching styles and learning styles improving college instruction. *College Student Journal*, 27, 509–513.

Sapona, R. H., A. M. Bauer, and L. J. Philips (1989). Facilitative stance: Responsive teaching of students with special needs. *Academic Therapy*, 25, 245–252.

Schwartz, G., D. Merten, and R. J. Bursic (1987). Teaching styles and performance varlues in junior high school: The impersonal, non-personal, and personal. *American Journal of Education*, 95, 346–370.

Factors Affecting Change in School-Based Systems: Resistance to Change and Strategies for Avoiding Resistance

Brown, D., W. B. Pryzwansky, and A. C. Schulte (1991). *Psychological consultation: Introduction to theory and practice* (2nd ed.), Boston: Allyn & Bacon.

Caplan, G. (1970). *The theory and practice of mental health consultation*. New York: Basic Books.

Fine, M. J., and C. Carlson (1992). *The handbook of family-school intervention: A systems perspective*. Boston: Allyn & Bacon.

Gray, J. L. (1984). *Supervision: An applied behavioral science approach to managing people*. Boston: Kent Publishers.

Gross, S. J. (1980). *Interpersonal threat as a basis for resistance in consultation*. Paper presented at American Psychological Association Convention, Montreal, Canada.

Havelock, R. G. (1973). *The change agent's guide to innovation in education*. Englewood Cliffs, NJ: Educational Technology Productions.

Kast, F. Z., and J. E. Rosenzweig (1974). *Organization and management: A systems approach* (2nd ed.). New York: McGraw-Hill.

Lin, N., and G. Zaltman (1973). Dimensions of innovations. In G. Zaltman (Ed.), *Process and phenomenons of social change* (pp. 93–115). New York: John Wiley & Sons.

Lippitt, G. L. (1982). *Organizational renewal: A holistic approach to organizational development* (2nd ed.), Englewood Cliffs, NJ: Prentice-Hall.

Randolph, D. L., and K. Graun (1988). Resistance to consultation: A synthesis for counselor-consultants. *Journal of Counseling and Development*, 67, 182–184.

Schmuck, R. A. (1990). Systems interventions in the schools. In T. B. Gutkin and C. R. Reynolds (Eds.), *The handbook of school psychology* (2nd ed.), New York: John Wiley & Sons.

The Development of Self-Regulatory Skills

Bandura, A. (1978). The self-system in reciprocal determinism. *American Psychologist*, 33, 344–358.

Gambro, J. S. and H. M. Smitzky (1991). Motivational orientation and self-regulation in young children. *Early Child Development and Care*, 70, 45–51.

Kanfer, F. H., and P. Karoly (1982). The psychology of self-management: Abiding issues and tentative directions. In P. Karoly and F. H. Kanfer (Eds.), *Self-management and behavior change: From theory to practice* (pp. 571–599). New York: Pergamon.

Quicke, J. and C. Winter (1994). Labelling and learning: An interactionist perspective. *Support for Learning*, 9, 16–21.

The Effects of Emotions on Reasoning and Behavior

Capaldi, D. M., M. S. Forgatch, and L. Crosby (1993). Affective expression in family problem-solving discussions with adolescent boys. *Journal of Adolescent Research*, 9, 28–49.

Duffy, E. (1962). *Activation and behavior*. New York: Wiley.

Easterbrook, J. A. (1959). The effects of emotion on cue-utilization and the organization of behavior. *Psychological Review*, 66, 183–201.

Knapp, A. and M. S. Clark (1992). Some detrimental effects of negative mood on individual's ability to solve resource dilemmas. *Personality and Social Psychology Bulletin*, 17, 678–688.

Malmo, R. B. (1959). Activation: A neurophysiological dimension. *Psychological Review*, 66, 367–386.

Martens, R., and D. M. Landers (1970). Motor performance under stress: A test of the inverted-u hypothesis. *Journal of Personality and Social Psychology*, 16, 29–37.

Yerkes, R. M., and J. D. Dodson (1908). The relation of strength of stimulus to rapidity of habit formation. *Journal of Comparative Neurology and Psychology*, 18, 459–482.

Zahn-Waxler, C., P. M. Cole, D. T. Richardson, and R. J. Friedmal (1994). Social problem-solving in disruptive preschool children: Reactions to hypothetical situations of conflict and distress. *Merril-Palmer Quarterly*, 40, 98–119.

References

Bloom, B., ed. (1964). *Taxonomy of Educational Objectives: The Classification of Educational Goals, Handbook I: Cognitive Domain.* New York: Longman, Gree.

Cline, F., and J. Fay (1990). *Parenting with Love and Logic: Teaching Children Responsibility.* Colorado Springs, CO: Piñon Press.

Covey, Stephen (1989). *Seven Habits of Highly Effective People: Restoring the Character Ethic.* New York: Simon and Schuster.

Covington, M., and R. Beery (1976). *Self-Worth and School Learning.* New York: Holt, Rinehart, and Winston.

Fay, J. (1986). *Helicopters, Drill Sergeants and Consultants.* Golden, CO: Cline/Fay Institute, Inc.

Fay, J., and F. Cline (1986). *The Science of Control.* Golden, CO: Cline/Fay Institute, Inc.

Gordon, T. (1975). *Parent Effectiveness Training: The Tested New Way to Raise Responsible Children.* New York: P. H. Wyden.

Kuhn, T. (1970). *The Structure of Scientific Revolutions.* (2nd. ed.) Chicago: The University of Chicago Press.

Mehrabian, A. (1972). *Nonverbal Communication.* Chicago: Aldine-Atherton.

Reasoner, R., and G. Dusa (1991). *Building Self-Esteem in the Secondary Schools: Teacher's Manual and Instructional Materials.* Palo Alto, CA: Consulting Psychologists Press.

Rosemond, J. (1981). *Parent Power: A Common Sense Approach to Raising Your Children in the Eighties.* Charlotte, NC: East Woods Press.

Index

Ability, 206
Abuse, 61
Acceptance, research and readings on, 374–375
Accomplishment, 208–209, 211
Accusations, from students, 228
Achievement, 80, 81, 214, 222, 223
  competitive, 59
  definition of, 205–207
  goal of, 204, 205–209
  indicator of worth, 59–60, 127–131
  optimal, 222
  related to self-concept, 117
Administrative hearing, 228, 246
Administrator, sending student to, 349–352
Advice, unsolicited, 169
Aggressive behavior
  See Behavior, aggressive
Aggressiveness, 80
Agreement, mutual, 92
Alcohol, 61
Alternatives
  See Choices
Anchoring, 184–187
Anger, 36, 83, 110, 136, 168, 169, 170, 262, 290, 361
  teacher's, 15
Apathy, 80
  student's, 219, 222
Appointment, setting an, 353–356
"Assumption of compliance," 323
Attention span, 62

Attitudes, research and readings on, 376
Authorization, need for written, 229–231
Autonomy, 68–69, 174–175, 211
  issues of, 330
  perception of loss of, 153
  restricting, 173
  teachers', 264
Avoidance, 43, 158
Awareness, field of, 78–80, 84, 210

Beery, Richard, 78
Behavior, 57, 61, 71, 78, 80
  aggressive, 75, 80
  changing, 85, 89, 91, 96, 131, 158, 163, 256–257
  consequences of, 110, 210
  guidelines for changing, 268–272
  higher standard of, 6–7
  interpretation of, 72
  management of, 321
  misplaced, 324–326, 360
  passive, 75, 158
  passive-aggressive, 151, 152
  passive-resistive, 74, 80, 151, 152
  principles of, 99–102
  reaction to, 84
  related to self-concept, 117
  research and readings on, 378, 379, 388–389
  rules for, 106
  See also Behavior modification
Behavior modification, 57–58, 67,

For a catalog of additional Love and Logic books,
Audios, DVD's, and training curriculums—
or for information on classes and seminars—
call The Love and Logic Institute at:
1-800-338-4065

The Love and Logic
PRESSInc.
2207 Jackson St.
Golden, CO 80401